LEOTARD – THE STORY OF JAZZ BALLET RODNEY

Leotard is an on- and off-stage story of dramas in an international ballet company. Set in the swinging 60's, it is a rollickingly funny tale of loyalty and friendship. Based on letters written home by two young dancers, Sally and Mary, Leotard is entertaining, effervescent, yet at times, poignant and heartbreaking. The dancing moves from the theatres and opera houses of Europe to casinos in Cannes, Cairo, and Teherān.

Sally Faverot de Kerbrech   -   Mary Spilsbury Ross

www.leotardthebook.com

Leotard is self-published by Sally Faverot de Kerbrech and Mary Spilsbury Ross, via www.createspace.com

Published in 2014.
Available in the Kindle Store and from world-wide Amazon sites.

ISBN-13 9781500161903
ISBN-10 150016190X

Leotard
PO Box 55057
3825 Cadboro Bay Road
Victoria V8N 4G0 B.C.
CANADA

The Authors

Sally Faverot de Kerbrech (née Seyd) was the soloist of the Jazz Ballet Rodney for seven years. Returning to England she opened a successful wine bar in Hampstead, London and thereafter two restaurants. She and her husband the Baron François Faverot de Kerbrech, restored an 18th Century wine estate and today, divide their time between England and France. Sally has one son and a step-daughter and granddaughter living in Australia.

Mary Spilsbury Ross was the only dancer from North America to join the Jazz Ballet Rodney and toured with them for three years. She is an artist, a former journalist, and the author of Doubleday's best selling cookbook Frugal Feasts. She and her husband, Michael Ross, live on Vancouver Island in Canada. They have two children and two grandchildren.

Dedication

Dedicated to our mothers who saved hundreds of letters written home which made this biography possible and to all mothers who encourage, comfort and applaud young, aspiring dancers of the future.

In memory of Rodney Stephen Otto Rudolph Felix Vas Choreographer, Teacher, Maestro and Creator of the Jazz Ballet Rodney (JBR).

LEOTARD is a work of non-fiction.

It is a true story of a modern ballet company, the Jazz Ballet Rodney and of people and events that took place in the 1960's. The facts have been taken from 50-year old letters, postcards, photographs, and publicity material belonging to the authors. If some of the comments seem to be a bit unkind, it is only a reflection of the young letter writer's views in the 1960's. It is not the intention of the authors to invade the privacy of certain individuals or to cause any embarrassment. Therefore many of the names have been changed. Events and times are accurate with the exception of the filming of 'Venus of the Lesbos' which took place in 1960 not 1964 and the appearance of Marcello Mastroianni' was also 1960.

At the very core is the story of a loyalty and a friendship that has lasted a lifetime.

The authors would like to acknowledge with gratitude, the support, encouragement and endless hours of editing by Michael Ross and François Faverot de Kerbrech. They have enriched the enjoyment of the memories. Without the energy and confidence of Simon Burrow, Leotard could have faltered. Thank you Michael, François and Simon!

Jules Léotard (1824-1878)

Jules Léotard, a French trapeze acrobat, was famous not only for his aerial feats but for his skin tight, knitted, one piece costume that made the ladies blush and the gentlemen envious. In 1867, George Leybourne wrote a song about Monsieur Léotard for the London vaudeville.

♫He flew through the air with the greatest of ease,
That Daring young Man on the Flying Trapeze♫

CONTENTS

Chapter One
Meet Sally and Mary

"Rodney and I became lovers in the eternal city of Rome at the Pensione Mignanelli', tucked behind the famous Spanish Steps.... I think Lesley was a little startled when I wrote that he is twenty three years older than me."

WORLD NEWS 1963
November 22 1963 John Fitzgerald Kennedy, President of the United States of America has been assassinated. The world is stunned into silence.

Sally

Bang on time, the Golden Arrow from Dover slows down and with a hiss of steam, shudders to a halt at Victoria station.   I pull soft leather gloves protectively over my new wrist-watch, wrap a shaggy mohair coat tightly around my chest against the damp chill of London and step onto the platform. This weary body has travelled from Lisbon to Paris to Calais, crossed the English Channel, heading home to Lesley for Christmas. Lesley is my mother, my friend and confidant and I always call her by name. A heap of luggage is somewhere in Paris with Rodney.

Although born and raised in London, the city is no longer my home.   For the past five years I have lived like a gypsy, dancing from city to city, country to country – from the capitals of Europe to small villages with unpronounceable names.   I am the principal dancer of the JBR, known throughout Europe as Jazz Ballet Rodney.

All my life I have never wanted to be anything other than a dancer. Ballet was my escape to an exciting world far away from London. As a little girl, I was happiest in ballet class, especially when my teachers told me I showed 'promise.' While still a teenager, Lesley encouraged me to enrol into the Hammond School of Dancing, a teacher's training college in Cheshire. I rushed through the course, got my qualifications but all the time I dreamt, not of teaching but of dancing on stage in front of an international audience.

Joy, my roommate at the Hammond School was almost six feet tall and beautiful with long blond curly hair. She came running up to me one day with the news that she had been accepted as a Bluebell girl and was moving to Paris to dance in the Lido on the Champs-Élysées. My heart was broken and I cried all night, I was so jealous. Not that I wanted to be a Bluebell girl but I ached to be dancing on stage too, in Paris, Rome, Brussels, Madrid, anywhere, everywhere.

When I was nineteen years old I moved back home where I fell in love with a new and revolutionary dance style that turned my life around. Martha Graham, an American choreographer came over to London giving workshops in her modern style of dance and I was besotted. All my waking hours I studied, practiced and mastered her fabulous innovative dance movements until I had the confidence to audition for a professional ballet company.

Martha Graham (1894-1991) was the most influential dancer and choreographer of the 20th Century. She has been immortalized as the "Picasso of Modern Dance".

An advertisement appeared in the London Stage Newspaper for a dancer to be part of a small ballet troupe in Brussels. After an audition, the job was mine and without a moment's hesitation I rushed off to join the Rainbow Ballet. Well, to be perfectly frank, they were certainly not the Bluebell's nor did they resemble the Martha Graham Dancers, but just an odd assortment of young and not terribly talented young girls. But, I was excited and joining them seemed a perfect way to begin my 'grand' career.

I should mention that I was engaged to be married to Peter at the time, but I was young and ambitious and set off on my own, not really knowing where I was heading and found myself dancing in a dingy basement nightclub on the main square of Brussels.

The Rainbow Ballet was a crummy little company comprised of four girls from various parts of France and Belgium and me. It was run by Xavier and Liliane Lavagie, a plain square-jawed Parisian girl with mousy blond hair and a gravelly voice. Liliane spoke only a few words of English and Xavier, who was Belgian, definitely did not. I learned French very quickly and was fluent in less than three months. After my advanced ballet training, I found myself performing a simple Cakewalk, the Charleston and three perky song and dance numbers reminiscent of vaudeville. Xavier sang beautifully in French with an accent like Charles Aznavour. Though our show was not really brilliant, it was a start and I was deliriously happy.

There I was, nineteen years old onstage in Europe, speaking French and surrounded by charming men who found me fascinating. The girls and I spent our days shopping and sitting in cafes sipping coffee, with only a brief stop in the afternoon for a short rehearsal. It all seemed so sophisticated. We unwound after the shows by drinking and eating until dawn, surrounded by admirers.

Lesley was delighted for me but my fiancé was not. Our engagement ended abruptly.

It was on the night of our last performance in Belgium that Rodney entered my life. I was onstage with the rest of the dancers rehearsing, when an extremely handsome man emerged from the gloom toward the footlights at the front of the stage apron. I knew immediately that he was somebody special in the theatre world as he made a confident, effortless entry. Although he was not too tall there was definitely something about him with his chiselled face that was aristocratic and at the same time sensitive. He had salt and pepper hair and blue grey eyes that, when they fixed on me I didn't know if he was laughing or flirting. As he walked across to speak to Xavier I followed his every step and could not take my eyes off him.

I should explain at this point that I was not looking my best. My nightlife had taken its toll. So when Xavier informed us that this man, Rodney Vas, the choreographer of the famous theatre cabaret in Brussels *'Le Boeuf sur le Toit'* wanted to engage the whole ballet for a tour of Germany and Italy, I was ecstatic. This was short-lived. Rodney was prepared to take the whole troupe with the exception of me. Thank God, Xavier was steadfast and said firmly, *"Tous ou rien!* You take us all or no one at all."

Rodney laughed and said "OK, I'll find something for that girl." Then he changed his choreography to ensure that I was hidden in the back row where the audience would not see me. *Bloody cheek*! I was furious and thought to myself, I will show him!

A few months later we were appearing in a theatre in Cologne, Germany. He finally noticed me looking absolutely smashing. I had been rehearsing every night between the two shows in the empty green room behind the stage, practicing modern dance movements that I loved.

During one of these private moments, I became aware that Rodney was watching me intently from the back of the studio. I slowly turned around, *"Daahlink"*, he whispered, "you are fantastic! I love this, you must show me," and we started to dance as if we had been partners our whole lives. I explained all that I had learned of Martha Graham's fresh exciting, almost geometric movements. In return Rodney took me under his wing and taught me about stage presence, projection and self-confidence. This was his gift to me. It wasn't long before he moved me from the back row to the front where I jolly well intended to stay. What I hadn't realized at the time was that Rodney was grooming me to be the soloist.

We became lovers in the eternal city of Rome in the *Pensione Mignanelli'*, halfway up La Rampa a small staircase tucked behind the famous Spanish Steps. I think Lesley was a little startled when I wrote to her, that he was twenty-three years older than me. "I don't care about the age difference, or that he has a son exactly my age, living in Amsterdam. Rodney is the most fascinating man I have ever met. With him I feel I have just awakened from a dormant state and alive in a new way. I am over the moon in love and in turn I seem to inspire him. He needs me and that is the greatest thrill of all."

Rodney's enthusiasm is like a magnet's attraction. He has us all working on his new creations until we can hardly stand up. From morning till night he is tapping out rhythms, leaping from his seat dancing and talking to his agents, stage managers and people on the street. He is curious about everything and wants to know what makes people laugh or cry and what makes them shout for joy

Once, just to impress me he did a handstand in the middle of a busy pavement in Brussels. He then walked the length of it upside down, dodging wobbly bicycles and startled bystanders. Who could resist a man like that?

Rodney and Sally performing at the 'Boeuf sur La Toit', Brussels, Belgium in 1960. Rodney was 43 and Sally 20 years old. The club was founded in 1938 and ran continuously even during the Second World War presenting song and dance revues. The Boeuf Sur La Toit closed in 1967 when the building was condemned and torn down.

Christmas 1963.

I have arrived in London at last, excited to see Lesley after a long, long time. For the past three months the ballet has performed two shows a night, every night on our tour of Spain and Portugal. We have become quite famous and our name is now Jazz Ballet Rodney shortened to JBR and painted on our suitcases and costume skips with our logo designed by Xavier. I am travelling alone because Rodney and his girls are spending Christmas in Paris in the *Pigalle* where all *les artistes* hang out. Many don't have any family to go to but I have Lesley waiting for me at number 9 Lyme Terrace, on the Camden Lock. She is my comfort and I haven't seen her in a year.

Rodney's last words to me were, "Please Sally Anna, find us another dancer in London and bring her back". He was holding both my hands in his and looking at me with his intense blue grey eyes. Well of course I would promise him the world. Christmas is not the best time to hold auditions but we must find a dancer to fulfill our contract in Switzerland where we begin our new season.

An ad was placed in the London Stage Magazine.

> "WANTED, FEMALE DANCER WITH CLASSICAL AND MODERN TRAINING FOR EUROPEAN TOUR WITH INTERNATIONAL JAZZ BALLET."

Not wanting to let Rodney down I arrive at the old and rambling Max Rivers Rehearsal Studios on Great Newport Street, earlier than my appointed hour for the audition. This ancient building with its memories and musty smells of sweat, stale cigarettes and rosin is like a second home to me. Climbing up the steep and narrow staircase I can hear sounds of muffled tap shoes, a piano tinkling behind closed doors and the voices of teachers, correcting, shouting and encouraging students.

Max himself is waiting at the top of the wide landing slouched behind his desk like a centurion guarding the gates to Rome. He peers over his glasses at his watch, pushes his hat back off his forehead with the stub of a pencil and runs his forefinger down a list in a battered ledger. "Three pounds ten shillings for three hours studio nine" he burbles all in one breath. Max doesn't look up but slowly stretched out his hand for the money. Then, with a vague nod in the direction of upstairs he disappears behind The Daily Express.

The door to studio number nine is ajar so I walk right in. Number nine is one of the smaller studios with a dusty window and a '*barre*' running along one wall. Opposite the door in the corner a rather plump pianist is sitting at an upright piano wearing a brown dress and bulky, hand-knitted cardigan. She has a bored expression on her face and an unlit cigarette in her mouth. "Good morning" I say very politely for she has the look of a woman not to be crossed. She nods in my direction, "Mrs. Briggs" she offers and I sit down to wait.

At least half an hour has passed and I am beginning to panic. Perhaps it is so close to Christmas that all dancers are already hired for pantomimes. Maybe no one wants to go abroad in the middle of winter. At last the door opens wide and a rather sweet-faced young girl enters wearing shocking pink shorts and plimsolls. I give her a simple '*enchainment*' to follow and Mrs. Briggs plays a lively tune. The girl looks panic stricken. She can't follow, can't remember what I have just told her. I think she is going to cry. Audition number two. I am aghast. She looks older than my mother and has on a thick layer of pancake makeup, her lips outlined in scarlet. "I have been in several shows in the West End," she said hopefully. This time, it's me who feels like crying. I want someone young and fun. The third girl looks about nineteen but she is too fat and has pimples. Number four is a great tap dancer but doesn't know the difference between an *arabesque* and an *attitude* and number five looks like a tart.

Feeling more than a little discouraged I am about to leave when there is a polite tap on the door. "Hope I'm not too late for the audition" asked a voice with an accent that was clearly North American.

A tall, slender redhead, with a charmingly freckled face walks in, slips off her coat to reveal a classic black leotard and tights. Although she appears nervous, her sensitive but very determined mouth breaks into a wide smile. She opens her holdall, takes out pink satin pointe shoes, puts on well-worn black ballet slippers and warms up at the *barre*. I watch carefully and see a really good technique. This is encouraging. We introduce ourselves. "Why don't you just improvise and show me what you can do, Mary, and I nod to the pianist? "Start when you are ready."

This time Mrs. Briggs plays from Gershwin's 'An American in Paris' but at top speed. *Crikey*, she must be late for her tea! Mary looks a bit startled but gamely takes off in an explosion of energy and enthusiasm, wild leaps through the air, spins, arms and long legs darting here and there with twists and bends as flexible as a piece of rubber. Half way through the music, her ponytail escapes from the elastic band losing the battle to contain a frenzy of thick, wild, fiery red hair. She stops a little out of breath gasping, "Do you wanna see some classical '*pointe*' work?" She's perfect, though I suspect that Rodney will have quite a challenge taming this one.

I will send a telegram tonight and tell him "I have found our dancer."

Mary

"I got the job, can't believe it." I want to yell from the rooftops of London from Leicester Square to the South Kensington tube station. When I was seventeen I came to London with my parents to audition for the Royal Ballet and left again, my hopes dashed. "You are too tall to be in the '*corps de ballet*' and not good enough to be a soloist" I was told coldly by a mean old witch. And now I have a job in a ballet company. I can't wait to write home.

I am still in a daze from the moment Sally pulled the contract from her purse in the coffee shop across the road on Great Newport street and signed the bottom of the sheet with a flourish Mary Spilsbury, no fixed address. Sally is exotic. She has an oval almost heart-shaped face and long neck, a little like a Modigliani painting, very dark auburn hair casually tucked under a paisley scarf and an elegant English nose. Sally is very sure of herself and a little aloof but that might be shyness. She looks sophisticated yet sexy in her leather boots, tight black pants and avocado green sweater. All eyes look up and follow her as we take our seats on the leather banquettes facing each other. When she speaks, her hands speak too, with the grace and flow of a dancer. Her dark eyes are ever so slightly almond-shaped, my mother would say 'come hither' eyes, and they sparkle at some inner joke.

I light a cigarette and casually blow smoke in the air, trying to look worldly. "Sally I don't really have an address in London but live at the moment in a cupboard in Queens Gate Gardens." My room is a Victorian wine cellar with a metal door like a prison cell with three holes for ventilation. It stinks of rising damp, perfumed with gas. At night my cupboard is so cold that I wear two sweaters under a flannel granny gown, knitted socks on my freezing feet and a fur hat that mother designed for me in case I am invited to tea with the Queen at Buckingham Palace. "You have to be prepared for any eventuality," she warned.

Two months ago I left Vancouver Island on the west coast of Canada to study modern dance in London with Madame DeVoss as it was clear that the Royal

Ballet did not want me. I didn't know a soul except a *Kappa Kappa Gamma* sorority sister, from the University of British Columbia, Sandra Browning. She groaned when she saw me standing at the door of their basement flat, in the pouring rain looking lost and almost teary. "NOT another one" Sandra said, implying that she and her flat mates take in strays every weekend. "Come in, but I warn you, there is really no room and you'll have to sleep in the cupboard." She was joking but I took her literally, moved in and stayed.

Sally tossed back her head and laughed, "SW7 is a very posh address for a closet. Just put down 53 Queens Gate Gardens, Kensington." And so I signed on to dance for five weeks in Berne, Switzerland. We went our separate ways and I promised to be waiting at Victoria Station on December 26th at eight in the morning.

With my toe, I push open the door to the lounge brandishing a bottle of cheap, sparkling wine in one hand and two chipped teacups in the other. "We are celebrating," I announce, "meet the new dancer of the Jazz Ballet Rodney." Sandra is curled up with a stray black cat named Schwartz, in a tattered wing-backed chair by the gas fire, reading Ayn Rand's 'Atlas Shrugged,' "Wonderful news," she put down the book. I pour the plonk into two cups, "To your career in dance" she holds her drink in the air, we clink and I reply "and to your career as the best soprano since Maria Callas."

Sally

I think this is one of my best Christmas' ever! Our townhouse on Lyme Terrace looks enchanting. Lights twinkle from the boats on the canal below the front windows and Lez has decorated a little tree using only our most precious ornaments. Branches of pine scent the sitting room. There is a fire flickering in the grate. Last night we cooked Christmas dinner for my brother and an elderly neighbour we call Old Bert. He is very frail but managed to stagger upstairs and join us for roast turkey and Christmas pud.

Boxing Day comes far too quickly. Once more I gather my belongings, the cabbie is at the door and Lesley and I hug in the downstairs hall. I hold her tightly and inhale her fragrance deeply, because I don't know when I will see her again. "Ta ta, I'm off." I hurry down the passage into the taxi before she sees my tears. The faint smell of *l'Air du Temps* lingers on my coat collar. I press it to my nose as we drive away.

Arriving at Victoria Station I spot Mary by the main door bundled up in a heavy coat, green knitted hat and suede lace ups. Her suitcase and various parcels are piled at her feet. She is shivering, but breaks into a cheerful smile as soon as she sees me. I stare at her feet. "Fruit boots, she retorts following my gaze. "They are the latest fad in Canada! Do you like them?" No I don't but, we'll deal with them later and we set off to find the boat train to Dover, known as the Golden Arrow. The first part of the trip is uneventful and I snooze most of the way to the coast waking up just in time to board the ferry.

I must have crossed the English Channel a million times in my life but nothing compares to our crossing this time. The boat is chock-a-block and the wind is getting stronger by the minute. Almost as soon as we leave port, the ship begins to roll, at first, a gentle almost loving side to side motion, then as we get out a bit, the wind picks up and we pitch backwards and forwards and then toss from side to side, port to starboard and the bow smacks the water with a huge *whomp* and it all begins again but more vigorously and faster. Waves are breaking over the rails onto the deck and with a crash we hit the bottom of a watery trough. Immediately we are lifted up and then *Wooooosh* are dropped again into a void. Passengers are falling over, crew members are tying the doors shut with thick rope and glasses and plates are flying off the tables in the bar where we are clinging to chairs. A most primly dressed lady, quite without warning, vomited over her lovely blue wool suit and started to weep. Oh Lord, I am starting to feel very unwell and want to go on deck to get some air but we are locked in. Children are now wailing. With eyelids half open I can see Mary through a blurry haze. She is the only person standing. With her legs braced for balance, she is knocking back neat rum laughing like some sort of mad pirate and puffing on a cigarette. "This little blow is *nuttin!*"

Well, we survived the crossing. In Calais I stagger down the gangplank with my luggage and followed the other passengers to the train bound for Paris. We climbed aboard '*La Fleche D'Or,*' the French version of The Golden Arrow happy to find empty seats. Around noon the train clattered into *Gare du Nord* and we were tossed into a mob of people all pushing and shoving like a tidal wave toward the exit and taxi rank.

It seemed like hours but finally we fought our way to the sidewalk with our luggage searching for a taxi. I was a wreck but Mary seems to be enjoying the chaos. She didn't realize that we could miss the last train to Switzerland if we didn't get cross Paris to the *Gare de l'Est* and quickly. Blimey, there was a queue a mile long waiting for taxis. As each one pulls up people flung themselves in and slam the doors. The taxis came in dribs and drabs. Panic was now rising as we edged ever so slowly forward. Finally, it was our turn. I hustled her dripping wet into the next one that screeched to a stop in front of us, and clambered in after her. The taxi, a battered old Citroën, was darting in and out of the traffic, changing lanes and swinging round corners. I was begging the harassed chauffeur to go *"plus vite, plus vite."* *"Oui, oui Mesdemoiselles, ne vous inquiétez pas."* Don't worry.

He hunched over the steering column, put his foot on the accelerator and drove like Stirling Moss. We made it, just!

Mary

Sally is practically dragging me down the platform towards the reserved carriage while I struggling with a huge overstuffed suitcase and my beauty box. That small leather case is filled with my most valuable possessions: pointe shoes, sewing kit, cigarette lighter, soft brown teddy bear whose name is Teddy, eye lash curlers, giant pink plastic hair rollers, and my U.B.C. graduation photo.

Panting and with perspiration trickling down my back, I met my future ballet master, choreographer and maestro, Rodney Stephan Otto Rudolph Felix Vas. As soon as he saw us he rushed forward and embraced Sally and searching her face nuzzled closer and whispered something in her ear before turning to me. I reached out to shake his hand but he took both my hands in his and kissed me, first left then right on my surprised cheeks, *"Bienvenue* Mary." Mr. Vas seems charming, sophisticated and very European. He looked me squarely in the eye for the longest time; his head held at a slightly bemused angle and then inspected me, from the top of my head to my soggy shoes as if he were judging a prize-winning cow. I tried to look confident but inside I am filled with self-doubt.

All around us, the members of the ballet were tossing suitcases through the windows, climbing on and off the train, arranging boxes, and trunks, and shouting in multi languages, hugging and kissing. Hands waved to me in greeting. In the midst of the pandemonium Rodney was calm, issuing instructions in French to one group, switching to English, Dutch and German with complete ease. He has an ever so slight lisp that is endearing. Blue eyes twinkle boyishly but he is a man in charge. There is no doubt about that. He gripped my arm firmly and guided me to the steps of the carriage. "Come on, quickly, quickly, *vite, vite, schnell bitte, kom op vlug opschielen.*" And we were off.

The compartment in the train has two leather-covered benches on either side, a fold up table under the window, metal racks overhead and a sliding door to the corridor. It is all highly polished wood. While the train is pulling out of the station the bags are stowed overhead, and everyone settles on the benches in a sort of 'pecking order' like chickens. Those playing gin rummy need the table and so grab the window seats. Those in the middle stretch their legs onto the laps opposite and Yvette, a French girl from Strasbourg, takes the place by the door and the one across from her for the sewing basket. In the next compartment there is a dog, a boxer, sprawled across two seats. "That's Pén-é-lope" Sally informs me, "Liliane and Xavier's boxer."

I am in the swaying corridor with Sally and Mr. Vas trying to balance and learn steps from the ballet *'Les Années Folles'* – which I think means The Roaring Twenties. Faster and faster we cross through eastern France toward the Alps. "Mary," calls Sally over the *clackety clack* of the rails, "You have to be on stage tomorrow night. If you are not *'en scene'* there is no *'argent.'* My French is good enough to know what that means, no work - no pay.

Yvette, with a tape measure over her shoulder and a little box of pins in her hand, slides open the door of her compartment and corners me. She is the costume mistress as well as a dancer and a bad tempered one at that. She quickly measures me, sucking in her breath in exasperation, whirls around and storms back into the compartment. I don't know if I am too tall or too skinny but she is not pleased. As the door snaps shut, I hear the words *"sale anglaise."* I am now a member of the filthy English. Officially I belong!

The train is just pulling into the *Bahnhof* in Berne when a petite blonde girl who must have been sitting in another compartment, comes up to me, *"allo* my name is Elizabeth" she says with a cockney accent. "Do you want to room with me in Berne?" I did, and she turns out to be a lively companion – full of gossip about everybody. In street clothes, Elizabeth wears no makeup at all, her hair hangs naturally to her shoulders and long bangs cover most of her face. She could be lost in a crowd. Later when I see her in full stage war paint, false eyelashes glued on with spirit gum and a hairpiece she is a knock-out. Elizabeth is happy to point out everybody and give details of their private lives "Over there" she points to a girl arguing with the desk keeper at the Wildenmann Hotel, "is Liliane. She is the only one in the company who is truly *'Parisienne'* Her mother is an usher in the cinema on the *Champs-Élysées* she adds with just a hint of snobbery. "Liliane, sometimes shares digs with Tanita but, usually with Xavier." Later I would learn that, on occasion, Elizabeth is also Xavier's 'roommate'!

Xavier appears quite the gentleman when we are introduced. I say that because he speaks not a word of English and we are uneasy together, stiff and formal. He is not at all handsome but has an interesting chiselled face with a haunted look. When I see him on stage he is mesmerizing, a cross between mimist Marcel Marceau and crooner, Charles Aznavour. At the dress rehearsal I watched him portray Charlie Chaplin from the silent movies and he was entirely believable. He trots on stage twirling his cane like a baton, sits on a bench and proceeds to annoy a young lady in distress. This is Sally.   It could have been Charlie Chaplin himself and they were both hilarious.

Xavier playing the role of Charlie Chaplin, in The Little Tramp" 1963. Sir Charles Chaplin was the most influential comic actor of the silent film era. He was born in London England in poverty and died one of the richest and most famous men of his day. After being accused of being a communist he was forced to flee the U.S.A. Charlie and his wife Oona settled in Corsier-sur-Vevey near Berne Switzerland.   While the JBR were performing at the Mocambo, he was seen twice in the audience, enjoying the character he made famous.

Opening night was terrifying.   My heart fluttered like humming bird wings and I could hardly breathe.   Not only have I never danced on a round stage of glass with the audience within spitting distance but I have had only one day to learn the Prologue which is about fifteen minutes in length and the Finale which is very fast to music from Stan Kenton's '*Artistry in Rhythm.*'   When I first heard it I thought that's not dance music! It sounded as though a 33rpm record was playing on 78 revolutions per minute.

The Prologue went without mishap. Our costumes are turtleneck sweaters in various colours and sheer black tights. Our hair is tied back in ponytails like Audrey Hepburn. Best of all we have really cool white boots that feel fantastic to dance in and make *pirouettes* easy. You can spin like a top with your ankles held in a vice like grip. The audience was hushed at our entrance snapping our fingers to the beat of a solo drum. Then *ta ta ta BAM*! The music erupted and we danced like crazy. I love the choreography. Never have I danced like this in my life. It's sort of 'West Side Story' meets 'An American in Paris' and is just wild. The audience thought so too.

There is a long wait between the Prologue and my next appearance as a flapper in '*Les Années Folles.*' I crept backstage and watched the next ballet from the wings, trying to pick up the steps. It is called '*Les Fourrures*' which translates to the fur stole or wrap or something like that. The ballet is a love story as old as time, of longing for something that is unattainable. A young girl from the wrong side of the tracks wants to be rich. Her boyfriend steals a fur coat from a mannequin in a shop window and gives it to her. Of course the inevitable happens, police sirens, boy runs off and girl is left holding the stolen goods learning too late that happiness was right under her nose. Sally is the girl and the boy is Rudy. This ballet seems made for them it all looks so believable. They dance as one with such intensity and passion that you expect him to rip off her clothes right there on the stage. Yikes.

I am studying the way Sally moves, lyrical and effortless and long to dance like her. Rudy is the perfect partner so cocky and confident. He has long black, kind of messy hair, and flirty eyes. I have barely said two words to him. He is married to Anke who is a beautiful blond with pale flawless skin. We both were a bit shy when we met and just said hello. Like our ballet mistress Tanita, he is from Amsterdam but Rudy is Dutch Indonesian, full name Rudolf Canesius Soemolang Wowor. The JBR is quite an international group.

1963 Rudolf Canesius Soemolang Wowor, 22 year old Soloist with the JBR.

Rudy

Rodney and I hang out in the Mocambo in Berne, Switzerland after the show. Everyone gone - talking, analyzing, and criticizing - trying out new music - how can we make this have more VA *VOOM* !!! you know??? Great new ideas - "Just do it" he always says. FAR OUT MAN! *Gewoon doen*" We talk in Dutch *ja!* I am from

Holland too. Anyway Rodney, my friend as well as everything said "careful what you say even in Dutch. Most of the staff and yes! Herr Manager all understand." I *LOVE this man*, his creativity, Wow, we do things no other dancers are doing and music, Stan Kenton on FIRE!! I get to dance with Sally, his woman in '*Les Fourrures*'. She is mine on stage. When we dance we make love - the vibes and thrills are there - Does she notice??? Does anybody notice that we are ONE? Off stage she is OFF limits *JA, JA*. Anyway, I am not alone. We have a new girl from Canada. Oh Yes, with leeeegs, gorgeous legs, long, long sexy legs. ......
Grrrrrrrrrr!!!!

Mary

'*Les Années Folles*' is a ballet of little vignettes from the Roaring 20's. Our costumes are sequined sack dresses of the flapper era and mine is peachy pink and weighs a ton. Yvette snarls that she will tear me apart with her teeth if I lose so much as one sequin. What a bag! As soon as we finish the '*Charleston*' a park bench appears and Sally and Xavier perform a sketch called '*Le Charlot*' the little tramp and then the '*Blackbottom*' with Tanita and Susannah a dancer from Germany. They both are spectacularly tall, almost six feet in heels, and dressed in jet black bodysuits with snow white collars and cuffs, topped with black Bowler hats. Without a pause the scene swings to Paris with Yvette who sighs, puts down her sewing hurries on stage into a single spotlight to sing '*Non, rien de rien*' exactly like Edith Piaf. She actually has a remarkable throaty voice, so very French. Who would ever guess that off stage she shrieks like a fishwife or as Rudy says a 'Horny Crow' but not to her face.

After Yvette's rendition of '*Non, rien de rien*', while we are all frantically changing costumes, Ronáld saunters onstage very at home, very self-assured. Ronáld is pronounced with the accent on the second syllable making his single name sound more debonair. Like Xavier, he is *Belgique* and sings in seven languages.   His costume both on and off stage is a raincoat belted around his waist with fedora pulled over one eye.   A spotlight casts a shadow on a lamppost, which has miraculously appeared from nowhere. Leaning on it, Ronáld lights a cigarette cupping his hands like Humphrey Bogart in Casablanca, blows smoke rings and starts to sing *'La Mer'* made famous by Charles Trenet. During that song, we change into our costumes for the *Finale*.

My *Finale* costume is horrible and I hate it. It looks only marginally better on the hangar than on me, this yellow satin, one-piece sleeveless leotard which is almost ten sizes too big. Yvette has stuffed the sagging bodice with rubber falsies to give me some cleavage but it makes it more ridiculous. I pray that no one who knows me is ever in the audience or it will be necessary to dye my hair jet-black and change my name to Agnes Gooch.

"Well," how do you say 'hopeless' in Dutch?" Tanita translated for me. I was a "*WAARDELOOS*" The orchestra played the music so damn fast I couldn't keep up. My arms were up when they should have been down, everyone looked left and I looked right. One of my rhinestone earrings flew across the stage and Yvette hissed "*merde*" as it whizzed by. The only thing I didn't do was fall on my *derrière*. Oh, the humiliation! Elizabeth had a satisfied smirk on her face as we went into the dressing room. She seems to resent me but I don't know why. Rudy laughed and said "you are very funny lady." Ha ha ha! Mr. Vas just patted my arm "tomorrow we will work on it." That was very comforting and I was grateful not to be criticized in front of the whole company.

Sally

Hotel Wildenmann, December 29th 1963
Darling Lesley: The opening night was REALLY GOOD and we have packed houses. It was reported in the Swiss paper to be the 'best show ever seen in Switzerland' and believe me they've had good stuff. There is a queue for hours to get in - apparently the word is out that we are doing 'West Side Story' our 'Asphalt' ballet to Leonard Bernstein's music. Last night the management from the Casino Montreux came to see the show and they loved the ballets. I think we have the contract for the Golden Rose Film Festival in Montreux which will be shown internationally on EUROVISION. Wow! I HOPE SO!

Today we were meant to have photo stills taken in the streets for the Front cover of Sie und Er Magazine (the Paris Match of Germany). The police blocked off one street for photos, but it snowed. Instead we went to the Rathaus (that's the town hall) and had them taken there. Rodney has been so passionate since I got back from London. He hardly lets me out of his sight and we are inseparable. Such fun! It looks like a good year for us– touch wood. Lots of love Sally

31

Die Beatles kommen — rette sich wer kann!

Sie and Er Magazine 1964 featured Rodney and the Ballet in the lead story. On the following page was a small photo and article about the Beatles a new band on the music scene. On January 1ˢᵗ, 1964 they released their first album Please, Please, Me.

Mary

Every morning between eight thirty and nine, the entire ballet assembles in a rented rehearsal studio. Tanita is our ballet mistress and gives us a good work out for at least two hours. There is no fooling around. Tanita is unrelenting and works us till we drop. Even my hands are aching. She insists that every part of our body must be expressive right down to the fingernails. Now here I have a problem. I am a nail biter. Tanita is determined that my hands will be an exquisite extension of my limbs and covers my stubs with a poisonous concoction. "Suzanna" she informs me, "receives a monthly cheque because her lovely long fingers are on billboards advertising hand cream, all over Germany." I vow to grow my nails. Susanna does have the most beautiful hands and arms. I like her immediately because she has an infectious laugh and is very kind to me.

Slowly I am getting used to Mr.Vas' style and don't feel like such a klutz. His choreography is very different from what I am used to but he is patient and tells me to listen only to the drums. Ready or not I have to be in every ballet tonight or I won't get paid. "*Dahlink*" he calls all his dancers that, "be calm, you will be *vonderful.*" He would extract a cigarette from his pocket, light it, inhale deeply and then disappear in a cloud of smoke.

Sally

It has been snowing for the past two days and Berne is exquisite. It looks like a glittery Victorian Christmas card. Mary, Liliane and I went to find Albert Einstein's house on 49 Kramgasse. Big disappointment! There was nothing to see and it wasn't open. We wandered back to the famous medieval clock the *Zylglogge* to wait until four minutes to the hour when the evil little puppets pop out sending Pénélope into fits. She barks until the last one disappears and then the cock crows the hour. She is trying to steal the show. As we went off down the street chattering and gossiping Liliane dropped a bombshell. "*La nuit de la Saint Sylvestre, J'ai baisé le garcon du Mocambo, you know Sallee. I have eet off, uh beeeg foouk*" and she threw back her head and laughed. I was with a waiter from the Mocambo on New Year's Eve. Mary did not quite understand what she was saying in French and stuck her head in a guidebook reading "In 1256 the Zylglogge which was the town gate became a prison for prostitutes who serviced the clergy." "Oh be quiet Mary, *Tais toi Mareee*! I give you beeg histoire and you read book. *Leesen,*" Liliane continued, "Xavier he find out. *Et bam, bam, bam.* He make scandal – break room, grab Pénélope and go." "Of course he return *thees* broken man," she said dramatically in her quaint English. Liliane blew a smoke ring in the air, "*et maintenant,* he follow me *comme un chien, mes chères* never to stop make love*"* and the result is that she can't stand him.

I can't wait to write to Lesley. She will find this very funny, absolutely brilliant!

Sally, Pénélope the boxer, and Liliane
January 1964, Berne, Switzerland.

Mary

There are lot of intrigues and funny business going on that I never suspected. Various people have filled me in on details that I will definitely not write in my letters home. Xavier seems to have three girlfriends fighting over him at once and I do mean fighting. Liliane flies into screaming rages and resorts to fisticuffs. My roommate disappears in the middle of the night and the next day has huge dark circles under her eyes and Yvette makes sly remarks and calls Xavier a *connard* which translates as 'you bastard' or worse. He laughs and teases her. Most women find him irresistible.

The multi talented Xavier in 1960. Singer, Actor
Mimist, Dancer, and Lady Killer.

I suspect that many of the girls in the ballet
would change places with Sally if they had half a
chance but Mr.Vas is almost as old as my father, for
Heaven's sake. Maybe age doesn't matter in Europe
but it would raise eyebrows back home. I really like
Ronáld. He looks like a young Harpo Marx with piles
of curly hair and a fedora perched on top. Ronáld
doesn't seem to flirt with any of the girls but they all
adore him like a brother. He often vanishes quite
mysteriously soon after the show and we don't see him
again until curtain time the next day. I really get along
well with him and envy the fact that he is fluent in so
many languages. Rudy is a little intimidating. His

talent is enormous. Onstage he is wild, sexy, confident and dances with fire. Offstage he plays the fool. *C'est un caractêre adorable* but married.

My roommate seems to be in name only. By the time our show has finished and we have had something to eat I stagger into our room, undress, put on my granny gown and with every muscle burning, toes blistered and sore, gently drift into oblivion. After the cupboard in London, this soft warm bed is paradise.

Very close to the hotel is a marvelous old restaurant called the *Ratskeller*.   Our first visit coincided with a massive snowfall and we slipped and skidded there after the show. Trooping out the stage door we stumbled into eight inches of the white powder.   In an instant the entire ballet turned into a bunch of kids, throwing snowballs, wrestling, shoving ice down necks and clowning around.   Much to my surprise Mr.Vas did a handstand and walked upside down across the square to the door of the Ratskeller. Then he straightened up pulling off his gloves and glided serenely through the door. The *maitre d' hotel* bustled forward all smiles grasped Rodney by the hand and said in perfect English, "Ah the ballet. Welcome Rodney, we are honoured. *Bienvenu, welkommen.*"

Almost as if the *Ratskeller* were waiting for us, we were ushered to a long table in the center of the room and there was a general stampede to find places. I found myself sitting next to Remo an Italian dancer from Milan. He is extremely good looking, almost like a movie star and not at all like any boys I know back home.   Fortunately he speaks English and with an irresistible Italian accent. I'm not sure if he is flirting with me or not. Everyone ordered the entrecote with sauce béarnaise and so did I. One bite told me that it was the most delicious sauce in all Switzerland. *Mais non"* - pipes up Mireille from across the table *bearnaise* is not Swiss at all but French, from Saint-Germain-en-Laye near Paris." Mireille is not terribly bright so I am a bit surprised that she knows this. Sally leans over and says that the French know about everything they stick in their mouths – there is general hilarity. Everyone argues immediately. Mireille may not be a genius in all things, but, she is strikingly beautiful and the audience adores her - tall, blond, curvaceous, and sexy, she has the mouth of a truck driver. She uses words that no one will ever find in the *'Le Dictionaire Français.'*

Sally

It doesn't matter where we go, Rodney seems to know everyone; the manager of the restaurants, impresarios, head waiters, stage managers and they all greet him like they are the best of friends. This is such a surprise to me but when I ask him about this connection with strangers he just smiles mysteriously and distracts me by changing the subject or nuzzling my neck. Perhaps he is a member of some secret organization that recognize each other by some look or perhaps it is just the way he is, confident, handsome, and in command. As soon as we enter any room, everyone reacts. Within minutes we are surrounded and Rodney starts telling funny stories in French or German or a mixture. Round of drinks arrive as if by magic as he takes center stage. Being with him is never dull.

Darling Lez: January 1964
We are leaving for Milano – you know how I LOVE Italy. I have exciting news. The real Charlie Chaplin that is Sir Charles Chaplin and Oona came to see Xavier and me in Le Charlot. Rodney saw them and they clapped and clapped. I couldn't see anything with the spotlight directly on my face but, as we took

our bows, Xavier whispered, "le vrai Charlie". I am thrilled. Love Sally xxx

Mary

    I am getting more and more depressed pondering my future back in foggy London town and cannot bear to leave this wild troupe of gypsies. I am having the time of my life and tore my five-week contract that I signed with Sally and tossed the scraps of paper in the air shouting... "Italy here I come!"Yvette sighed *"Mon Dieu."*

Chapter Two
Da Vinci, Di Vino, il Duce

.... It's called "a Turk's Head" informs Tanita peering over my shoulder, disgusted. This is a childhood fantasy come true, a wacky old theatre straight out of the pages of history.

WORLD NEWS 1964
PUSH UP PLUNGE BRA INVENTED BY
CANADIAN DESIGNER, LOUISE POIRIER'

Sally

Darling Lesley:

CHAOS! Absolute bedlam leaving Berne! I am a wreck. Fortunately I have found a seat alone so I don't have to hear Liliane wailing and moaning as only the French can. Her beloved Pénélope has been sent back to Paris to live with her mum, Madame Lavegie. At the moment of parting Liliane screamed and threw herself at the dog, clinging to him.
What a scene!!!Xavier tried to comfort her but she scratched him then Rodney dragged her off to a taxi -

we almost missed the train. ....must stop now and will write when we get to Milan.........

....Now in Milano, Italia. Brilliant! I have a big room to myself at the Hotel Residenzia at 68 Corso Garibaldi which is owned by an old friend of Rodney's. I want my room to feel like a proper home with my photographs on the bureau, clock by the bed and my clothes in the wardrobe with the luggage out of sight. I am feeling the need to be on my own. Rodney is down the hall so he can be as independent as he wants. Sometimes he sleeps in the same room with me but when he has a new ballet in his head he gets fits of creativity and disappears to the rehearsal room trying out new steps, new music and organizing our future contracts with his agents. We are just much happier like this. Some may think our living arrangements weird but no one questions. Our private lives remain just that, private. You, Lez, are the only one who really understands us. Love Sal xxxx

I am not at all sure about things with Rodney, our personal relationship I mean. I keep thinking about Rudy and can't get him out of my mind. When we dance together I am on fire and he is too. But then I feel guilty because, *'Les Fourrures'* is really Rodney's love song. He choreographed that ballet especially for me.

Mary

When I was seventeen, my sister Allie, mother and I had a whirlwind bus tour of Italy. We shot through Lake Como, Pisa, Florence and Rome in four days. On the first bright sunny afternoon, Allie and I were strolling across a piazza, wide-eyed. Like a scene in a movie a boy was standing and crooning an Italian love song at an outdoor café filled with beautiful people. Unruly black hair flopped over a tanned face. He was young, swaggering, confident and adorable. I stared and stared at him and WHAM, walked straight into a lamppost and almost knocked myself out cold. Everyone at the café howled with laughter, clapping their hands together with glee, including him. My sister of course wanted the sidewalk to swallow her up she was so mortified and ran off wailing. "Momma, do something with her".

I loved Italy from that moment and knew I would return. Throughout my years at university I would fantasize about the outdoor cafes, cobblestone streets filled with bronzed elegant people and singing. I dreamed that I would someday be sitting at a linen covered *'tavolo'* with an adoring waiter hovering, napkin in the crook of his arm waiting for *"uno caffè espresso per favore"* from my quadrilingual lips. I would peer over my enormous sunglasses like a near-sighted Audrey Hepburn, ready to charm the pants off, well not literally, but maybe later, Marcello Mastroianni my hero. He would be seducing me with his deep, dark Renaissance eyes.

February in Italy is not a sun-drenched fantasy at least not in Milan. Arriving at the main train station was dismal. Rain cascaded down soaking our cases, and the precious *'paniers'* of costumes, as we ran for taxis. The freezing rain mixed with sleet kept falling day and night that first week. I sloshed about ruining my new Bally boots from Switzerland feeling like a bedraggled alley cat slinking from the steaming rehearsal studio to the draughty, smelly theatre. Relief arrived in the form of letters waiting at the American Express Office. My mother, bless her, sent a money order to 'help tide things over.' I must have told her that we made the equivalent of ten dollars a day only when we are actually performing, but, in between we are paid zilch *niente di niente,* not a penny. Sally told me in confidence that her mother often sends her money or she would never survive. Most of the other dancers are not so fortunate so we keep this to ourselves.

Again I am sharing a room with Elizabeth. There is no choice of roommate. Our room with two iron beds, called a *'camera con due letti singoli'* is cramped with no room for suitcases let alone a chair. It has a tiny terrace that overlooks the wet pavement below and the bathroom is down the hall with a window the size of a book. On the ground floor there is a reception desk and a narrow bar/café that serves a coffee and *'tosti'* - a toasted ham and cheese sandwich but squished flat. It tastes a bit like cardboard but is cheap and we are constantly hungry. Late at night most of the ballet gather around the reception desk spilling into the street drinking Stock 84 to keep warm. It is a wicked brandy that sets your throat on fire and acts like cough syrup, which everyone needs.

The *Teatro Smeraldo,* just off the *Bastioni de Porta Nuova,* is like no theatre I have ever seen. It is enormous but the stage is quite small. High overhead lurks a movie screen hoisted up into the 'flies' with thick nautical ropes. The ballet for the next two weeks is the *'avanti spettacolo'* before the film. We do our complete ballet repertoire by nine in the evening and then a giant screen descends and the audience watches a spaghetti western on it. That works perfectly. We have a job and the moviegoers get a little culture. Often the leading man is Clint Eastwood dubbed in Italian with English sub-titles. The audience is a rough lot a bit like the spectators of a Shakespearean comedy. They are mainly Sicilian workers who travelled to the north for jobs repairing war-damaged buildings. The *'Milanese'* call it *'la boom.'* We are happy with the *avanti spettacolo* because it gives us time to work on our new ballet in the daytime and go dancing after the performance.   After the show we are far too wired to return to the hotel and Remo has been escorting me to a discothèque called *'Whiskey a Go Go.'* We can't afford to drink anything but it costs nothing to dance. We are good at that.

The only drawback of the *'avanti spettacolo'* is the filthy stage covered in globs of grease from the mechanics of the movie screen. We dance in bare feet and wear all white costumes in the 'Afro Cuban.' Yvette snarls and hisses at us if there is so much as a pinprick of dirt on the pristine costumes.   They are difficult to see anyway as the ballet is in a blue fluorescent light, with thunder, lightning and a tropical rainstorm.   Like the Cheshire Cat in Alice in Wonderland, the audience sees only big, smiley white teeth. Intermittently during the lightning are flashes of fringe bikinis, one legged pants, ruffled tails, and white umbrellas. A little grease here and there would not be seen.

Publicity still 1959 Lisbon, Portugal. The Afro Cuban Mambo. Jazz Ballet Rodney. Music was a medley of music by Cuban musician, composer and band leader Pérez Prado

Last night during the Prologue, someone from the audience yelled out loudly *'troppo magra'*. "It means you are too skinny dearie," translated Elizabeth in a particularly bitchy tone of voice as soon as we were offstage. It was as though she had whapped me in the face. I am never going to share a hotel room with that cow again. '*Sale vieille vache!*'

Sally

We are always starving. Our days are long, very, very, long. A warm up class begins in the morning, then hour upon hour of rehearsal followed by another warm up class before the first performance. Like athletes in training we can hardly think of anything else but food. Most of us eat nothing during the day, certainly not breakfast before class. At lunchtime when Italian families enjoy their main meal, heaps of pasta and sauce mopped up with bread, we are dancing. Of course we never eat just before a performance. So as soon as the last applause dies down our bodies are screaming for food and we rush into our dressing rooms, slap cold cream on our faces, wash as best we can in antiquated plumbing and dress. There is a babble of voices while everyone discusses what they are going to order.

My favourite *trattoria* on *Via Rovello* has no name. The owner is a darling person who keeps the kitchens open for us and for other entertainers around Milan's theatre district. Tourists would never find this little hole in the wall. It is not really on a street but a *vicolo,* a passage linking two streets. I don't think there is even a signpost. Dingy grey buildings line either side and their walls are mottled with peeling paint and faded paper posters. The plaster on one exterior wall is cracked and perforated by what looks suspiciously like the spray from a machine gun probably from the Allied invasion. After fifteen years it is still not repaired and remains a constant reminder of that terrible time.

44

Heavenly smells of garlic and onions simmering in olive oil reach us before we even get to the door. Inside, customers, mostly older men, shuffle chairs around making room for us. Miraculously space is cleared for sixteen of us at one long table, a family gathering.

By now we are almost frantic with hunger and can see the steam arising from a giant pot of *zuppa* bubbling gently in the kitchen. The Mamma bustles in and snatches soiled white cloths off the tables and spreads new ones, still smelling damp from the clothesline, cluck clucking all the while like a mother hen. Pappa arrives with an armload of drinking glasses, chunky, hexagonal, and restaurant sized, and several carafes of '*vino rosso*' made by a cousin or an uncle out in the countryside. These he plonks on the table and Rodney pours my glass to the brim and passes the carafe down the table. "*Tchin, Tchin!*" We knock it back. Our exhaustion is forgotten. Mama is back with baskets filled with little bread rolls with holes in the middle. They are still warm from the oven. These are gone in a flash and she arrives with more. Oh the joy!

Like most family owned '*trattorias*' there is no written menu. Little bowls and platters of *antipasto misto* arrive from the pantry, slices of home-cured salami, mortadella studded with fat olives, baby artichokes, and *pepperonata* drizzled with olive oil are devoured with gusto. Ahhh! We are all beginning to feel much better. Tonight we are offered as the '*piatto del giorno,*' *osso bucco con risotto a la Milanese*' veal shin slowly simmered with tomatoes, garlic and herbs and finished with *gremolata,* anchovy, lemon zest, caper and parsley. Perfect *grazie!* That is for me. I have told Mary that it is best to order the *piatto del giorno* the daily special. It will always be good and cheap. She has taken my advice. Almost everyone is having the veal except Remo who is attacking *spaghetti*

Bolognese. Probably his mother makes the best *osso bucco* in Milano. The carafes of wine are replenished and I am feeling warm and fuzzy. It has been a perfect day.

Some musicians from a local club have arrived. Ronáld gets up from his chair to join them still wearing his fedora, glass and cigarette in hand. He seems to know them but then all artists seem to have a network of friends that continually appear and disappear on the theatrical circuit. Pappa returns with an accordion and within minutes Ronáld, is singing in Italian to Mama. She is beaming up at him like he is her son.

♫ *O sole mio , sta 'nfonte a te, O sole, O sole mio sta 'nfonte a te, 'nfonte a te ' sta 'nfonte a te* ♫

♫ *My own sun, shines from your face, The sun, my own sun, shines from your face etc.* ♫

Of course for the last stanza we are all on our feet singing at the top of our lungs, hands in the air like great opera singers. The noise is deafening. As we get louder, more people arrive. News that the ballet is eating here has quickly spread. Maybe the patron is counting on that for a full house. I suspect he charges us less, hoping that we will come again. We pay almost nothing for an enormous meal and lots of wine.

Italian women do not wear trousers, at least not in public and I know that because last year Liliane and I went to the *Piazza del Duomo* wearing boots and trousers and almost caused a riot. The square was absolutely empty when we arrived and within five minute of us wandering around gazing at the shop windows in the glass domed *Galleria Vittorio*

Emanuele II we were surrounded by whistling and men of all ages pushing and shoving against us. It was quite unnerving because there were so many of them.

Yesterday, Mary, Liliane, Elizabeth and I set out incognito to the same piazza wearing skirts and sweaters with raincoats and dark glasses, no trousers. We took the bus and got out at the *Piazza del Duomo* just as the sun broke through the clouds and the vision of the enormous fairy tale cathedral with the sun hitting the wet spires and turrets was enchanting. "I had no idea it was so, so…" For once Mary is speechless.

We walked right past it through the arch into *Galleria Vittorio Emanuele II,* a massive glass covered shopping piazza and then into the best department store in Italy, *La Rinascente.* We are on a mission, 'Operation Underwear.'

Piazza del Duomo in 1964. A triumphal arch (on left) leads from the piazza into the largest glass covered shopping arena in Italy, Galleria Vittorio Emanuele II, built in 1861. In 1917 Italy's oldest department store, La Rinascente, opened its doors for business. British and American bombs destroyed the store in 1943 during the German occupation and it was not rebuilt until 1959.

Mary cannot go on wearing her ridiculous huge white knickers and a girdle that she indignantly describes as 'a very expensive Playtex long leg panty girdle.' It is a frightful thing.

The first time she took off her street clothes for rehearsal in Berne, all the girls sniggered and then pointed in disbelief. "What is it?" She was mystified and looked around. *"Mais, qu' est que tu porte?"* Mireille asked pulling at the elastic girdle and then, when it was removed and Mary stood there in plain cotton bloomers we all hooted with laughter. The noise was loud enough to bring the boys in: Xavier, Remo, Ronald and Rudy came through the door to inspect the offending undergarments while Mary stood stiffly like a school teacher and snapped "Oh grow up." That produced even more hilarity.

After a month with us, she completely changed her attitude and is rummaging around piles and piles of lacy panties in every colour, size and shape. They come with matching underwired push-up bras that give even the smallest breasts a cleavage. The three of us lark about holding up outrageous choices – black lace, sheer white with tiny flowers embroidered in pastel colours, cotton eyelet with little ruffles and satin woven with tiny bows. An hour later Mary has chosen seven pairs of bikini panties, three push-up bras and she has smile on her face. "I feel liberated at last."

Having spent most of our lira on knickers we barely have enough money for a cup of tea. Undaunted we troop next door and climb the stairs to the most expensive tea salon in Milan. The tall glass doors open into a vast room with walls the colour of Devonshire cream, ornate ceilings and chandeliers.

On each linen covered table sits a Venetian glass vase of tiny spring flowers. This is the room the crème of Milanese society eat fancy cakes and meet their lovers or so we have been told. We are feeling very genteel sipping our tea in china cups in such a grand setting and look around to see if we can spot anyone famous. The room is almost empty. When the bill comes we can see why.

Mary

One thing I have learned being a part of this crazy troupe is that there is no room for modesty, at least not backstage. We all have some very fast changes of costume and Sally has taught me to master the art of the ninety-second change. From the Prologue, exit stage left – costume for the next ballet *must* be hanging on a rope just out of view of audience – slip out of white turtleneck, never dream of putting it on the floor or Yvette will stab you to death. Then struggle out of boots – black tights off – bottoms of Afro Cuban on – do up 3 large hooks or lose it on stage – turn with back to stagehands - remove padded bra and put on fringed top, - hook up neck piece, wrist fringe, release chignon into a pony tail....60 seconds, music is beginning –wipe off red lips, smear on pale pink –take a puff of ciggy, listen *only* to the drums, do deep '*plie,*' breathe and blow out, flex back – OK!. Stage hands clear the entrance with ten seconds to go, starting on the right foot: one, two, three, four strides and then "*fly through the air with the greatest of ease like the daring young man on the flying trapeze.*"

At home, mother dresses and undresses in a cupboard in her bedroom. I don't know why she is so shy. She is a very beautiful woman with dark wide-set eyes and has a tiny waist and curvaceous hips. We never discuss curves. Mummy has set ideas about what is 'proper' and what is not. We, meaning my two sisters and I, have never discussed 'girl issues', sex is out of the question, and boys want one thing only. She is a black and white person but never, ever, grey. You are either a virgin or a tramp, your manners are either regal or they are peasant, you are brilliant or you are an irreversible moron. Mummy, I know, lives through my letters and I am very, very, careful what I write, describing only what I think she wants to hear.

Life in the ballet is sometimes not as glamorous as one might think. After our shopping excursion at the *Galleria* I really do not have any money. Back in London, one hundred pounds waits for emergencies but I am trying to live on what I earn. Tonight, Sally announces, "we will cook at home," home being the Hotel Residenzia. We pool our meagre resources and come up with enough liras for two pork '*salsicce,*' two buns, a small piece of *gorgonzola*, in other words two baby bangers for dinner. I still have a little *Toblerone* chocolate left over from Berne, hiding in the bottom of my suitcase and head to Sally's room.

"I didn't know the hotel had a kitchenette for guests" I say, pushing the door open. "Kitchen is over there", Sally is pointing to a rather faded greyish green suitcase sitting in the corner by the doors to the terrace. 'Kitchen' is opened to reveal one small electric hot plate, one saucepan that fits in a frying pan with no handles, which fits two bowls, a one-cup emersion heater, an espresso coffee pot, can opener, cork screw, cheese grater, strainer/sieve, multi-headed plug that converts electricity from country to country, a lid, two plates, two cups, salt, pepper, oregano, basil (all dried) small bottle of olive oil and a tea towel. I am instructed to memorize how it all fits in.

This is the first of many meals that we prepare together. Unfortunately the hot plate is either red hot or barely warm so we have to be a little creative with the sausages or they are either burnt or raw. The rolls we halve and toast over the bare unit on the end of a fork. Sitting on pillows on the floor we drink hot tea and discuss the ballet, our ambitions and families. Sally confides in me some aspects of her life with her stepfathers and half brothers and sisters, but not a word about her father. We both like our privacy. Smoke from the sausage fat and the cigarettes are filling the room so we open the terrace doors and look into the magic of the Milanese night. It has finally stopped raining.

I thought that the *Teatro Smeraldo* was pretty grand but *Teatro Puccini* on Corso Buenos Aires where we are dancing for the next fortnight is an absolute gem. It is a textbook pre-Edwardian gilded opera house complete with ghosts. The whole thing looks like the set from an Alfred Hitchcock movie. It is dim and dingy with faded velvet seats and chipped gold plaster designs on the proscenium arch. The orchestra pit can seat about fifty with grand piano and the stage is raked at a fifteen-degree angle. How you hold your balance, I have no idea. There is even a trap door and it reminds me vividly of a movie *"The Unfinished Dance"* with Margret O'Brian playing an evil brat who pulls the lever sending her competition hurtling down below stage. There are times I would love to try that on Elizabeth.

Backstage has got to be seen to be believed. There are three floors of crumbling private dressing rooms, each with a sink and all the floors are hand-

51

hewn rock. Even the stairs are stone with many going nowhere but bricked up doorways. The one toilet is up a steep flight of steps at the rear of the stage and lo and behold it is a smelly old hole in the floor with a tap on the right with two footprints in enamel to balance precariously above. It's called "a Turk's Head" informs Tanita peering over my shoulder, disgusted. This is a childhood fantasy come true, a wacky old theatre straight out of the pages of history.

Sally

Most opera houses built in the nineteenth century have a raked stage with anything from a five to seventeen percent slope. For the opera this is perfect because the singers can be seen and can see the conductor from anywhere. But for dancers it is like performing on a gangplank heading straight downhill into the pit.

The Puccini where we are performing for the next fortnight, not only has a steep slope but is full of gouges and splinters, in fact, the stage is a wreck. From the audience it looks very luxurious with lots of gilded plaster and plush velvet curtains that are worn but still regal.

Rudy and I are having trouble with our 'grande lift' in *Les Fourrures*. We have rehearsed for hours and are feeling a little giddy. It is a special, poignant moment in the story, the climax as it were, and there can be no wobbling or stumbling around. The music reaches a crescendo. I run across the stage to him, arms outstretched fling myself into the air Rudy catches me by my thighs and slowly I slide down his chest until we are standing face to face.

Usually we end up panting with exertion and relieved that no mistakes were made. This time however, I am standing pressed against him, his heart is pounding and I have an overwhelming urge to wrap myself around his steaming body, drenched with sweat and make love to him, right here, right now on stage. We are both trembling with desire. I pull away and cannot look at him. It is only my loyalty to Rodney that prevents me from tearing at him like an animal. Is it possible to love two people at the same time?

Mary

Sally and I are becoming very close friends and complement each other's personalities. We both like our own space and sometimes want to be left alone but, basically, we are very alike. After the show is over we both have fun at the local bars and during the day we like to explore art galleries and museums. Not all the girls are keen to be tourists. We both adore spaghetti, any kind at all and certainly we like flirting with the boys who hang around the stage door in order to escort us home. Of course I think they want to escort Sally home and I am just tagging along.

For days I have been talking about seeing Leonardo da Vinci's The Last Supper, 'Il Cenàcolo' before we leave Milan. I wrote an essay about the painting in an Art History course and long to see it firsthand. Sally and I set off to find *Piazza Santa Maria delle Grazie* which is a little outside the center of Milan. It took forever to get there and we had to change trams three times. Sally was beginning to grumble and threatened to go back to the hotel because everyone stank of garlic and she was fed up. The other passengers on the bus gave us confusing directions, pointing opposing ways until the driver finally stopped and shouted, *"Ecco qui* Here, Here"* and pointed across a square to the Church of Santa Maria looking fragile and wounded with war damage.

We splashed our way across the *piazza* and entered through a single door into the dark interior. Far off we heard someone mumbling in prayer but otherwise the church was deserted. We crept about peering at paintings trying to find the famous long table of disciples in flowing robes. It was eerie stumbling around in the gloom with only a candle for light. "Here it is," Sally called *'Shhhhhh'* came a whisper from the darkness on the other side of the monastery. I have seen photographs of this masterpiece in books but standing in front of the real thing all twenty nine feet was overwhelming. I didn't expect it to be so big. It is not a painting on canvas but a fresco painted on the wall. A lot of it is crumbling and faded but the impact is fresh. The figures are so lifelike, the faces alive and expressive. In 1943 the church was bombed and it is a miracle that the sandbagged wall stayed intact. I drank it in taking in all details because I may never be here again. In the dim light a feeling of calm settled around us. Isn't it uplifting that something so exquisite, so peaceful could survive through generations of battles, bloodshed and intolerance? I glanced at Sally's profile with her scarf over her head. She's holding a candle up high, her head tilted as though gazing to Heaven. Just for a fraction of a second she looks like one of the saints.

Sally in the JBR ballet "Black Saint and Sinner Lady" 1964 to the music of Charlie Mingus.

Outside it was still pouring and so we dashed over to the nearest bar to have a cigarette and a coffee and a sip of '*Stock 84*' to warm our innards. "I think I am getting a cold sore" pointing to my upper lip, "ain't I luuvely?" We both cracked up. I had wanted to go on to *Piazza Loreto* to see where the bodies of the fascist leader Benito Mussolini and his mistress were hung upside down on meat hooks but Sally thinks that is gross and refuses to go.

In many ways, we are all sorry to be leaving Milan. Yes, it is a sprawling industrial city, a construction site that is being torn apart and rebuilt but we are happy here and many people have treated us like family. That is the problem with being in a touring company, the minute you start feeling at home it is time to move on.

A new French girl, Nadine, has just joined the ballet, well, I mean new for me. She was with the ballet last year but disappeared somewhere in Portugal. Nadine is very cute, '*mignonne*' in French, with short blond hair cut like Peter Pan. She is very sure of herself and knows some terrific swear words. The problem is I don't know what they mean. She can't believe that I am a Canadian but speak appalling French. Yvette doesn't like Nadine very much, but then, I don't think she likes anyone at all, except Rodney.

Chapter Three
Marble Statues and Strega Liqueur

... I'm leaving part of my heart behind in Florence. The French say 'partir, c'est mourir un peu' to leave is to die a little, and I agree...

WORLD NEWS

February 7th 1964   The Beatles arrive in the U.S.A. for the first time. Pan Am Yankee Clipper flight 101 was met by 3000 screaming fans. Two days later they were featured on the Ed Sullivan Show and watched by an estimated 73 million viewers.

Sally

The train pulls into the railway station *Santa Maria Novella* in Florence. I stick my head out the carriage window, hug myself and smile. The warmth of the sun greets us. We have only a few moments to unload before the fancy new diesel engine leaves for Sienna so I toss my belongings through the window to Remo and jump to the platform amid the heap of luggage, bags and satchels. Farther down the track I can see Yvette and Rodney. She is frantically counting the costume skips and Rodney is paying the porters to haul the costumes to the *Teatro*. Off we go, this time to the *Pensione Tenti* on via Porta Rossa where Mary and I are going to be roommates for the first time.

Our room is palatial and we even have our own bath. Unfortunately it is on the fifth floor and the lift, a creaky old cage, only goes to the fourth but we don't care about little details like that – just so excited to be here. As soon as we registered and handed in our passports we set off in search of the *Teatro Verdi* on via Ghibellina.

Firenze is like a medieval maze. Streets and alleyways go in all directions on either side of the River Arno. The *via Porta Rossa* where we are staying seems to be the heart of the town. It is very narrow almost a lane but packed with people chattering in groups, kissing, arguing and smoking. Across the way I spy a *trattoria* that looks just my cup of tea. I think I am going to like it here.

On every street and *passaggi*, there are posters advertising the JBR and every few minutes someone stops us and asks if we are from the ballet. It must be a very small town or else we must look like exotic birds in a zoo. Of course Tanita and Suzanna tower over everyone. In heels and with their hair pulled into chignons they are well over six feet. Tanita has bleached her hair dazzling white and Suzanna's is the colour of garnets. An awestruck street urchin staring up at them points to the stage door on an oddly named passage, *via Dell'Isola Delle Stinche*.

The old Teatro Verdi is rumored to have been built over the fourteenth century *Trecento* Prison and Mary is in Heaven at the thought of tunnels to the prisoner's cells right under the stage. I must admit the dear old Verdi is priceless. It even has a Royal box and six levels of *loges* and stalls, with gold plaster swirls, and silken velvet hangings. Standing on the empty stage looking out at eight hundred seats I can feel that show business buzz and can't wait for the first night. From the exterior, the theatre doesn't look imposing at all, just another black and sooty building in an ancient medieval street.

I can hear the others arriving through the stage door and turn to give the dressing room a once over. Upstairs there are private dressing rooms for the stars but they are unusable and smell of mould. There is only one loo for everyone but thank the Lord it is not a hole in the floor. Our costumes have arrived and Yvette is bustling about from room to room, fussing, folding, hanging and ironing them. Mary is prowling around trying to find a way into the dungeons. On stage I can hear Rodney starting to rehearse Nadine into the ballets. She has only one day to learn her part as tomorrow night is the opening. Immediately I set off to the wings to watch. Hey presto! It's just as I suspected! Nadine is flirting like the French bitch that she is, with pouty lips and fluttering eyelashes. She wants my roles and she wants my man.....not bloody likely. I went back to the dressing room, put on my leotard and a sweater to start my warm up before the main rehearsal. I am keeping my eye on that girl.

Opening night, Rudy and I stole the show with our *pas de deux* in *Les Fourrures*. The boxes, the *loges* and the auditorium were standing room only and we finished to thunderous applause. Rodney is elated. The long hours of rehearsals have paid off and our show is a hit. I still get that aching feeling all through my body being so close to Rudy and having to pretend that he is just a dance partner. During our bows he holds my hand and the electricity is excruciatingly exciting. He still fancies me.

The newspapers said it was the first really modern ballet to perform in Firenze. Success feels fabulous. Rodney and I are stopped in the street and people ask for autographs. After a few days we have a following of fans, who want to speak to us and are desperate to hang out with the ballet. I'm not quite sure why because off stage we are people like everybody else.

Mary

Florence is not just another Italian town. To walk along the streets is like being transported back in time. The whole city is a medieval museum where past and present live together. The narrow streets are filled with the sound of a swarm of wasps. They are *'vespas'*, small Italian motorscooters that don't go very fast but make a racket. Cobbled alleyways, *vicoli* are crowded with children playing and old men shouting and arguing politics. Archways lead into *piazzas* with medieval houses leaning against each other like gnarled old crones in a church pew. Ancient bridges crisscross the Arno River that curves and twists like an exotic dancer. I am inspired. I want to see it all; the towers and spires that dominate the skyline, the statues standing in public places so close you can touch them and everywhere you look there are churches: *Santa Croce, San Giovanni, Santa Maria Novello*, and my favourite of all, tiny *Santa Spirito*, a hop, skip and a jump from the Arno River.

Each one is more beautiful than the last. Sally and I walk about in wonder exploring the shops and the museums, the palaces and the bars. We want to buy things; leather purses, embroidery, and gold jewellery.

We can't afford to buy anything but there is no charge for drooling.

The Abduction of the Sabine Woman, by Flemish sculptor Jean Boulogne, known as Giambologna. He settled in Florence in 1553. The Medici family, fearing he might accept commissions outside their realm, forced him to remain in Florence for the rest of his life. The sculpture stands in an open air 'loggia' in the Piazza della Signoria, for everyone to see, but not to touch. NON TOCCARE!

Time is so precious that I have been dragging Sally out of bed before rehearsal for flying tours of the city. We have a map and are trying to visit every '*quartieri*', this is of course impossible. In the early morning the streets are usually quite deserted with very few Italian *signores* and never any young girls to be seen. The elderly women are found in the market dressed in mourning, in black skirts, sweaters, with scarves covering their heads. They carry baskets of vegetables, bread and cheese. If you say, really politely, '*Buongiorno signore,*' they glare at you and look the other way. Maybe our voices remind them of the war and bring back painful memories.

I've begun to notice that Rodney walks with his feet slightly turned out. On some men this might appear a little effeminate but on him it is the stance of a person ready to burst out dancing at the drop of a hat, which he does with regularity. One night after the show, Sally and I went with the others to '*Trattoria La Bussola*' just down the *via Porta Rossa* from our '*pensione.*' As well as a restaurant, *La Bussola* is sort of a clubhouse for musicians, nightclub artists of all types, painters, and eccentrics. They come late at night to eat *calzone* and *pizza,* washed down with strong *vino rosso.* The room buzzes as everyone discusses and argues about show business and the arts. Autographed photos of international artists cover the walls like wallpaper, including a great photo of the Jazz Ballet Rodney. We love it here.

At about 2 a.m. we left with arms linked like baby cygnets in Swan Lake, and danced down *via Porta Rossa* toward the '*Mercato Nuovo.*' We were a little tipsy and started to sing old English musical hall favourites to irritate the French girls. Rodney was prancing along with his characteristic walk and started fooling around with some dance steps. He often creates his choreography in the oddest places. By the time we reached the deserted '*loggia*' of the straw market he was doing his interpretation of Gene Kelly tap dancing around '*Il Porcellino*,' the wild boar, leaping on and off the fountain. We all cheered and clapped encouraging him to do double back flips and hand springs like he learned at the Budapest Circus School. Rudy joined in dancing a wild flamenco banging his heels like drums and charging the brass pig like a matador. Crash! Shutters flew opened from above. "*Basta, silenzio,*" yelled an infuriated voice.

Sally

This morning I awake in Rodney's room feeling a little dizzy but supremely happy. Rodney is sitting smugly at the foot of the bed, which is covered with lots of little parcels all wrapped in coloured tissue. "Happy Birthday my dahlink Sally Anna" and we kiss. I am twenty-four years old today but I feel about sixteen as I rip through all my parcels. He is grinning as I unwrap a box of lacy knickers, a silk scarf, and chocolate kisses, *'Baci'* from Perugia, a leather folder embossed in gold leaf with the Florentine coat of arms, a book of paintings from the Uffizi Gallery, a bottle of Capricci by Nina Ricci and the prettiest gold charm of my Zodiac sign Pisces the fish. Brilliant! I am going to have a perfect day. Happy Birthday to me! *'Tante Auguri.'*

Mary

It is seven in the morning in the *Pensione Tenti* and my head is like jelly. I am not really used to drinking so much wine in fact I am not used to drinking much at all. In college we drank horrible sweet loganberry wine that makes you ralph after a few glasses or homemade *saki* that was even worse.

I crawl out of bed and stumble over last night's discarded clothes. Yesterday was wash day and Sally and I have hung wet bras, panties, g-strings, stockings, garter belts and towels over the back of chairs, the shower rack, out on the balcony rail and on hangers dangling off the chandelier. All clothes are washed in two inches of tepid water in our bathtub. The ballet has a special rate in the *pensione,* which precludes maid service so no one sees this pigpen. My roommate is nowhere to be seen.

Five minutes later I teeter into the *piazza* in my sling back heels, with my hair in two ponytails, and order cappuccino while I wait for Sally. I hope she isn't late because we have only forty- five minutes to be tourists before class. Ahhh, here she comes sauntering serenely down the street looking like she has all day. "Hurry up!" People on the sidewalk stop and stare at her. Sally has that confident indescribable 'look' both offstage and on that everyone reacts to and I am sure that she is not even aware of it.

The ticket taker at the Uffizi Gallery is a cute young guy who recognizes us '*Buongiorno belle signore*' flirtatiously leaning close while he stamps our two free passes – we do not feel very '*belle*' after only four hours sleep. Two flights of stairs later we hurry through the first three chambers of Madonnas and some pious Saints in scarlet robes, past gilded masterworks by Fra Lipolippi, Fra Angelico and Giotto and do not stop until we reach the Botticelli Room and flop dramatically across the leather covered benches. Usually we are alone. Sally gazes at "Primavera" that enormous allegorical scene of the three innocent, dancing maidens in peek-a-boo diaphanous gowns, protected by the sword- wielding mythical god Mercury and I ponder "The Birth of Venus". Both are painted by Alessandro di Marinao di Vanni Filipepi, famously known as "Botticelli".

Venus has long reddish blonde hair, pale almost anemic white skin and is rising out of a giant clam shell her right hand to her heart and her left covering her snatch. According to the brochure she represents 'physical passion transcending to divine love,' whatever that means. Her lovely face reminds me of

Katie, my roommate at university. Suddenly home is very, very far away.

Our contract at the *Teatro Verdi* finishes at the end of the week and we will be unemployed. Rodney is leaving for Rome to find work. Realistically I should return to London for the summer and then go back to Canada. My parent's letters are filled with anxiety. "Come home and go back to school," father advises. "Find a proper career." But dance consumes me. At last I am truly a professional dancer and can to do whatever is required for any choreography. *'Pirouettes'* are no longer a matter of luck, balance is never a problem and my legs will go exactly where they are told. Now that I have reached this level, I can't just throw it all in and go home.

Sally

Darling Lezy:
Thanks a million for the birthday money and the belt you sent me. I shall wear it with my new 'blue jeans' (they are American trousers made of French denim cloth from Nîmes.) It couldn't have arrived at a better time. No contracts are lined up but please don't worry, Rodney has gone to Roma or Milano to see what he can do about it. Finally we have time to discover the 'real' Firenze, the city that tourists never see. Mary and I have eaten in fabulous unknown cheap restaurants or dives where only the Florentines go and hanging out like 'normal' girls and I am learning to speak fluently. I've met a group of boys who work in Florence and then in the evening spend their time picking up American girls, students from the villa on the hill who are getting finished off (ha ha). I am seeing a lot of a very talented artist named Paolo who is gorgeous. He

is engaged to a student from New York but he claims he doesn't really love her. Mind you he is a bit of a bastard and a liar like all of them but I just love him for himself. When it is time to go I will be leaving a part of my heart here. As the French say "partir, c'est mourir un peu" and I agree.
Love from your Sal xxx

On our last night in Firenze the temperature suddenly dropped. It was as if the city itself was unhappy that we are leaving. Mary and I wanted to prolong our departure for as long as possible and decided to stay up all night and oh what a night it was!

We started out on bar crawl at about 9 pm. with a rather buxom blonde named Cherry - a stage name for sure. She is an old friend of Rodney's and looks a bit like Diana Dors, the film star. I think she is the bees' knees. The three of us were all very sedate and sophisticated until someone introduced us to a liqueur called '*Strega*' which translates to witches brew or something like that. Well that set us off and we made the rounds of all the places we knew sipping the magic potion and saying goodbye to everyone we had met in the city. On our final stop, perched on tall stools in a chic, modern bar - who knows where – I looked around and Mary was gone. She had quietly toppled over into a heap on the floor, wild red hair all over the place, long legs tangled like Pippi Longstockings and killing herself laughing. '*Basta*' No more *strega* for her.

Just as dawn was breaking, it started to rain. Cherry had disappeared somewhere along the way and we took cover in the flower market where I knew we would find Paolo and his friends. Sure enough he was there and I hugged him and said '*Arriverderci*' knowing full well I would never see any of them again. Ignoring the drizzle, we both staggered back to the

Pensione Tenti for the last time feeling very nostalgic. We got into the lift and rattled up to the fourth floor. As doors opened like the parting of stage curtains, Mary swayed backward and forward, fell flat on her face in the corridor right in front of the astonished night clerk who couldn't believe his eyes. It was brilliant.   I laughed until I cried.

Two hours later we awoke, to a pounding on the door, honking horns and shouting from down below in *via Porta Rossa*. I put the pillow over my head and said 'bugger off' until I realized it was Rodney. I thought he was in Rome. "Please, Dahlinks we are waiting for you two. The bus is holding up all the traffic." Pandemonium, I had completely forgotten that we are leaving this morning and nothing is packed. "Mary" I holler "Get up!" I ripped open my suitcase and snatched clothes off the backs of chairs and she staggered out of bed and started flinging everything willy-nilly into her holdall. Kitchen is scattered all over the room; the hotplate, knives and forks, pots, plates, what a mess. I rushed into our bathroom and pile everything into a bag to sort out later. There is more banging on the door and a pleading voice, "Dahlinks please Hurry Up," more honking in the street, everyone is yelling. "Quick empty the cupboard" Mary shrieked. She is hauling up her drawers, pulling stuff out from under the beds and tossing books and maps into a giant handbag. We fling open the door and shove our stuff into the hall. A chain gang from Rodney, to Remo, to Rudy pass our belongings down to the 4th floor lift. "I forgot Teddy," Mary moaned, holding her head, dashing back into the room. "All clear" she calls disappears down the stairs without a backward glance. I follow clattering down in my high heels, dying for an *espresso*.

Outside the owner of the *pensione*, Maria Tenti gives me a motherly hug and nudges me onto the bus.

The driver is waving his arms in the air and shouting at everyone who cares to listen *"porco miserio"* my life is as miserable as a pig's - something like that. I agree with him. We leave Firenze in a cacophony of horns and utter chaos.

Mary

Have you ever had the feeling that you may never, ever have such fun again in all your life? The most historic, romantic, fantastic medieval city in the world is receding into the dust behind us. I have tears in my eyes, not because I am heartbroken but I think I might have broken my nose last night. I haven't had any coffee, have a *"strega"* hangover and to top it all off, bleeding gums. Stupidly I wrote to mother about the state of my mouth, and she writes that I have trench mouth from 'kissing too many boys' and "such behavior should stop immediately!" From now on, all letters must be censored! Marcello Mastroianni will not give me a second glance if I smile like Count Dracula. Perhaps it is the lack of fruit and scurvy has set in. Certainly we never see so much as an apple at this time of year and eat mostly bread and pasta, *'cucina povera'* food of the poor.

I have just discovered that we are not heading directly for Rome but doing ten days of 'one-nighters,' taking in La Spézia, Viareggio, Grosseto, Lucca and other coastal towns along the Tyrrhenian Sea before turning south to Rome.

The last 'one-nighter' we did, several weeks ago, in Rimini was a disaster. The contract was for three performances and we travelled eastward from Firenze in a bus even worse than the one I am in now, winding around steep hills and roller-coastering into valleys with every window rattling and suitcases, boxes and belongings slamming about. Only Mireille and

Shirley, curled up like kittens, slept through the madness. Tanita was trying to paint her long finger nails a shocking pink and kept swearing in Dutch every time the bus veered around the corner at breakneck speed. Like a racehorse, the driver had the bit between his teeth and was determined to set a new record, hollering out the window at anyone who tried to get in his way, careening around *piazzas* in tiny villages sending chickens and children into doorways. Old men in caps shook their fists and grannies genuflected. It seemed like forever but finally we exploded into Rimini by the sea, and were dumped at the stage door of a fine old opera house.

There was no time to explore or even try to find a cup of cappuccino so we all unloaded the costumes from the skips or *panniers* that arrived by truck and set up the stage, found our dressing room and got ready for the first performance.

I was just starting my makeup, fortunately wearing a cotton smock, when the door burst open and the room filled with the *polizia italiana*, beaming and winking and having a good look. Those who were half naked scurried for cover, except Mireille who giggled like a coquette and placed fingertips over her nipples. Sally indignantly pushed the cops out, berating them marvellously in Italian for not knocking. I was so proud of her and wished my Italian were more fluent.

Apparently, our agent had not signed the proper work permits for the stage hands, nor paid the orchestra their 'up front' money, in other words the' bribe' and, instantly the show was cancelled. In all the places we perform, a full orchestra must be paid even though most of the time the musicians are not capable of playing our music, in fact, they cannot even read music. Our entire show is on a reel-to-reel audiotape recording. Usually the orchestra can play the finale and 'The Charleston" by James Johnson. Otherwise they just sit like lumps and collect their paycheque.

Backstage in the girls' dressing room in the 'teatro' in Rimini just before the police raid that closed the show. (Feb.1964)

Lordy, Lordy, it's back on the bus. I can't believe it but the crazy driver looks drunk. Rudy glared at him and said "take it easy on the way back" or words to that effect. The driver slurred *Non preoccupatevi amici.*" (Don't worry) so we didn't, we prayed and passed a bottle of brandy around like a 'communion cup.' Hail, Mary, full of Grace, please get us back to Firenze in one piece. The return trip was beyond description. Almost everyone threw up and the ones that didn't had raging headaches from the exhaust. We staggered out, once again, on the *Via Porta Rossa*. By some incredible good fortune some of our rooms at the *Pensione Tenti* were still available and we moved back in, four or five to a room and passed out in a heap. Yvette refuses to share a room with anyone.

Sally

Our ten-day tour of Italy's west coast along the Tyrrhenian Sea began in the opera house in Pisa, another *Teatro Verdi* only this one on *Via Palestro*. It was every bit as elaborate as the one in Firenze with burgundy velvet curtains fringed in gold and a stage the size of a ballroom. The *'Pisani'* loved our show especially 'Asphalt' probably because the music is so dramatic. We dance to the overture of West Side Story. Our coach arrived in the historic center too late for us to be tourists for even a moment. Early the next morning, we dragged ourselves back onto the rattling wreck and headed north. The twelfth century leaning tower of Pisa was a sixty-second glimpse out of the window.

Only a few kilometres out of town our bus splutters to a stop. Our driver seems quite unconcerned. Lifting himself out of his seat he lumbers down the steps, lighting a cigarette and stands in the middle of the road, scratching his head waiting for help to miraculously appear. Rudy, Ronáld and Xavier leap out and with a flourish throw open the bonnet and start clowning around like the Marx brothers, pulling cables, kicking the tires and prodding the innards. They don't know a thing about the mechanics of the combustion engine. We are all rolling around in our seats in hysterics. Yvette does not find this funny and sits with a face like a bulldog. It's going to be a long day.

Hours later the repaired coach limps into town and belches to a stop in front of the opera house, *Teatro La Spézia* in the *Piazza Mentana*. Like robots we unpack the costumes and begin the rehearsal. The stage is much smaller and many changes are made to new entrances and exits. Will we remember? Just before curtain time Rodney announced that he is off to Rome to try and find more work. I am crushed because Rodney and I had planned to see La Spézia together.

Teatro La Spézia built in 1846 is squeezed between more modern buildings, one of the survivors of the Allied bombings of 1945. The town of La Spézia is famous for its harbour, a natural fortification and refuge in the north Mediterranean Sea. Between 1945-49 ships of mercy carried 23,000 Jewish refugees from La Spézia harbour to Palestine.

Sometimes I feel like the White Rabbit in Wonderland, running around singing 'No time to say hello, goodbye, we're late we're late, we're late.' On goes the makeup; up goes the hair, pull on clean tights, and boots. The orchestra is tuning up, the tension builds, show time once again.

The rest of the week flashes by, winding roads, glimpses of the sea peeping through scrubby pine trees, little fishing villages, heavy velvet curtains, smells of sweat, dust, basil, salty air and stages stops for the loo, stops for coffee and petrol until all meld into one glorious blur of another day, another show, another town: Viareggio, Lucca, Livorno Piombino and finally Grosseto a town whose roots go back over two thousand years to the mysterious Etruscans. Our chariot dumps us onto *Via Mazzini* in front of the *Teatro degli Industri,* then Mary and I bolt.

Mary

It is so quiet inside the museum. No one is screaming and swearing. What a relief. Sally and I had escaped from the others into the *Museo Archeologico Della Maremma* and are lost in our own thoughts as we wander from room to room looking at the treasures of a lost civilization; funeral urns, gold and other metal jewellery and dozens of coffins.

Why did the Etruscan race disappear when they were stronger and more advanced than the Romans? The Etruscans developed an alphabet, decked themselves out in brooches and bracelets and created walled townships. Then, *poof*, they just disappeared and all that is left are *sarcophagi*, toys for their dead children and odd rock formations up in the hills. It is very mysterious. "Time to go" Sally touched my arm and reluctantly we retraced our steps to the stage door. We have two shows to do, a seven o'clock and a nine o'clock, both to sold-out houses before we continue south. All roads lead to Rome.

Chapter Four
The Eternal City of Rome

...and she stays for 'la dolce vita.' " I think she looks better with her clothes on...

WORLD NEWS
1964 Vatican City: The Vatican condemns the female contraceptive pill.

Darling Lez: I can hardly believe it! I am sitting in a bar at the film studios just outside Rome called Cinecitta. Rodney has found a marvelous, really well-paid job for some of us in a film called called Sappho Venus of the Lesbos and it is directed by Pietro Francisci who is world famous at least here in Italy. The stars are Tina Louise, Kevin Mathews and Elke Sommer. If you could have seen me yesterday you wouldn't recognize your Sal! She had the whole 'do' – Fantastic make-up, hair pulled in Grecian style swirls wound with jewels and face and body painted dark brown. My costume is a lovely pale blue, drapy thing with matching knickers. When Rodney came in and saw me he nearly collapsed. Yesterday we worked from 8 o'clock in the morning until one o'clock the next morning. Must get back on set! Love - your film star daughter, Sally xxxx

Being in the films is not as glamorous as you might imagine. Rodney is loving it though, because, for once in his life, he is making masses of dosh. In elegant new clothes, he swans around Rome and dines

in some of the poshest places. He has developed such a taste for 'the *Dolce Vita'* that he has got Liliane and me a second job in some third-rate flick where we seductively dance around a phony swimming pool set. For this he is going to earn a fortune. So I am working all night on 'Lesbos' flitting around in a gauzy drape and all day in a swimsuit under hot lamps. There is no time to rest.

From time to time Rodney appears with some sandwiches and little white wake-up pills. One morning, Mother Nature took over, my eyes got heavier and slowly I drifted off to sleep right there on the set draped across the chaise longue like the Sleeping Beauty. Clearly the pills didn't work.   I was woken by a roar of rage from the Director and he yelled, *"Siete Licenziati"* you're ALL fired. Sod it. There ends my hopes of a career in Hollywood and Rodney's moment of financial euphoria.

Saffo Venus of Lesbos was released in the U.S. as the Warrior Empress and one of a series of Italian films called "peplum" or sword and sandal adventures. Some of the Jazz Ballet Rodney dancers including Sally appear in several scenes.

The main dance sequence was cut in the American edition as being too risqué for the 1960's. It is now a cult film with an enormous following worldwide.

We must have the most amazing luck or else Rodney knows just the right person to telephone because only one day after we got fired, he has come up with a contract for a week in a cabaret. The money is a joke so it must be a bit of a dump. The entire ballet will be dancing two shows a night for a pittance. It could be worse. At least we have a job.

Mary

It appears that Sally and I are roommates in a brothel. I thought the *pensione* was a little odd when we arrived. Our room is at the end of a corridor that lists to one side like a sinking ship. The room is clean but reeks of smoky, antiseptic soap. The most bizarre paper, orange and red roses climbing up a trellis, adorns the wall. From upstairs water pipes come right through the ceiling down to the floor and gurgle and gush every few minutes. There is a sagging double bed and a sort of single day bed with a missing leg. Guess who got the latter? Tall shuttered windows look onto lines of laundry stretching across the alley to the buildings opposite and in the corner there's a tiny washbasin, a water jug, and a large plaster crucifix hanging over a nasty-looking tin bidet. Through a small door into the guesthouse next door, is a communal bathroom, a very peculiar set up.

Roma 1964. Our room with a view.

"This is what one thousand lira gets you?" Sally is not impressed. We are earning six thousand lira per performance, so we really cannot stay in a fancy hotel. Our concierge is a hoot, an ex-dancer or so he claims. He knows everyone in Italian show business from Sophia Loren to Claudia Cardinale and has plastered the walls with autographed photos. With '*grand jétés*' and '*pas de bourées,* he cavorts down the halls, draped in a long silk scarf like Isadora Duncan. When the telephone rings he answers with such an exaggerated lisp, garbling in Italian, Spanish, German and English that we dissolve into fits. Rudy did a perfect imitation of him on stage last night just before the curtain went up and we howled with laughter until Rodney came scurrying back to tell us to 'keep it down' the audience could hear us .

We are performing for a week in a sort of supper club, cabaret but with a full stage, proscenium arch and curtains. I feel quite out of place here but at least we are working. It is hard to keep focused with the distraction of people drinking themselves silly but I am trying to ignore the whole scene. Like most dancers, I would perform in the middle of the street for nothing, rather than not dance at all because once the music starts the surroundings don't really matter that much.

My mother however, would drop dead of a heart attack if she knew her daughter slept in a brothel and worked in a nightclub. Tomorrow I will send her a postcard of the Pope and tell her not to worry about me.

Pope Paul VI 1963-1978. The Vatican condemns the female contraceptive pill in 1964.

And worry she might, if she knew about '*La Salle.*' Doing '*La Salle*' is not a type of dance like the Frug or the Twist but a sneaky little obligation written in small print in an artist's contract that means all entertainers, especially the females must mix with the audience after the show and accept 'drinks' to pad bar bills. The boss of the Roma nightclub decided that if we wanted to be paid our wages, we would be obliged to do '*La Salle.*' There was a lot of arguing after the Finale on opening night. I'm sure the audience could not fail to hear the shouting match but one cryptic telephone call from Rodney to his unknown 'friend,' simply referred to as Sciavoni and the whole matter was dropped.

Sally

I don't know if it is my imagination but it seems that the further south we go in Italy, the more our bottoms are pinched and blimey it hurts. These are not little tweeks of the cheeks but fingers trying to hurt. Some little urchins sneak up behind you squeeze and run off like rats. Others, egged on by friends surround and pinch hard waiting for an outraged reaction and then laugh. Mary has an enormous handbag with metal studs on it that she uses like a club and whacks the little buggers around the ears screaming '*va via cretino!*' in foul Italian.

Remo has been appointed to be our tour guide and protector in Rome. I'm not sure he is entirely pleased with this role as he would rather be alone with Mary. But I am her unofficial chaperone as she is completely naïve to the obvious. During the day Remo, Mary and I tour the sites: the *Trevi* Fountain, Spanish Steps, Pantheon, and visit the *Piazza Navonna* without being molested. And Remo is in his element. He struts along like a film star with two ballerinas, one on each arm. Life is a bit of a fantasy for all of us.

At night after the show everyone goes dancing or else to late dinner in the *ristorante* at the train station. It stays open all night. The station restaurant is the haunt of all the musicians and artists because it serves the best and cheapest *spaghetti carbonara* in all Italy. Even ex King Farouk of Egypt goes there after hours to mingle with showgirls or maybe just to eat his fill.

King Farouk of Egypt was forced to abdicate the throne in 1952. For the next thirteen years he lived an extraordinary life, loafing in luxury, throwing money around, drinking and eating with a harem of mistresses. On March 7, 1965, at the age of forty-five, the once all powerful King of Egypt ate himself to death in a Roman restaurant, the 'Ile de France' on the Aurelian Way near the Vatican city. There was talk of poisoned lobster but it was never proved. He was forty-five years old.

One night at the station some very sweet guys joined our table and two of them, brothers I think, invited the whole ballet to a party up in the hills just outside Rome. Nadine, Mary and I thought that was a grand idea and we left the others in the '*trattoria*,' squeezed into the back seat of a new red *Alfa Romeo Giulietta* and roared off. We wound up the twisting hairpin bends, past really big mansions encircled with walled gardens. After being cooped up in our shambles of a hotel, buses and backstage dressing room we felt exhilarated, like caged birds being set free if only for a moment. The Alfa swung into a park through wrought iron gates and down a long winding driveway before screeching to a halt in front of a darkened but enchanting villa. It looks like a film set.

We giggle and whisper together wondering if we are appropriately dressed. Under my A-line yellow mac, I have on my black wrap around skirt and a new pink blouse given to me by Rodney, Nadine and Mary have pencil skirts on and sling back heels so we decide we look very with it. Roberto and Enzo, link arms with us and the five of us make our grand entrance. I don't know what I expected but it certainly was not the scene before me. The room, sort of a library or concert hall is sumptuous, quite *'magnifique.'* There are dozens of candles lighting every corner. At one end are floor to ceiling windows opening onto a terrace of stone. A piano sits in the corner and a man in a white suit is playing songs by Noel Coward. The people, maybe two dozen, look like models, quite perfect, silhouetted in the flickering candlelight. A most beautiful man sidles up with a tray of sparkling white wine. Mary whispers "Wow! This is straight out of a Somerset Maugham novel. I hope we are not murdered."

The other guests are languid and sophisticated, tittering at nothing and glancing over at us. I wonder why the three of us have been invited to join this very private group of friends. We are offered long, slender cigarettes that smell a little odd. We prefer our own. Roberto is chatting to Mary and I in English as Nadine disappears into the group chirping away in *Frenchified* Italian.

We have more drinks, probably too many, people are lounging, others dancing, everyone very dreamy. I am feeling very tired as we have been doing two shows a night and racing around Rome all day and

I think I must have nodded off for a second. Now people are kissing and fondling each other. I am feeling lousy and suspect Mary is tipsy because she is flitting around the room in her own little world singing along to the music.

Suddenly I am uneasy. There is something very odd happening. People are slowly taking their clothes off. At first it looks funny and then I see Nadine is topless and unzipping her skirt. "Blimey, I must rescue Mary before she makes an ass of herself. "We've got to get out of here. NOW! Let's find our coats." Roberto appears alone. "Come, I drive you back to Roma, O.K." I guess he could see that Mary and I are not hip enough for a Roman orgy. Nadine? She stays for '*la dolce vita*.' Mary sniffed, "personally, I think she looks better with her clothes on."

Mary

I don't know what we did last night; I am not at all well. The disgusting roses are whizzing around the room, I can't remember where the bathroom is and I am about to explode. Oh God yes, it is through the Alice door to the nut house in the next building. I make a dash for it. Sally is groaning "I am never going to smoke again." Being part of the JBR has its drawbacks but also can be very comforting. There is no privacy but everyone rallies around in a crisis. Yvette of course does not rally very well.

Rodney was very sympathetic as I staggered through the morning rehearsal. Ronáld made me drink several pots of herbal tea. Pills and potions arrived to stop the trots, to no avail. Even Elizabeth fussed over me offering useless bits of advice and medical quackery although to tell you the truth she looks sicker than I do, very pale and weak as a kitten. When I asked if she should see a doctor she panicked and said, no, no I shall be fine. We will all be on stage even if we have to crawl and the boss man will get his full quota of dancers in his horrid nightclub.

Most theatrical companies have understudies but not the JBR. The last place I danced in Canada was at the Theatre Under the Stars in Vancouver. I was the unsuitable understudy for all three of the strippers in the musical Gypsy. The strippers were: Electrified Electra, Tessie Tura So Demura, and Bump It With A Trumpet. Luckily for the audience, the strippers never got sick.

The final disaster was the last night of our contract. Still feeling fragile, I saw a 'peeping Tom' trying to peer through the window in the stage door. I flushed hot with rage and flew at him like the Wicked Witch of the West, pushing him aside then flounced through the door and slammed it shut. There was a horrifying crash. The frosted glass panel with beveled edges and etched with the words *l'entrata di artisti* smashed into a zillion pieces. Oh no, there goes my pay cheque for the next three months.

A verbal agreement was made between Rodney and me that I will receive half wages until the repair bill is paid. The equivalent of five dollars per day will have to cover food, cigarettes and hotel. I don't think I am going to be living in luxury for quite some time.

As the bus was pulling out of town after our last show Elizabeth turned around and asked, "did you see who was in the audience?" No I queried. "Your hero Marcello Mastroianni in person. He was sitting in the front row with Sophia Loren. Pity you missed them." I could have killed her.

Marcello Mastroianni in 'La Dolce Vita,' an award winning film produced in 1960. Translated as the Sweet Life, it is widely considered to be one of the greatest achievements in world cinema. The film won the Palme d'Or at the Cannes Film Festival that year and made Marcello Mastroianni one of the most popular actors in film. When he died in 1996, the Trevi Fountain was draped in black as a tribute to the love scene in La Dolce Vita that made him famous.

Sally

The frantic pace picked up again once we left Rome on our next marathon of one-night stands. In the weeks that followed our journey became like a kaleidoscope; the villages, audiences, theatres, coffee bars and dressing rooms an exhausting blur. Can we keep up this grueling pace? No one complains we just keep on going. Notices have been over the top from Napoli, Sorrento, Al Berobello, Taranto, Foggia, Pescara, to Téramo. In Bielle, the manager of the theatre said, he had never seen a ballet work so hard and have such an attentive audience. Of course there are very few television sets in homes in this part of Italy. That is a luxury that few can afford and so travelling shows are the only entertainment. In every tiny town, and village, we are welcomed with throngs of excited little girls and boys and teenagers, longing to be dancers, waiting for autographs. There are posters on every street, and always a restaurant is held open for us to eat after the final show, no matter how late. Cooks and artists have a lot in common especially the hours they work.

Mary and I buy postcards at every stop because there is no time to see anything except the inside of a theatre. We spend our days packing and unpacking the skips of costumes and props, climbing in and out of the coach, writing postcards home and dancing. Perugia, Cortona, Arezzo, east to Pésaro Bologna, Modena and finally in Verona we stop. Ahhh, our contract ends in the city of love, the city of Romeo and Juliette. It is end of the tour before we open again in Milano in forty-eight hours. We are long overdue for a fiesta. Rodney has found us a 'ristorante,' quite cheap, that looks warm and inviting and arranged with the chef to include us in a family gathering. The chef is making his specialty 'pastissarda de caval' with lots of Hungarian paprika. Horsemeat stew is a favourite of Rodney's. "We ride our horses in Canada not eat them," Mary huffed. Not for me! I have a double portion of the ravioli in browned butter and pass on the 'caval.' Our host proudly comes out of the kitchen bearing a platter of spicy pork sausages called 'tastasal' for us to sample. They are super. We toast him with Valpolicella. "Tchin, Tchin."

Rudy

Ja Ja Ja! There is some SHIT about my visa being in '*over stay*', whatever that is and somehow, someone knew about this. I was told YOU stop dancing now! Immediately and leave the country. Impossible! There are a lotsa of dance troupes here that are very jealous - oh yes! - of JBR's success and would do anything to stop us. Rodney, he has a big network of friends that he rings up and Ja, I am allowed to finish this contract and then rush, rush, rush to a small Swiss town on the Italian border and get renewed. After the last show in Verona, we had a '*groot feest*' as only the ballet can do....lotsa of food, drink, song and dance and I poured myself onto last train heading for the border.

After BEEG snooze in the corridor of the train we are at Italian border where I hide in men's toilet. The inspector passed but did not open the door. So I *grand jete* off at little village early, NOTHING is open. At a small house I see a sign hello, here is Italian Consulate. The door opened and a man in slippers greets me " come in" Surprise! It was 'Il Signore Consul' himself who knows me. How? I dunno. Had he received a telephone message?

86

Nice café and croissants and other stuff and soon I have a stamp in my passport AND NEW VISA. Back to the station I dashed in time ....just in time..I catch the morning express - head south for Milano.....but will I be 2 late.... to open show?

Mary

My last sight of Rudy was hanging out the rail carriage with a foot in the air while we shouted *"Romeo, Romeo wherefore goest thou Romeo"* before finding our way back to the bus for the final drive overnight to Milan and to bed for a few hours.

The JBR is ready and waiting. Our rehearsal this afternoon was interrupted by many telephone calls to Rodney from agents in Italy, Switzerland and Germany, sorting out contracts for the next few weeks or months. We are back at the *Teatro Smeraldo.* the curtain is about to go up and RUDY IS NOT HERE. We can handle the prologue with a few changes but '*Les Fourrures*' without the leading man? Our music is already spliced on the reel to reel and there can be no changes at this last moment. We are all unbearably tense. His costume is laid out like a corpse, Remo is at the stage door ready to pay the taxi driver and push Rudy into the dressing room. Ronald will guide him to the stage. We are in position, warmed up ready to go. The orchestra is in the pit.

Always before I perform I start to yawn and yawn and get a squeezing in my chest. I feel like a racehorse ready to crash through the gate. Curtain opens, a rustle in the audience, the drum roll and we are off....

Rudy

I leapt off the train onto the platform before it came to a stop and fly into nearest taxi, slam door CRASH!! Hey driver .... Address of *Teatro Smeraldo*. Casually he looked at it and did nothing at all ...relaxed as a German on a beach in Bali... "You know *Piazza XXV Aprile*?" I ask calmly, "Hey, Imaa Milanese, I know everything, the best ways too, Hey, you got that, Milanese, allright? "Yes, yes, I pleaded but I am in a hurry." "Hey, no good this hurry, hurry all the time, must relax in Italia" "Fuuuuck!!! I looove Italy, man, but I am artista and I am on stage NOW. Jazz Ballet Rodney, *Teatro Smeraldo*, opening night blablabla. He gazed at me through the rear view mirror and his face lit up. "I see show *que bene que cosa*" and he started the cab and said something, who knows what, and we shot into the street like an enraged bull.

I had multiple heart attacks as we tear down one-direction streets, traffic lights, no way and we fly through Milano.....as we screeched to a halt his face had huge smile, "you see, you BELIEVE, si, si, *I'mma Milanese*, I know all streets."

Remo is at the stage door and threw some money at the happy driver, I undressed on the fly, hear our MUSIC no no no wait...YANK on pants, shirt, jacket, shoes...Someone grab me and shove me to stairs towards stage... Where is the public?.   Where's the public I shouted. Damn it. "On the right" Deep deep breath, calm calm and 5, 6, 7 and 8 - big smile. Yes indeed, the public was on my right side. Ya. Ja. The public is on my right side. Hooray, what excitement!

Sally

Rudy leaped on stage like a gazelle, no makeup but costume on and grinning like a monkey. As soon as his face was turned toward us but back to the audience, he chirped "I'm legal" and we all sighed with relief.

For about one week all went well. The shows were sold out and the press was lavish with praise for the 'avant-garde' edginess to our dance style that is both sophisticated but fun at the same time. Newspapers write that we are the top touring dance troupe in Italy and we are justifiably proud. We have worked night and day to get where we are. However such praise has provoked other companies. Last Wednesday someone was hired to steal our costumes from the Smeraldo. Just as we were leaving for the night, the stage door burst open and two guys rushed into the first dressing room and started scooping up armloads of costumes off the racks.

Yvette saw them first and went beserk shrieking like a mad woman seeing all of her darling costumes disappearing. The next moment there was a battle led by Yvette, Liliane, Nicole, Nadine and even timid Shirley. They started bashing and kicking the thieves, tonking them over the head with their high heels and anything else within reach. It was a good ol' punch up, a right old barny. Without our costumes, there is no illusion, no fantasy, there is no show.

When everything had settled down, Rodney hired one of the older stagehands a big, broad chap with a scar on his chin to be 'guard of the wardrobe' for the rest of our contract. Yvette is still suspicious.

Mary

Mother wrote that perhaps it would be a good idea if I were to enroll in finishing school in Florence to improve myself before coming home. She also delighted in telling me of all my friends who were now married and having babies, implying that I am now officially 'on the shelf' in other words, a spinster at twenty-two. I sent a postcard of Leonardo da Vinci's 'Last Supper' and wrote "Dear Mom and Pop: How calm it is to be back in Milan. Everything is going so smoothly. Thank you for my Easter present. I will buy chocolate *'Baci'* that means kisses in Italian and think of you. Love Mary. P.S. I think perhaps I am already 'finished' whatever that means."

She would have an absolute hissy fit if she knew that we slept on the smelly old bus between performances on the last tour, or that Sally and I and sometimes Elizabeth, cooked our suppers of eggs and toast on a hotplate on the floor of the dressing rooms. Every few days we would meet an understanding hotel manager, who would rent us a room with bath for the day and eight or nine of us would take turns, bathing, washing our hair and underwear. The soggy washing would then be hauled backstage and hung on any hook or rope that was handy to dry before we moved on. The audience imagines that our lives are so deliciously elegant. If only they took a peek beyond the velvet curtains and smelled the unforgettable combination of laundry soap, fried eggs, Chanel Number Five, mould, dirty feet and latrines their fantasy would be shattered. I am having the best time of my life.

Teatro Rossini in Pesaro was built in 1818. Only two years after the JBR performed there the theatre was condemned and closed for 14 years before it was renovated and reopened to the public. It has been the site of a theatre since 1637. Today it is home to the annual Rossini Opera Festival held each August.

Chapter Five
'La Belle Vie' in Montreux

...The noise was deafening when the Rolling Stones burst through the door of the casino with an unruly mob of fans...

WORLD NEWS

**April 1964 U.S. President Johnson –
Approves the bombing of North Vietnam.**

Sally

Switzerland is such a contrast to Italy. Montreux after Milano looks as picturesque as a postcard and our hotel is a palace. We arrived by train and hung out the windows gazing at the snowcapped mountains surrounding this beautiful lakeside town. We are all as excited as children because this is probably our best contract ever, dancing at the Casino for the world famous Festival of the Rose d'Or.

Darling Lez: Rodney and I are over the moon that you are coming for a visit to Montreux. The Rose d'Or is a bit like the Cannes Film Festival but for television shows. April 24th is the big day and we will be live on EUROVISION, all over the world. I have sent an open ticket to you from London to Geneva return. Montreux is about an hour from there. Lez, you should bring a nice dress for the evening, perhaps the one you wore to The Establishment. I am going to be on stage with Sacha Distel. You know him Lez, he is quite sexy and sings "La Belle Vie as his signature 'hit'. Mireille is faint with excitement. Must close now and Happy Easter to all of you. Love to Judy & Richard Kisses. Sal xxxx

Mary

The famous old Casino on the shore of Lake Geneva is absolutely gigantic. Endless ballrooms, music salons, nightclubs and gaming tables sparkle in all directions. In 1881 it was built as a glamourous health spa for the filthy rich and deathly ill of Europe to rest and recover from excesses. Today the whole lake front salon has been converted to a Ye Ye Club named after the Beatles new song, "She Loves me ye ye ye." Not exactly restful if you ask me.

The Rolling Stones seen at their first performance outside of Britian in Montreux, Switzerland. April 1964 filming 'Ready Steady Go. for British television. The JBR were the resident ballet in the Casino Montreux and filming for EUROVISION the Festival of the Rose d'Or.

Television crews are everywhere setting up cables and cameras for an English pop show 'Ready, Steady, Go' that I have never heard of. Everyone is in an absolute tizzy and there are lots of Swiss police milling about because on the program is a new rock group called the Rolling Stones – never heard of them either. So it is mayhem both here and at our usually calm and elegant hotel, the Grand Hotel Excelsior. Tanita, Susannah and I have landed in the lap of luxury in an immaculate room leading right on to a stone terrace that stretches the whole length of the hotel. It overlooks acres of tulips, daffodils and pansies with the lake beyond. We have been given an artist's rate or we would never be staying here.

Sally

Rodney and I are together again. He is a very sloppy roommate and I seem to be continually picking up clothes, newspapers, letters and mess off the floor, the bed and the dresser. This morning I was on my hands and knees reaching under the bed for Rodney's socks when there was a tap on the hotel room door. Someone with a cheery voice and a Dutch lisp opened the door and called "Hullo! Is anyone here?" I scrambled to my feet, banging my head hard on the bedside table. "Oh sod it," I muttered wincing in pain and squinted up to get my first look at Rodney's son from Amsterdam. I looked a fright, no makeup, my hair all over the place and in my dressing gown. "Hi Mom," he smirked, "Very amusing," I sniffed as haughtily as I could. He gave me a wink. Rodney Junior is the image of his father but exactly my age.

He has made the journey from Amsterdam to introduce Francis who is standing behind him just inside the door. His wife Francis is stunningly beautiful with a face like Claudia Cardinale. On the short walk through the gardens to the casino people stop and stare at her. They nudge each other and are convinced she must be a famous film star or model. She remains aloof and seems unaware of the effect she has on strangers.

Rodney is relaxing in the main ballroom of the Casino when we arrive. He seems surprised see his son, and like everyone else, gob smacked by his wife. Rehearsals start in earnest with everyone focused. Over and over again we dance the same three minutes of The Afro-Cuban that will be filmed. Rodney is pacing back and forth muttering in Dutch as tense as a cat stalking a sparrow. This contract is huge for him and success here could change his fortunes. In the audience will be impresarios from all over Europe seeking an exciting new company. Last year the ballet appearing in Montreux was Roland Petit with the famous Zizi Jeanmaire directly from Paris. We just have to be as good or better!

I must confess that I am rather put out that Rodney is making such a fuss about Francis. He has insisted that she make an appearance in *La Fourrures* and given her a 'walk-on' as the mannequin in the shop window. That is my ballet and I am feeling more than a little peeved. Here I am soaked with sweat, looking like a hag and Francis is floating around fresh and dewy as a rose petal. In the front row watching the rehearsal intently is the famous Sacha Distel. He has eyes for only one person, Rodney Jr.'s wife. Hah! Meanwhile Rodney Jr., a professional drummer is oblivious to all. He's more interested in joining the orchestra for the filming of the Afro Cuban and practicing in a frenzy in a corner. Our tapes, at top volume are shaking the chandeliers. The ballroom is in chaos, a typical rehearsal.

♫♫ Ô la belle vie, sans amour, sans soucis, sans problème ♫♫
♫♫ It's a good life, without love, without stress or problems ♫♫

Underneath the glass stage are the dressing rooms. What a difference from the Roman nightclub. Here our dressing rooms are spotless and they even have sinks with hot water. Such luxury!

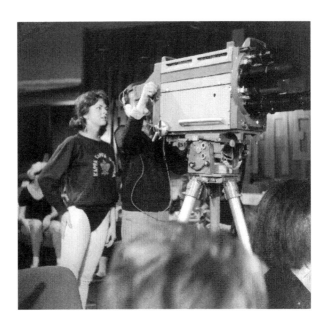

Montreux 1964 Mary during JBR rehearsals for Eurovision filming.

Mary

Tonight is the night and I am dizzy with excitement. We are filming live across Europe. I spit on the black cake of mascara to moisten it, swipe the brush across and with shaking fingers paint on my cat's eyes from the corner of the eyelid almost to my hairline. There is a knock on the dressing room door and a giant bundle of red roses is thrust in. The whole room is fragrant with a glorious scent for just a moment. Mireille with a grin pounces like a tiger onto the small white card tucked within the blooms and reads *"Ma chérie Francis"* signed Sacha. The smile vanishes. Francis is hardly the star in fact she is not even a part of the JBR but, for some unknown reason, is going to appear for a few seconds on stage. There is a pregnant pause and Sally whispers in a low voice "My new daughter-in-law is living *la belle vie*" and we stifled giggles and then laugh uncontrollably until tears run down our cheeks wrecking our careful makeup. Now, we're ready to dance circles around the famous Roland Petit and Zizi Jeanmaire.

JBR performance of 'Afro Cuban' filmed live for the opening of the Festival of the Rose d'Or, April 1964 in the Casino Montreux.

Sally

As soon as the performance was over, I changed into a black cocktail dress for the presentation of awards for the best television productions of the year. Sacha is the master of ceremonies and I was chosen to present the first prize. In the cramped corridor waiting to go on, I am pressed against Sacha with only a rose between us. As the orchestra played a medley of his songs and seconds before his entrance, he is flirting with me. Wow, I am having a good time.

Mary is hurt that she was not chosen to present the silver or any rose at all. She hasn't said anything but I know because she made bitchy remarks about Yvette's dress, "She looks like she is wearing a curtain with a dead cat sewn around the hem."

Sacha Distel, the M.C. at the Festival of the Rose d'Or in 1964. The awards are presented each year for excellence in television production each year and filmed live on Eurovision. Sally is on the right and the 'dead cat' dress is centre stage.

Mary

I spent the next few days sulking. For the life of me I cannot understand why I was not chosen to present one of the damned roses. Sally of course I understand but Elizabeth, Shirley and Yvette presenting the other prizes? Why, why, why? I am a better dancer than the three of them and I thought Rodney liked me. There was never a word of explanation and I am an outsider all over again. 'It just ain't fair.'

A few days ago on the 20th of April, 'Ready Steady Go' was taped. I went along with the others to see what the fuss was all about. From the moment the cameras started to roll, it was more like a party than a television production. The whole casino was swamped with kids squished together doing the 'French Twitch' to The Surfs, a family of tiny people from Madagascar with powerful voices. Then everyone in the room danced while Petula Clark sang in a sweet innocent voice 'Downtown' and we all started to bounce around and unwind.

Suddenly, noise was deafening when the doors burst open and the new group from England, The Rolling Stones came in with a mob of fans, pushing, shoving us around and screaming in our ears. At what? Five skinny boys, who looked extremely uncomfortable and stood there wondering what to do. I thought they looked messy, certainly not my type at all with long greasy hair down to their shoulders, scruffy 17th century cavalier boots on their feet and horrible baggy blue jeans. Tanita turned her nose up offended "they have dirty fingernails," she sniffed.

As soon as they started to play the room began to vibrate and the kids went berserk. They flung themselves about howling like animals and rolling their eyes in ecstasy, mugging for the British television cameras. It was quite embarrassing. We were horrified and quickly left feeling very superior speaking in French so that no one would think we were part of the scene. As it turned out we weren't!

The next morning the waiters in their smart uniforms and polished shoes regaled us with discreet gossip about the invasion that moved from the casino to the street and went from raucous to a riot. In the small hours, the pimply brats were so sloshed, loud and puking that the police arrived. They were herded like sheep into paddywagons and taken to a train station out of town, and told to go home and stay there.

Sally

We have almost been thrown out of our hotel like the Rolling Stones fans, but not for drunken behavior. Mary and I decide it would be a super idea to make *croque monsieur*. We shop for the ingredients, Swiss *gruyere*, ham slices, eggs, butter and milk and plug in our hot plate. The doors are open onto the huge terrace outside my room. '*Croque* Monsieur' is a sort of cross between a ham and cheese sandwich and French toast - absolutely fab. Our hot plate is a little tricky so while Mary butters and assembles the sandwich I dip them in egg and fry them in hot butter – not easy with a hot plate that has to be unplugged every few minutes as it gets too hot and the 'medium' knob doesn't work.

First *croque* is ready and Mary rushes down the terrace into Tanita's room. "She LOVES it" – next one is ready and Xavier whose tiny balcony is just above us comes flying down through the open French doors, poised, fork in hand. The *croques* are a grand success. I get a little creative and toss a clove of garlic or two in the butter and slip the next sandwich into the pan – the smell is heavenly – wafting up to all the hotel rooms above. Heads peak out of windows and over balconies. Next! Without looking up I hold aloft a plate with a perfectly golden, crispy *croque,* oozing with melted cheese and dripping garlic butter, right into the face of the hotel manager. Oops! *Monsieur*, wearing an immaculate morning coat is looking very cross. He draws himself up to his full height, which is only up to my nose, and sniffs "*Mesdames*, L'Excelsior Palace, eet ees hotel deeee luxe, no camp for zeeee gypsies" turns on his black patent heels and disappears through the French doors. Kitchen is quietly packed away, not to be seen again in Switzerland.

Unfortunately Lesley didn't stay long enough to see the awards nor did she have time to really get to know Rodney Junior and Francis. When it was time for the two of them to return to Holland, I was quite relieved to see them go. I am going to miss Rodney junior but Francis spells trouble. Even Lesley noticed the attention she was getting. All the guys including my Rodney have fallen under her spell. He hasn't said anything to me but I know him so well. He can be very seductive and women are attracted to him even the married ones.

Mary

Mother is getting all steamed up about the company finances and why we never have any money. I tried to explain in a long letter that Mr. Vas is just one man trying to establish something new and different out of his own pockets. Other ballets, the Royal Winnipeg in Canada for instance went broke and had to be bailed out by the government. Sadler's Wells in London has been verging on bankruptcy for years so I don't know why she should be surprised that our little ballet has money problems. I'm not sure that Rodney is much of a financier except that he seems to come up with just enough money at the last moment to keep us afloat. I admire him enormously even though I am still annoyed about the award ceremony.

102

The grand casino in Montreux was built in 1881 and was host to many famous artists including Igor Stravinsky, Coco Chanel and Maurice Ravel. Only seven years after the JBR was featured at the Festival of the Rose d'Or, the casino burned to the ground. On December 3rd 1971 Frank Zappa and the Mothers had a gig in the main ballroom when someone in the audience fired a flare gun. The ceiling ignited, fire spread and the grand old casino was destroyed in minutes – gone forever. In 1975 a mega complex was built on this once serene lake.

Susannah is leaving the ballet. She cannot bear the thought of heading north to Sweden and is taking the train back to Roma to become a star in *Cinecitta.* That seems rather unlikely to me. Susannah is six feet tall and speaks Italian with an almost unintelligible German accent. But she does have those lovely long fingers on all the billboards in Germany so she will not starve.

Chapter Six
♫ On the road again

...Time stood still, stunned silence, no one moved which is just as well because I think I am about to die...

WORLD NEWS

June 4th 1964 Beatles World Tour begins in Copenhagen, Denmark. June 11, 1964 Queen Elizabeth orders Beatles to attend her birthday party.

Sally

After months of travel can you imagine a collection of eighty-four pieces of luggage, record players, trunks of costumes, boxes of props, bags, kitchen, and parcels all being loaded in the four minutes that the northbound train stops in the station at Montreux?   Up and through the windows and doors we pass the bags like a chain gang. Yvette is snapping *"merde alors"* because there is a skip missing and Rodney is dashing to and fro like a referee in a soccer match, Liliane and Xavier are in the midst of one of their famous brawls, screaming and spitting like cats, and we are all tired but relieved to be on the road again. *Finalmente,* we are all aboard for a long, long ride across Switzerland, the length of Germany, through Denmark to the docks in Copenhagen bound for Sweden. All, except Susannah looking lovely but forlorn standing on the platform with Rodney. He hates it when any of his girls move on. They are his family. She clings to him for a moment and then he jumps aboard. Good bye, good bye, *au revoir, alles gute, hals und beinbruch,* break a leg and she is gone forever.

Mary

Sally has snuggled into the corner of the wagon-lit and is feigning sleep. We have all paid a little extra to be in the first class car because the seats turn into beds at night. The entire trip should take twenty-seven hours if there are no breakdowns. Do I want to play gin rummy in the next compartment? "Non *merci, peut- etre, plus tard."* With my well-worn map spread on the fold out table, I am inking in our route to Bâsle, Fribourg, Strasburg, Karlsruhe, Mannheim, Frankfurt, Leipzig Hanover, Hamburg, Copenhagen and finally Malmö in Sweden.

As we travel farther and farther into Germany I am frustrated because trains always seem to go through the poorest parts of town filled with filth, graffiti, garbage and clotheslines. Each hamlet, *die kleinen dorfer,* all looks the same. In my imagination the ballet is a company of wartime soldiers getting carted back and forth, clickety, clack, clickedy click, whistles tooting, people sleeping, playing gin rummy and drinking beer. We pull into a station with no name and Herr Porter rumbles in a low monotone "*acht minute.*" The JBR crew pile out to stretch.

Most normal people would take a brisk walk up and down the platform, but not us. We are doing '*grand battements, jetés en l'air,*' tap dancing and running around like children at recess. All aboard and we march like soldiers back to our steel chamber on rails. People push and shove, trying to take our seats. No one speaks English. All my German words seem to have vanished. I try to conjure up my lessons from Professor Herr Kriegle, German 101, but all that comes to mind is '*Ich habe einen bleistift*' I have a pencil when what I really want to say is "get outta my seat you blubber butt." Order is finally restored with multilingual bickering and we settle once again like chickens on a roost until the next stop.

Sally

The rhythm of the wheels on the track is like a drug and after a couple of hours of lazy gin rummy with Shirley, Nadine and Liliane I returned to my compartment next door for another snooze. I looked up as two uniformed guards entered our wagon-lit at the end of the corridor to inspect passports and tickets. *Merde*! My heart beat a little faster and I whispered to Rodney and nodded in their direction. "Inspectors!" Nonchalantly he slid into the corridor as if to have a cigarette and disappeared in the opposite direction into the *'toiletten.'*

Since the age of fourteen Rodney has been stateless, a man without a country. Although he was born in Dresden Germany where his father, a Hungarian Jewish lawyer worked, his childhood was spent in Hungary. He was a student at the famous Budapest Circus School studying acrobatics, trapeze and ballet until, that is, the pro-Nazi Arrow Cross Party, reared its anti-Semitic head and threatened anyone with Jewish blood. Rodney and his friend Brady from the circus school took off one day not for school or over any of the patrolled bridges crossing between the twin cities of Buda and Pest but, dove into the Danube and swam to freedom. With nothing to identify them, they walked, rode the rails and worked their way doing handstands and backflips in the street for over seven hundred miles to Amsterdam. On Oct

15, 1944 fifteen thousand Jews were rounded up in Budapest. Rodney never saw his father again.

That is why he prefers to use the loo instead of spending hours with the local railway police in useless explanations of his stateless passport and lack of travel papers. Crossing borders can shatter one's nerves.

Rudy

I am just beginning to fall nicely asleep to the rhythm of the train in my classy wagon-lit when a GOD-AWFUL RACKET erupts in corridor right in front of our door. Voices, louder and louder and I am irritated!!!! "This wagon-lit is for *schlafen* NOT hanging around Herr big mouth," I grumbled and open the door. Not one meter away stood three, fat, noisy and very drunken giants just asking for trouble. One lurched forward, stinking of schnapps slurring, *"Ach mensch schlafen sie mal?"* Haw haw haw." I am diplomatic, very, very nice indeed and told them in a sort of German/Dutch language that a noise was not wanted in corridor. They laughed very rudely not at all diplomatic these three *Schmugelglumpfs*. I jump up and down like Peter Pan having BIG FIT! 'Look you,' and my fist landed on a big red nose and my left leg executed a krakaboom into a beer belly. *"Das ist für you mein Fuucking Herrens."* I waited; time stood still, stunned silence...no one moved which is just as well because I think I am about to die. But no, I turned slowly around and went back to my compartment to sleep big *schlafen*.

This is not the end of my tale. Hours later, I don't know how long, there was a knock on the door and as I stepped out, I was surrounded by Herr Offizier of Immigration and the trio *Schmugelglumpfs* now sober, serious and indignant. Something in my head snapped and I became the 'Führer,' haughty, arrogant and barked out nice loud orders in perfect German about rights, discipline, shame and other bullshit, all the time standing erect, head held high and gesticulating like Herr Hitler. *Ja,* I give commanding performance and believe it or not, it worked. Herr Offizier clicked his heels spun round and left.

Sent from Copenhagen before crossing to Malmö Sweden April 30, 1964

Mary

I fell asleep in Hamburg and didn't wake up until we were at the docks in Copenhagen. Seagulls and salt-laden air again, I could have cried myself to death with homesickness. Smelling the sea, listening to the seagulls cry, the white painted ship and chimney stacks, it was all so familiar. The ferry could have been a twin of the midnight Princess Ships going from Victoria to Vancouver: identical mahogany paneling, polished brass, leather sofas and of course the smell of the engine fumes.

I hope there is mail waiting for me at the *Kron Princen*, where we are going to appear. I am very lonely and sometimes think I should chuck this whole adventure and go home. My first impression of Malmö is stainless steel push buttons for everything, very modern, a bustling city but with a sweet little river running through a park right in the middle. I read my letters from home beside the stream and felt peaceful at least for a moment.

Seven of us, eight counting a nameless cat decided to share a two-room apartment and try to save some money. Sally, Elizabeth, Tanita, Nadine, Mireille, the cat, Shirley and I are living at the unpronounceable *Wassberg Soderforstadsgatan* 7. Our set up is like an English girls boarding school, St Trinian's according to Sally. There is constant noise, singing chattering, banging of pots and pans and a blaring radio, bumping into one another, seven cooks in one tiny kitchen and a bathroom like a Chinese laundry. I don't know where Rodney, Remo and Ronáld are but Anke and Rudy have a spacious modern apartment on the 25th floor of some tall luxury tower and Liliane and

Xavier have called a truce and taken a room somewhere nearby.

Sally

We have the most stupendous news. The JBR has been chosen to be the resident ballet at the world famous Palm Beach Cannes in August. Rodney got a telegram from somebody who saw us perform in Montreux. This is it! The moment that Rodney has been waiting for has come; a chance to make a name for himself as a great choreographer and perhaps end up in the Olympia in Paris. He is a new man fired with energy and passion.

There is a snag though. Palm Beach demands that we open the season with all new ballets, fully costumed and never before seen in Europe. That ends our gin rummy games. We have exactly three and a half months to accomplish the impossible. As well as two performances a night at the *Kron Princen* cabaret we work from morning until curtain time on the new ballets.

Kron Princen, Malmö, Sweden May 1964

Darling Lez

Life here is dull! If we weren't so busy working on the new ballets, which are the best ever, I wonder if I could stick five more weeks. No one speaks to us. Just walking down the street for example there is no eye contact whatsoever, no sympathy. Pale faces march by like mannequins all lost in their own world. No wonder they all commit suicide. Thank you so much for the loan. I know Rodney will someday pay you back. All the new costumes are ordered and we will have fittings in Amsterdam sooner or later. One more thing darling, we need sixteen pairs of knee-high boots, white (you have the sizes) and one pair of thigh-high black leather size 36. Could you please dash down to Agnello and Davide and have them sent over. Lots of love Sal xxx

I really don't know what we would do without Lesley. One ballet '*Black Saint and Sinner Lady*' has lots of costume changes. I play a bride, a nun, and wear a robe and long black wig for the Old Testament bit and then end up a machine. The new prologue costumes "Adagio, Allegro and Beat are breathtaking with nine yards of chiffon in each one. For our comic ballet "*La Rue Verte*", which is a street in the old Red Light quarter of Paris, all the girls are dressed as flirty French '*putains*' and wear sexy, skintight red or green satin sheaths with fuzzy blond and red wigs. This ballet is going to bring the house down. '*La Rue Verte*' is based on the story of the Happy Hooker Irma la Douce. Rudy and Xavier play two pimps, Johnny and Arthur Le Marquis and their comic duel with billiard cues is brilliant. Nadine got the role of Emilie the new girl being lured into the trade and Yvette sneered, "*Pouffias,* it suits her to a T," or words to that effect *en français.* I agree in English.

The JBR's comic ballet La Rue Vert was based loosely on the story of Irma La Douce, a French musical that opened at the Théâtre Gramont in Paris on November 12, 1956 and ran for four years. In 1958 it opened at the Lyric Theatre in the West End of London and two years later on Broadway at the Plymouth Theatre in New York City. Xavier in the middle, Sally on his left and Mary on the extreme right of the photo.

Mary

Hour after hour we sweat it out in a large rehearsal room painted the most bilious green. There are windows all down one side but only one seems to open. The air is stifling. Rodney is creating to Dave Brubeck's 'Take Five' in 5/4 time, the accent beginning 'and one TWO three four.' It is a very difficult rhythm to dance but he is determined that we shall get it right. "*Non mes chéres, attention, encore* ta ta TUM ta ta. *Daahlinks*" he smacks himself on the forehead in exasperation "*leeesen to za music. I vant you to feeeeel it inside.*" We try again and again.

Sweat flies through the air and lands on whoever is in its path. Necks ache, arms feel paralyzed and feet are bruised but still we keep going. "O.K. *pirouette, eins, zwei, drei, fier and stop! Basta, basta.*" Rodney skips from one language to the next automatically without even thinking about it. "Now one more time daahlinks." *"Merde."* Yvette has mutinied. She can't understand why we don't just do our same old ballets with new costumes. In the middle of rehearsal she stopped dead and sat like a stone on the nearest chair and refused to budge. Well really! In any other company she would be fired on the spot. The problem is Yvette is getting old. She is almost thirty and this new choreography is too difficult for her. Rodney pleads and cajoles her to get up and try again. Finally we break for the day.

My birthday is in two more days and it is so depressing. I will be the only twenty three year old virgin in the entire world and I could just scream. I feel like I am on the wrong side of a locked door without a key. At this rate I will end up a sour old spinster looking after my dad until I die of boredom. Nadine asked Sally if I was a lesbian or something and she said, "Oh no, she's a Canadian."

On the twenty second of May at one in the morning the JBR celebrated my birthday in a basement room at the *Kron Princen*. We invited everyone we knew in Malmö, which was really pathetic. The guest list included: the Portuguese janitor and his sidekick, three German stage hands, two Italian waiters from the supper club, a melancholy Spanish singer who always looks like he is about to burst into tears, a Swiss ventriloquist whose stage name Remy Martin was inspired by a bloody bottle of brandy, his long-suffering wife and finally Frank a tall, swarthy strongman from Paris who is nuts about Tanita. Rudy

113

calls him the gorilla because his body is covered with curly black hair. Not one guest was actually Swedish.

The girls in the ballet presented me with a carved wooden chicken for some odd reason. Sally gave me a pale pink negligee, which I immediately put on. It was a real whoop-de-doo not at all like my birthdays at home with cake and candles. At three a.m. the night watchman begged us to go home before he got fired. Happy Birthday to me.....'*Grattis på födelsedagen*".

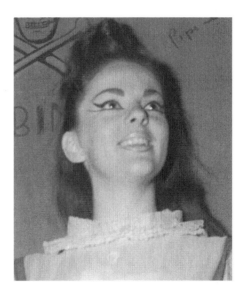

Mary on the eve of her 23ʳᵈ birthday backstage at the Kron Princen, Mariedalvagen 32, Malmö, Sweden.

After a lot of searching Sally and I have found a canteen that we can afford. It is all shiny stainless steel with no cook just one cranky old lady who takes the money. She wears a plastic apron, rubber gloves and wears her hair in a snood. We were ravenous the first time there and had to choose food from a billboard with numbered photographs of open-faced sandwiches lying seductively on plates almost begging, choose me, choose me. There was a wall of stainless steel doors, like a post office all numbered and when you press your choice a red bulb lights up. After a few minutes the light turns green, the door unlocks and there is the food on a little plate in the chamber, just like magic. Before you eat however you must pay your *kroner.*

On the second visit, the whole ballet trouped in. Rudy had us in stitches running back and forth pretending to push buttons, changing his mind and dancing from the front of the line up to the back. I pushed the cheapest button which was a boat made of bread with sails of ham floating on a brackish pond of pâté. I waited, eyes fixed on the green light like a cat by the mouse hole. There! As soon as it lit up I ripped open the door and peered in and saw a hand, just for a second before the back door slammed shut. "Hey, there are human beings in there I yelled, "I saw a hand, a real hand." Peering in I called, "allo, allo! It looks very good, thank you   *"tack sa mycket"* to the empty box. Madame Rubber Gloves was not amused. She scowled but at least I got a reaction.   No wonder the Swedes get sloshed all the time!

Rudy

Anke and I have a big apartment on the 25th floor, with a great view of Copenhagen across the water. Hey!!!!! Power failure NO GOOD!!! I WALKED down emergency stairs to get ciggies, and found a kiosk of magazines and a HUGE woman with a cigar in her mouth straight out of Marx Brother's film. Ha Ha Ha. She is selling newspapers and stuff – HOLY MOLIE!!!! WHAUUUUUUHHHHHH– pictures of naked ladies, many colours, with legs *NOT* crossed, in many positions. I take a long, long, time buying one little package of fags before I climb 25 flights. Anke and I don't really get to know anyone here in Malmö but are looking ahead...where??? I dunno. My future is always tomorrow. The constant "HELLO" and "Bye-bye" forces me to carry a mental shield, so I don't cry and feel lonely things in my chest. Beyond the horizon more travelling, more stages and another performance. We have to keep Goin', don't we?

Sally

Living in Malmo was like a month in a tunnel, endless work with no relief. I was constantly lonely. When we boarded the ferry for Copenhagen en route to Aarhus, Denmark, I did not look back but concentrated only on the future and our hopes and dreams of what is to come. Often I ponder about my life with the ballet, rushing here and there. Is this really how I want to live? I do love to dance, it is part of me but, oh, to settle somewhere and not be like a vagabond without a home would be absolute bliss. I have begged Rodney to find us a little nest, not big, not grand, but somewhere just for the two of us but I doubt he ever will. The JBR is his life and the ballet is his home.

Mary

There was a police escort waiting to guide us into Aarhus late yesterday afternoon because Soviet Premier Khrushchev is in town and they, the Danes, or perhaps the Russians want to know where every stranger is staying. We signed millions of papers in a frenzy of bureaucracy. The whole town seems to be in a nervous state. Rodney stayed in Amsterdam to audition more dancers or something. Who knows what he does, he appears and disappears like the Scarlet Pimpernel.

This morning at ten o'clock, we left our hotel the *Rute Hoteller* and walked to the rehearsal studio near the old Aarhus Theatre. I changed into leotard, tights and leggings with bare feet and went to the *barre* to warm up. Tanita began class, *'battement tendu, grand battement en avant, a la second, en arriere.'* Legs in unison kicked to the front, to the side and to the back. "Turn" called Tanita and we began on the other side. *'Ronde de jambe en l'air, arabesque ponché,'* I was getting warm and perspiration was prickling my skin as I walked to the center of the room to work on some turns and balance. Second, forth, turn, turn, turn, turn, finish. Start again, then again and again. From the back of the studio a door swung open with a crash. "Daahlinks, *Bonjour*, Hello, *Guten Tag,"* called Rodney and there he was with a smug grin on his face and two girls, one on each arm. On his right Puck, Remo's future girlfriend and Femina, Rudy's second wife as it turned out, on his left.

Mary

We have been rehearsing our new ballets for three weeks nonstop ever since Puck and Femina arrived. Puck as her name suggests is pert, petite and as agile as an elf while Femina is a more delicate lyrical dancer. They are both Dutch, which makes our United Nations ballet a little lopsided. That makes seven Dutch dancers to four French and three Belgian, two English and *moi la Canadienne*. The French do not like to be outnumbered.

Sally

Darling Lez, May 1964
Marselisborg Slot (that's the palace gardens)
A short postcard to tell you that our last Gala night here in Aarhus was quite wonderful. An overwhelming sea of bodies was gathered in the royal gardens-just masses of people in our audience. I think the entire population of Aarhus must have been there. In the quiet bits of "Les Fourrures" you could hear a leaf fall from a tree and at the end of the ballet the applause went on and on. We all had lumps in our throats and there were a few very moist eyes. This little town has a big heart. Rodney was so proud he just smiled and smiled (you know, the way he does)   Love Sal xxx

Mary

On our last night in Denmark, we went *en masse* to the film, 'Four Horses of the Apocalypse' dubbed in Danish with German subtitles. Everyone had a different interpretation of what it was all about. Our discussion went from calm to an emotional shouting match in minutes. Everybody talked at once and rehashed the war and the aftermath. Hunger, the occupation by the SS troops, Nazi cooperation, the roundups and execution of Jews called *'rafle'* and all manner of skeletons were brought up. The only time everybody stopped fighting is when Rodney quietly told us about his scrape with death.

It was in the center of Amsterdam somewhere near a bridge. Rodney and his friend Brady from the Budapest Circus School were in a street. Suddenly the sound of marching boots was heard, getting closer and closer, louder and louder. There was an ominous hush among the throng of people gathered by the bridge listening. He and Brady stared at one another tense, waiting. "Under the bridge, quickly, *gyorsan*". As one, they dashed to the rails, dove off in a somersault over the top and grabbed onto the girders under the bridge, hanging on like trapeze artists under the big top. Overhead people began to run in all directions crying and calling for their children, their wives, their fathers and mothers. True Hell broke out as the sound of gunfire echoed round the square, deafening any other sound. Rodney's arms and hands went numb with pain as he tried desperately to hang on and not lose consciousness. He could hear bodies slumping onto the bridge overhead. Screams of pain and terror were silenced by another burst of bullets until the sound of retreating boots was all that was left. Muddy water rose up to meet them, sucked them under, and carried them away to safety.

Tomorrow June 1964 we are off to Germany. A contract is a contract and we are entertainers first and foremost.

Sally

It was at the Casino Lübeck-Travemünde that the JBR almost came undone. The historic building once the playground of Russian and German royalty was two hundred years old when we arrived on a really cold June morning. We were scheduled to perform in the large and glamourous outdoor theatre but icy winds blew across the Baltic Sea forcing us inside to a very small cabaret. We crowded in to inspect a shabby but ornate theatre. There was no orchestra pit and at one end stood an oval platform that served as a stage with a grand piano taking up most of the space. No footlights, no backstage, no dressing room but a small curtain covered a door to the next chamber that was to serve as a makeshift change room for our whole company now eighteen dancers. There was an unhappy rumble.

I was sitting at a table with everyone else putting on makeup when he stuck his head in the door. He had a whiskey clutched in his hand otherwise all was normal. "Full house daahlinks." The orchestra, crammed to one side started the music to the prologue and we filed through the door one by one like prisoners out for an airing.

Somehow we managed to dance the Prologue, *Les Fourrures* and *Les Années Folles* without anyone tumbling off the platform.

Sally made up for the "Afro Cuban" ballet. Jazz Ballet Rodney 1964

Next on the program was the Afro Cuban in dark florescent lights. With white fringes, smiling white teeth and hair twirling we danced to the wild rhythm of the drums until the moment of the storm with lightening, thunder and rain, in other words, the crescendo the big climax. Suddenly NOTHING! No sound, no lights except for one miserable blue spotlight. We must have blown most of the fuses. My heart didn't stop, it started to race, then in a split second, Rudy burst into action and picked up the rhythm with Spanish '*palmas*' a type of hand clapping and finger snapping and his heels stamping a sort of '*zapateados*' in bare feet. We all just kept up the rhythm and continued dancing, ponytails whizzed round and around and we whirled and leapt. Rudy let out a blood-curdling yell like mating jungle monkeys and we took it up from one part of the stage to the other, bird calls, growls, and shrieks. No one faltered. It turned into a jungle romp on stage, and we spun and screamed like savages. In the semi dark, Liliane took her position, center stage beside Remo, Rudy stepped behind and then together they hoisted her up, into '*un grand-ecart*' the splits upside down and we finished. For a brief second there was a shocked silence. Then like a bomb they exploded cheering and stomping on the floor.

Backstage we all jumped on Rudy hugging and kissing him to asphyxiation. Ronáld then sauntered onto the stage in his trench coat looking like Humphrey Bogart in Casablanca flicked his lighter and chattered away in '*Deutsche*' to the audience, telling jokes and singing favourite songs. The orchestra hastily grabbed their instruments. The rest of our music was on tape so 'Asphalt' was cancelled. Rodney was in a state of shock trying to figure out what went wrong with the mass of antique wiring. We danced the Finale in candlelight, clustered like moths to the flame. Miraculously no one caught fire or tripped in the dark.

Mary

Dear Mom, Pop, and Granny: July 1964

Please excuse the messy handwriting, I am on the train whizzing through the entire length of Germany and into Italy. Destination? Venice! We are performing on an island called Lido on an outdoor stage hanging over the Adriatic Ocean. It's called the Casino Excelsior Palace. It is very posh! Also on the program is Gilbert Bécaud, a French singer who is world famous at least in Europe. You may have heard his song, "What Now My Love." I am so excited that I am almost sick. Well, actually I am sick or maybe just a little bit rundown after long rehearsals and not much food. Everyone in the ballet seems to be coughing and sneezing. The French girls love suppositories. No one takes cough drops or vitamins the normal way by mouth but pushes waxy torpedoes up their bottoms. VERY KOOKY eh!

I had a raging toothache in Travemünde and went to the local dentist. He spoke very little English but said "root canal" and I almost fainted. A little money was left from Sweden but not enough for a root canal. I wanted to buy a fancy bathing suit for France. The dentist's room was tiny and looked like a Victorian torture chamber. The drill was actually operated like a treadle sewing machine with the feet. If the pain had not been so intense, I would have run away. Well to make a long story short, he was as gentle as a lamb and even made me laugh.

As he approached my open mouth with the archaic drill, pumping with his feet, he leered "I am very bad Nazi, ja," trying to look fierce and then he threw back his head and cackled. I had to return for a second appointment to finish AND he didn't charge me "ein pfennig." He kissed my hand, just like the movies and said, "Das ballet ist sehr gut und du bist ein schönes Mädchen." Wow, he thinks the ballet is great, I'm beautiful and there is still enough money for a bathing suit. Write soon, I miss you all. Love Mary xxxxx

Chapter Seven
Venice...we came, we conquered but saw nothing.
With apologies to Julius Caesar: "veni, vidi, vici"

...on this sublime night with the moon dancing over the Adriatic and phosphorescence trailing from fingertips, twelve or so naked bodies, twirling and slithering like silver fish, hair plastered to scalps, spouting water like nymphs, buttocks, balls breasts and legs entangled, I felt delicious...........

WORLD NEWS

123

| July 1964 U.S. Congress give President Johnson authority to wage war against Vietnam |

Sally

After thirty-six hours on this torture train we pull into the *Stazione Centrale Venezia* and as one we all stir, stretch awake stand, and prepare for the inevitable. The wagon-lit jolts suddenly, I lose my balance and Rodney catches me around my waist pulling me close to him. Hmmm, that feels good. I put my arms around his neck and our lips touch and as we kiss I feel the warmth of his body. Seconds later we pull apart and he jumps to the platform and grabs the bags as they are flung out of the carriage windows.

What a commotion as eighteen dancers, stiff and groaning, stumble about dragging valises onto carts. People are shouting, "*'Allo allo, per favore, mie bagagli sono qui*" (Excuse me, listen my luggage is over here). I feel so alive to back in Venice. The stink of the canal, flirtatious porters, pious nuns in flowing robes slithering by as though on silent roller skates and kids darting in and out, their mothers shrieking "*raggazzi raggazzi*, it all makes me dizzy with happiness.

What! There are no hotel rooms. Where is the impresario who was supposed to meet us? Rodney is rolling his eyes. "*Merde*" hisses Yvette. I glance over at Mary gazing over the water, her long red hair shimmering in the sun. She is oblivious to any of our problems.

Rodney and the boys take off in different directions to find somewhere for us to stay for a few days before we go to the Lido where there are rooms waiting for us.

Like a tigress guarding her litter, Yvette sits on the costume skips. "Come back in an hour, someone calls." After thirty-six hours cooped up on a train, Tanita, Mary and I escape. Stepping aboard the nearest *vaporetto* we ply through the water toward Venezia, the Queen of the Adriatic Sea.

From left: Puck, Remo, Tanita and Mary aboard a vaparetto in Venice July 1964. The vaparetti, little steamers have been churning up the waters of the Venetian canals since 1881, when the first vaparetto, the 'Regina Margherita' was built. Twenty-three more steamboats followed quickly and by 1937 more than fifty were operating.

The *vaparetto* veers into the Grand Canal where palaces from another age stand like tall soldiers on parade. They are exquisite with lacy pillars, Juliette balconies, arches and turrets. Murky water is sloshing into the sinking doorways as we chug along under bridges and past narrow waterways leading nowhere. "Rialto Bridge," An English voice calls to a group of students and we are literally pushed off onto a small dock and carried along with the hot and sweating bodies. They are moving as a tidal wave to the bridge but the three of us escape to a side street café and plop onto sturdy wrought iron chairs.

It's stifling hot, my blue and white cotton sack dress is clinging to me and I breathe in the welcome scents of coffee, real coffee, oil, garlic and oh glory, melting cheese. *'Bene,'* we order *café latte'* and bask in the sunshine.

Rudy

For a whole week we change rooms. First, Ronáld, Anke and I together - one room over a FISH shop. Yeah! That's right! Five a.m. and EVERYONE screams at one another. Anke says, "No fish ever again." Then, a small hotel but at least I am alone with my wife and Ronáld gone, into the streets. He will turn up at rehearsals, immaculately dressed - grinning as though he has done something bad. Hah, very good ya!!!!!

Now we are in STAFF quarters of Excelsior Palace and it is very, very good. A private launch carries elegant patrons to the 'Excelsior ONLY dock' with guys in uniforms helping beautiful ladies in big hats and glasses step out of private launch. Lots of legs! I think a very good job for young Italian lads. This is a 1001 night's dream come true. Ja!! Fantastisch!!!

Sally

I could not be happier. The Excelsior has rooms for us in the staff quarters, an annex right across the street from the Palace and the famous beach. There is a private beach for guests of the Excelsior only. On the public beach, I am working on my tan wearing my new swimming costume, a pink bikini, very mod. Rule number two is 'no tan lines' and so I might take my top off. Cruising by in trousers rolled up to his knees, Ronáld tips his trademark fedora. Remo has wandered off flirting with Puck. Anke, Rudy and Femina are splashing in the briny chattering in Dutch. No one is aware of the drama about to unfold.

Rudy

Hey. The JBR is a HIT and we are *NOW* allowed on their private fancy hand-raked beach. We see much more than legs. OH YES!!! I rent one of those paddle boats, all bright colours, yellow, blue, pink, etc. with seats and two foot pedals, like a bicycle to propel through the water. My legs are very strong so this should be very nice and easy. I cruise along at the shoreline, past the huge sunglasses and bosoms, then out into the Adriatic. Further and further, the sea inviting me to swim naked, very sensual in the warm water. Oh yes – this is paradise. I climb back onto my green boat and lie down to dry, so relaxed and oh so happy. Zzzz, I am gone into a beautiful space.

" HOLY SHIT, *MERDE*," the sun is low on the horizon, 360 degrees of blue sky turning pink. Where am I? I gotta show to do and this BEEG nightmare. Rich, fancy people waiting in their finery full of champagne, smelling of Chanel and I am lost somewhere on the coast of Italy. Like a madman I paddle around in circles-panic, where to go, I'm parched and think of 'water, water, everywhere and not a drop to drink'. Who the Hell said that? Doesn't matter, the sun is going down and I must get control. Ah a bird a seagull or something, it must be flying for land, of course. Pedal, pedal, right, left, right, left as fast as my legs will go, it's show time, pump, pump, pump, legs like Nijinski, lots and lots of muscles. I look down, burnt legs now on fire – and then I think, what if seagull's home is Greece...oh my God. Pump, pump, pump! Then I see land, and go crazy. Green boat flies through water and we hit shore. Boatman yells and points to me, naked. My swimsuit is on in a flash and I dash through the stage door and into the dressing room panting, muscles burning, skin burning, I am a lobster with '*no tan lines*'. A cool shower hurts but calms me. I saunter out ready for the show.

No one asks where I have been, no one, not even my wife. This will be the first time that my delicious *pas de deux* with my lovely Sally is going to be "ouch" rather than "aahh"

Mary

Sally and I are happily lounging in the warm sand on a long skinny island called the Lido, that overlooks the Gulf of Venezia. It's boiling hot and Sally is brown and me freckled but we look like a million bucks. Ha Ha! Please don't tell me about anyone else getting married this July.   It is all too depressing...Your spinster daughter. Mary. xxxx

What I didn't mention is that many of the guests on the private beach in front of the Palace are STARK NAKED. I suppose I was a little embarrassed for them at first, all that blubber for the world to see but then I realized that no one paid them the slightest notice. How different from back home. At night in the outdoor theatre the women wear exquisite silk gowns with flowers in their hair and look madly elegant. Who would know they look a fright in the buff?

An unwritten rule of the palace is that we are not permitted to see the rest of the show after our performance. The ballet is supposed to disappear until the second show and then mysteriously reappear. This is a ridiculous stupid rule, so the other night, I stole into the back row and watched Gilbert Bécaud perform. Backstage Mr. Bécaud seems to be just a nice guy, kind of cute but old. "He's thirty seven," said Elizabeth raising her eyebrows. He hangs around laughing and chattering especially with Nadine who is from the same part of France near Toulon. To me, a bit of an outsider, with a French vocabulary limited to food, whining and swearing, he could be anyone walking down the street.

That night I got the shock of my life. There was a fanfare, the lovely ladies rustled and squirmed in their seats and then he catapulted onto center stage simply ablaze with energy bowing to roars and cheers. They don't call him Monsieur 100,000 volts for nothing. In a flash he was at the piano singing 'Nathalie' and then his famous theme song '*Et Maintenant*' with the audience going nuts. Who could have guessed that the rather ordinary man backstage would become larger than life onstage? I wonder if we are a bit like that, just people until we are in front of an audience and the music sets us on fire.

Gilbert Bécaud 1927-2001 singer, composer and actor. Many of his songs were translated and sung by Bob Dylan, Elvis Presley and Willie Nelson. "What now my Love" is known worldwide and has been performed by Shirley Bassey, Sonny and Cher, Judy Garland and Frank Sinatra. Gilbert Becaud is buried at the famous Pere Lachaise Cemetery in Paris, born Gilbert Léopold Silly.

Venice was burning hot that July and although we were dancing in an outdoor theatre our dressing rooms were stifling. Sometimes late at night we would head for the public beach with flasks of wine and food to go swimming, another unwritten rule broken. On one such night we must have consumed more than a little *vino rosso* and without warning we all went skinnydipping. Over the past seven months I must have seen every member of the ballet in various stages of undress and thought it perfectly normal. But on this sublime night with the moon dancing over the Adriatic and phosphorescence trailing from fingertips, twelve or so naked bodies, twirling and slithering like silver fish,

hair plastered to scalps, spouting water like nymphs, our buttocks, balls, breasts and legs entangled, I felt delicious.

In a few minutes it was over and we swam ashore suddenly modest again, put our clothes on and padded sheepishly through the sand to our rooms. The next day at rehearsal no one said a word we just smiled shyly at one another. "Oh for crying out loud," exasperated Rodney, "what IS going on?" Nothing at all!

Chapter Eight

Cannes

♫Unforgettable That's What You Are

...Only then did I glance at the maestro through my false eyelashes, sweat pouring like rain from gutters on a roof. He was looking directly into my eyes and I into his. There was no mistaking the message...

NEWSFLASH

August 23rd, 1964. Beatles perform at the Hollywood Bowl in Los Angeles.

Sally

I have to pinch myself. At last we are in Cannes on August the first as planned and our dream is about to come true. Rolling down the window of the taxi, I stick my head out to get my first glimpse of the famous *'La Croisette,'* the wide avenue that strolls along the waterfront like a pampered poodle. It is lined with tall Palm trees, hotels and royal villas. I know I will never forget this taste of Cannes as long as I live. All of us have worked ourselves silly for this moment. If hard work makes a great show then we will be a grand success.

It is early morning but the bright sun is already warming the early birds lying completely nude on the sandy beach hoping to be bronze by sundown. Liliane and Mary are crushed against each other hanging out the opposite side of the taxi. "Look at the flowers, Holy Cow," Mary whistled. *"Mais oui, c'est formidable et les voitures, les Rolls Royces, les Ferraris, quelle elegance!"*

The Promenade de la Croisette and the Palm Beach Casino were completed in April 1929. Between 1960-1963, the wide sandy beach and retaining wall was built. Underground tunnels linked the private beach to luxury hotels across the street. The original Summer Casino, renamed the Palm Beach Cannes, was built over a clay-pigeon shooting range on the tip of the peninsula. This is a Postcard from 1964.

Rounding the corner at the very eastern tip of *La Croisette,* our taxi smoothly swings into a large curved driveway lined with flowers and potted plants, to the entrance of the smart new Palm Beach Casino. We are the resident ballet for a whole month in their outdoor theatre called the *Masque de Fer.* It is all too exciting. A liveried doorman rushed forward, smiling in welcome and began to open the door. Mary is about to leap out and I called across, "we are the Jazz Ballet Rodney." The welcoming smile vanished. "You aaf to go round zee back," and he slammed the door. "Well that was some welcome," Mary snapped as the taxi moved around the corner to the *entrée des artistes.*

The rest of the ballet arrived ahead of us from the main train station in Cannes. Rodney was standing in front of someone who was blocking the way waving his arms frantically. "Oh Blimey, now what?" Rodney is shouting in French and English. "Today, August the first is the day we arrive *oui?*" "*Non,*" a head shakes violently and a hand appears with a handkerchief and mopped a brow. *"Demain, I am expecting zee ballet demain".* The stage manager of the Palm Beach Casino looked very confused. He is a lean and dapper fellow, a bit of a toff with a moustache that reminds me of Peter Sellers as Inspector Closeau. I got a fit of the giggles. After a lot of arguing Monsieur calmed down and extended a hand to Rodney and greeted him "*Bienvenue* Monsieur Vas,*"* and bent stiffly from the waist with a little bow of welcome.

Rudy

I got love and lotsa respect for Rodney but how in HELL could he get the date wrong. Disasterous, RAMPZALIGO - Here we are, high season in *MOST* popular beach resort in France - No ALL of Europe and not ONE single hotel room until tomorrow for whole ballet - 19 people, 20, with Jorge the maestro who has arrived from Lisbon with new music and one bloody CAT, and we hafta sleep on the *beach* just like bums. Posters of incredible, marvelous, JBR all over town and we slink around like we are invisible.   *Godverdomme!*

Sally

Darling Lez: Sorry to leave you hanging with no postcards. On our first night in Cannes your daughter ended up sleeping in the 'grand salle,' the gilded ballroom of the casino ON THE FLOOR. We, the girls that is, were lined up like sardines on sunbeds reeking of tanning oil. So tired, we didn't undress but slept in our tee shirts surrounded by a golden army of stacked chairs multiplied in a floor to ceiling mirror. The boys were left on the beach for the night even Rodney and Jorge. He is the Portuguese musician that we hired to compose the music for our new ballets and conduct the Palm Beach Orchestra. Don't worry Lez, I am now settled at the Hotel Residence in a pretty little room overlooking an enchanting garden with an assortment of old chairs in the shade of fruit trees. Love Sal xxx

Mary

Everything about Cannes is perfection, the tropical flowers bursting from tubs, the outdoor cafés, the mansions that line the main street and the sophisticated ladies gliding by like swans in sunglasses. Everybody is gorgeous except me. Another damn cold sore has erupted. I am supposed to look like a classical ballerina as delicate and lyrical as Moira Shearer in '*The Red Shoes*.' Instead I look like I have been punched in the mouth.

The JBR is on every billboard in town and although this makes us feel important, we cannot afford a cup of coffee on the *Croissette* let alone a proper meal. Our photographs are splattered in magazines all over France and I am living in an attic full of cast off mattresses and boxes of junk like a poor little mouse. The Residence Hotel is full except for an iron bedstead stored under the eaves. Rodney and most of the French girls are scattered about in the old town on a hill called *Le Suquet* where I could move but my garret is *artistique* and for now it is my home. I just adore the owner who spoils us at breakfast with homemade apricot jam and croissants and doesn't charge us anything, no matter how many we eat.

Sally

"*Et, un deux trois quatre cinq*, ta ta tum ta ta ta daahlinks listen to the drums" yes yes, *d'accord*, one more time." Rodney is standing in front of the orchestra with Jorge who has used the same 5/4 rhythm as Dave Brubeck to compose our opening music. The sun is blinding and making me feel faint. Tonight is the night. We have rehearsed our new repertoire at least a hundred times today. At the moment the theatre is deserted except for the waiters who are placing gold chairs all around the stage, setting the tables and bustling about with flowers and candlesticks. The backdrop is the blue, blue sky and the Mediterranean Sea. Later tonight at the *Masque de Fer,* the audience will be a very different crowd. Rumors circulate that the wife of the Aga Kahn, the Emperor of Japan, Elizabeth Taylor and Richard Burton are all coming to the first Gala in honour of the Polio Foundation. After our performance the show is to continue with Dionne Warwick from America.

"Take Five, '*cinque*' *minutes,*" Rodney turns to Jorge their heads together nodding at something and we scramble behind a curtain, down an iron staircase to our dressing rooms in the underground dungeon. It is cool here and we towel off and light cigarettes.

When we first saw the dressing rooms we were disgusted. I went in the door first and switched on a light. Elizabeth screamed. The floor of the corridor was a brown moving carpet of bloody cockroaches, millions of them. As soon as we all yelled and jumped up and down they scuttled down the smelly drains, into cracks between the floor and walls and poof, they were gone. All except the squished ones. It was truly disgusting, *'degoutant, vraiment dégueulasse.'*

Mary

I have never had a chance to dance with a conductor who gave a damn whether the music was too fast or too slow so it came as a bit of a surprise when I met Jorge. I had been rehearsing my solo for months with a recording of Benjamin Britten's *Petit Ballet* and was expecting his new music to be a challenge. To my amazement, Jorge has worked hours with me following my dance steps and making everything work together. He is quite fascinating and handsome in a European sort of way. I think he is older than I am and very serious about his music. He is probably married.

The costume for my solo is a sheer white one piece leotard, very classical, very naked. My *pointe* shoes darned so carefully are also white and the Moira Shearer hair is unfortunately, screaming orange. Sally and I decided to dye our hair red with a porridge of Egyptian henna leaves. This operation was carried out in the communal bathroom at La Residence because there is no running water in the attic. Boy, was that a mistake. Sally ended up looking stunning, so beautiful with hair the colour of polished mahogany. I look like my hair is on fire. We have a new dancer, Richard from England. He is just a kid, tall, scrawny and very homesick. As soon as he saw my hair he howled, threw back his head and laughed himself silly. Well, at least I made someone happy.

Rudy

What do you know? There is more sparkle and jewels in the audience than on stage. And the PERFUME aahhh *Nina Ricci* sponsoring this Gala. EVERYONE must have taken a *bath* in the stuff. And hundreds of security people are posted everywhere. I practically had to show my passport to get in the bloody stage door. Prince Rainier is here with all his bodyguards. I think I saw Elizabeth Taylor, WOOOOOW she looks *SUPERB* with gigantic décolleté. I love it. Ja! The Begam Kahn who is the Ali Kahn's wife or mother or someone has a necklace that must weight forty pounds. Holy Shit! The security guys all are ARMED, standing in a curve at the back dressed in bulging tuxedos like a semi-circle of lumpy penguins. Well this is a very big deal to benefit the Polio Society of France.

Sally

We are tense. There is silence for once, as we warm up in our rabbit warren beneath the stage. Everyone is thinking his or her own thoughts, maybe praying, maybe just trying to breathe deeply gathering strength.   The new chiffon costumes are lovely and feel so light, just how I imagined them when I suggested flowing dresses to Rodney. He came into the dressing room and I spun around modeling for him. "Beautiful my lovely Sally, *gyönyörő*" in Hungarian and he kissed me on the top of my head, his lips avoiding my careful applied *maquillage*. There is nothing more to say. "*Merde*" we whisper as we always do, to bring us luck. Our stage manager appears from nowhere and gives the signal. One by one we file silently up the metal stairs and prepare for our entrance. There is a hush in the house and then polite applause as Jorge takes his place in front of the orchestra. He lifts the baton... waits... someone coughs discreetly... there is the sound of a gong in a minor key, a slightly discordant sound and Rudy and Richard carry a classical ballet *barre* on stage horizontally as though they are invisible and it is fixed to a wall. The music starts and I peek through the side curtain as Mary drifts to center stage looking fragile, and every inch a ballerina. The audience gasps at this unexpected start. She takes her pose and '*Adagio Allegro and Beat*' begins.

We wait for our entrance, tense, alert, absorbing the music and waiting, coiled like steel springs '*and* one TWO three four, and one TWO three four... we are off. After months of rehearsal we dance with the precision of a Swiss clock. No one falters. Five times during the ballet, the audience burst into applause. And at the end when we took our bows, they stood up, clapping, men in black dinner jackets shouting "*bravo, bravo.*" I think they were astonished by Rodney's choreography. It was really very mod. All I can think of is, they love us, we are a success and Rodney has reached the top. Downstairs while I was changing for 'Asphalt,' Yvette snatched my chiffon frock from its hanger and examined the perspiration marks. "*Sale anglaise, putain,*" she spat as she hustled off to sew cotton pads into the armpits.

Mary

There is a faint breeze off the Mediterranean as I tippy, tippy to the center of the glass stage in my brand new *pointe* shoes. I am alone in the blinding spotlight dressed all in white, ready as I will ever be and suddenly I feel very fragile as though my body was made of porcelain and my feet of crystal. With pounding heart. I take my pose, arms *demi bras,* head held high looking to the end of the earth and pray that no one can see me trembling. Please God, let me finish my *pirouettes* and not fall off *pointe*. I will be so good it will really surprise you. The music began and I just danced, right from my very soul I danced. It was as though all my life I had been waiting for this moment to become one with the music. Every part of my body from head to arched foot, from my neck right down to my fingernails responded and I gave the performance of my life. Exactly on cue Richard came up behind me for the final triple *pirouette*, caught me around the waist and I finished in an *arabesque ponché* with my legs like an arrow at six o'clock. I did it! I really did it! Abruptly the music changes to 5/4 time and we move to the complicated rhythm of the jazz and take the final pose and BLACKOUT. The applause is like a clap of thunder. We all join hands, walk downstage together and bow as one. Everyone is elated. After all the tortuous training, bruised feet, aching limbs and fatigue we have pulled it off. Even the orchestra is clapping. Only then did I glance at the maestro through my false eyelashes, sweat pouring like rain from gutters on a roof. He was looking directly into my eyes and I into his. There was no mistaking the message.

Sally

August is the most perfect time to be in the south of France. The town is alive with people; Parisians from the north, rich English residents summering at their villas and students from all over the world here for the annual Ballet Festival. After the show we are intoxicated and just dying to "let off steam" as Mary says. We head to the *Whiskey a Go Go* and party until dawn with all the local boys. The management of the discothèque is delighted because word is out that we are regulars and the place is packed. Endless partners line up to dance with us, try out trendy new steps, the Twist, the Frug and to show off. Every night Rudy and I erupt into a sexy flamenco jive rock and roll style and the rest clear the floor and cheer us on. Well perhaps his wife Anke doesn't cheer very much. Even Jorge looking serious and a little out of place joins in the mob and we dance until dawn – driven unable to stop.

The daytime is a whirlwind too. Mary and I have been to fashion shows, art galleries, receptions and cocktail parties with Charles Aznavour holding court and the Aga Khan's wife and other ladies standing aloof and untouchable. There we are, the two of us, photographed wherever we go. Late one afternoon we were sent to a press conference at the casino. In our best cotton A-lines from Malmö we glided through the front door for a change rather than the *'entré des artistes.'* Almost immediately men who lit our cigarettes and handed around flutes of champagne surrounded us. We drifted around the room getting photographed with big wigs for a French magazine all the while searching for grub. Why does everyone want to give us drinks but no one wants to feed us?

At dawn one morning we went straight from a party at the *Whiskey a Go Go* to the casino swimming pool where we had a photo shoot for an advertising leaflet. Most of the morning was spent in our swimming costumes in front of a camera and we were not paid one flipping franc. It was a long morning and everyone was feeling a little hung over and grouchy. Nadine started to sway as if she was going to faint. She was holding her stomach and gasping. I looked in horror at her waistline. Oh no! She is very, very pregnant. I don't know who the father is but it better not be Xavier or Liliane will strangle him with her bare hands.

Sally

La Residence Hotel, Cannes, August 1964.

Darling Lez: Thanks for the money – I spent it on lots of little necessities. I am in a hurry but must tell you about my memorable life experience.

I think I told you in my letter the other day that the stage door is on the side of the building by the beach. Going round there we pass, a tiny 'hut' style beach restaurant with wooden tables strewn about 'willy nilly'. It is always packed full of 'les chic français'. You can imagine we just love it. It was here that I had this salad for the first time. It was amazing! Lettuce, tomatoes, tuna, hard boiled eggs, green beans (lightly cooked) anchovies, potatoes, capers and all this topped with a scrumptious vinaigrette. It is called 'Salade Nicoise". It is, of course, from the city of Nice that is only 25 kilometers away.

Even better! We have discovered this wine in a jug not red, not white but a pale pink - a beautiful summer colour -that tastes of sunshine itself. The French call it Rosé. We all love it. The whole ballet now eat and drink here, and it is cheap, about the only place we can afford to eat. All along the 'Croissette' Boulevard, a cup of coffee costs the same as our salary for a whole day. One cup of coffee. Imagine!

Yesterday, while I was having lunch with Shirley, Liliane and Xavier, I was looking around and my eye was caught by a French lady a few tables away, sitting with her family. I just couldn't take my eyes off her and I was not alone. It seemed that most people were looking at her too. She had long, naturally grey hair tied gently back to reveal a very bronzed, not beautiful, not even pretty but, strikingly sensual face. She had a still serenity and an aura that I shall always remember. I intend to be just like her. My inspiration! I do like to be at peace and serene but life with the JBR doesn't really allow that. Love Sal xx

Mary

I have met Dionne Warwick and she sang to me. It all happened quite by chance one morning in the casino. I was late for rehearsal and took a short cut through the upstairs salon, another rule broken and screeched to a halt in front of a grand piano. Leaning on it talking to her accompanist was Dionne Warwick and she turned to look at me. I was stunned and mumbled my apologies and she said "do you want to listen to me rehearse." Abruptly, I sat down on the edge of a dainty golden chair clutching my darned *pointe* shoes against my chest. ♪ If you see me walking down the street and I start to cry, Walk on by, walk on by, don't stop.♫

Her voice rang out clear and powerful, filling every corner of the ballroom from the floor to the *trompe l'oeil* painted on the ceiling. She threw back her head and sang from her soul. A tiny trickle of perspiration glistened under her eyes. I was frightened to breathe in case the spell was broken. She finished and gave me a wide friendly grin. I'll never forget how easy she was, so natural and willing to share her unbelievable voice with a homesick girl far away from her family.

Rehearsal finished early and most of the JBR and the orchestra have left for the beach. Only Jorge is standing there waiting on the terrace by the stage. I stopped short in front of him and just stood there, unsure what to do or say. He took me by the hand barely touching my fingertips and whispered "come with me?" He stepped closer waiting for my reply. I knew exactly what he meant.

It seemed the most natural thing in the world to follow him up the winding maze of streets of the old town, to a little villa on top of the hill where he was staying. From the stone terrace there is a calm and uncluttered view of the old fishing port and the vast expanse of the Mediterranean Sea trailing off to the invisible coastline of North Africa. I stood there acutely aware of him just behind me, waiting for me to turn around. Without a word I slipped off my sandals and walked barefoot through the door.

Perhaps I should feel guilt or shame or something but I don't. I am ecstatic. For the first time in my life I feel truly lovely and desirable and I want fling myself off the terrace crying "take off the red shoes." I was beginning to think that nobody would ever find me irresistible and make love to me over and over again. I thought I would end up a wizened old prune pouring over my scrapbooks.

Sally

Tanita's voice continues, "*plié* stretch, back bend and up, forward back *et grand battement, retiré* and turn." Crikey, it is scorching on stage in the full sun but we must keep on practicing. That is what dancers do. We are well aware that there are always young hopeful students lurking in the wings, eager to take our places on stage. And so we rehearse, we take classes and dance day in day out, month after month until we are as fit as any Olympian athlete.

We may be fulfilled on stage but offstage we fantasize about food or rather lack of it. Several times after morning classes Mary and I have been sneaking into the elegant casino dining room with its graceful bow windows hung with silk curtains billowing like sails on a yacht. We set a small table for two in the vast room and share a one baguette smeared with a portion of *lipatauer*, soft cheese, shallots, capers, pepper and Hungarian paprika. It is Rodney's favourite and mine too. Sitting on gilt chairs in our smelly old leotards we sip our Rosé wine from delicate crystal glasses embossed with the Palm Beach logo and pretend to be princesses, giggling and telling secrets. Over the past year we have become much more like sisters than girlfriends. I think our friendship will last forever.

Our season in Cannes is flying by and I wish it would never end. The critics have been very flattering for all our ballets except for the ill-fated '*Black Saint and Sinner Lady.*'

Sally, Principal dancer with the Jazz Ballet Rodney as 'the Bride' in Black Saint and Sinner Lady. In the background is Shirley as 'Biblical Eve.' The music, a Charlie Mingus masterpiece was written in 1963. 'Black Saint and Sinner Lady' has been described as one of the greatest achievements in orchestration by any composer in jazz history. Charles Mingus 1922-1979 was an ambitious and if true, bad-tempered, Chinese, English, Black American and first cousin of Abraham Lincoln. His music was hot and sexy, encompassing bee bop, gospel, classical and jazz.

Personally, I think it is Rodney's best choreography ever but perhaps it is more fun to dance than to watch. The critics and the audience just didn't get it.   The transition from biblical times to the machine age in dance went over their supposedly sophisticated heads. No one realized when the music and ballet was finished. At the end there was silence and then slowly a gathering of polite applause. I can't believe they are so bloody square. This music speaks to us.

We performed Black Saint again for the students and teachers of the ballet festival at the *Théâtre des Étoiles* in the old town and they were blown away. They adored the choreography.   But, the management at the fancy *Masque de Fer* in the casino pulled it from the program for the rest of the season and a more commercial ballet was put in its place. My poor Rodney was crushed. He wanted our new ballets to be taken seriously as a modern art form not merely entertainment. His dream of taking 'Black Saint and Sinner Lady' to the Olympia Music Hall in Paris was forever dashed. *The Contract never came.*

Rudy

Security guys with BIG guns are swarming for the Ray Charles concert. Well!!!!! This is a big deal to benefit the Red Cross and maybe Veterans of WW2.   Yvette went *BESERK* - NUTZ - when the back-up girls RAYLETS and band took over our dressing rooms without saying one DAMN word. They just BARGED in like we were the cleaners.   So lucky they don't dig French or there would be a big scene I can tell you maybe WW3. Jorge and I with some guys from Palm Beach orchestra are going to JAM with the band tonight FAR OUT MAN, Ja!!!!!! After Raylets and stuff - on the *plage*.   This is *gute* let me tell you.

CANNES

PALM BEACH

MARDI 11 AOUT A 21 HEURES

, DINER DE GALA

en accord avec JOHNNY STARK et HENRY GOLDGRAN
(en exclusivité)

RAY CHARLES

son grand orchestre
et LES RAELETES

LE RODNEY JAZZ BALLET

PALM BEACH ORCHESTRA

BENNY BENNET et MICKY MITCHEL

Prix du dîner : 250 F, comprenant : "Champagne-à-votre-volonté", taxes et service.
TENUE DE SOIREE   RESERVATION : 38.25.09

Mary

As soon as the first half of the program is finished, the JBR are expected to vanish into thin air. Of course we had absolutely no intention of missing the opportunity to hear Ray Charles. As the last notes of "*Artistry in Jump*" came to a crashing climax, we took our bows and flung ourselves down the stairs. The Raylets are using one of our dressing rooms and so Yvette with a scowl gathered up the piles of orange feathers, chiffon coats and gloves and sorted them in the corridor. We scrubbed all traces of stage grease paint from our faces, reapplied our going-out-to-party make up and splashed perfume over our sweaty bodies. As soon as we were dressed Sally and I stole past the guards at the stage door and ran around the outside of the casino to the beach, through the private cabanas and up the back stairs to the terrace. We know every nook and cranny of this place.

At the top of the stairs another guard eyed Sally up and down, winked and nodded toward a large urn of flowers and massive loudspeaker where we hid. "*I Gotta Woman*" was blasting into my ears. The fancy people at the back were standing and were roaring their approval. It was deafening. Amid the waving arms and wiggling jiggling hips, all I could see was the top of Ray's head bobbing up and down and the five back-up girls wearing black *putain* wigs. They were snapping their fingers and swaying dangerously, in their tight, shiny red satin dresses about to go down like dominos. The whole orchestra started to bob and sway again to "What'd ah say, Hey mama, don't ya treat me wrong come and luv your duddy all night long." The place went ape with everybody bouncing to the beat. Even the waiters were snapping fingers, shaking and twitching and having a blast. Sally and I wanted to bob and sway too but just then a gorilla of a guard sidled over and demanded to see our tickets. "Hit the road Jack and dontcha come back no more, nor more, no more no more" and so we did. Tickets would have cost us two hundred and fifty francs and so we ran off join the others at the '*Whiskey-a-Go-Go.*'

The next morning, Sally, Tanita and I went to reclaim our dressing room and found it had been trashed. And there at Sally's place on the long battered table was a small paper packet containing a tiny white pill. Ah hah! She popped it quick as a flash into her purse and snapped it shut. "This is my souvenir of Ray Charles" she said with a happy smile.

Sally

The midnight blue side curtain hides me and I am alone with my thoughts as I wait for my entrance. Deep breathes in and out as I struggle to calm myself. I have a lump in my throat because this is the last time I will ever dance with Rudy. I sense his presence rather than see him as he silently takes his place at my side poised like a bird for flight. Is he feeling anything or just anxious to leave, get to Paris and out of our lives? In the dark he takes my hand and squeezes it. We dare not look at each other or say anything. Here is our cue. We rush onstage, two young lovers joining our friends in dance. But I play a foolish girl who is discontented and longs to live like the ladies parading along the boulevard in expensive furs and fine clothes. Pushing her beau away she gazes longingly at a white fur stole on a mannequin in a shop window. She pretends to be rich and preens like a peacock in a wild orgy of dance. Her beau returns with a fur wrap that he has stolen and places it around her shoulders.

At this point Rudy and I dance our *pas de deux*, at first joyously and then more somberly as the girl realizes that what matters most is not the riches and trappings of wealth but true love. The final leap, my arms outstretched, I launch myself into the air confident that Rudy won't drop me but hold me high before he releases me to slide very slowly down his body inch by inch. Backstage the shrill blast of a police whistle is heard. The fur wrap lies in a heap, forgotten. Rudy's lips brush against mine and I can almost taste him. Then without warning we kiss, a real kiss that makes me feel quite faint. I don't want it to stop. Is this goodbye in front of everybody? BLACKOUT, exit stage left. As we take our bows smiling, gasping for air Rudy turns to me, cocks his head to one side and winks. I never see him again.

Darling Lez. I am coming home and bringing Mary with me. I long to be with you even if it is only for a few days. We are both absolutely knackered and need to sleep. Will arrive next Thursday at the latest. Love Sal xxx

Rudy

HELL I am going to miss my beautiful Sally. Dancing with her was like flying through time. In rehearsal and on stage it was spiritual, physically and emotionally thrilling. We danced with passion and love - not the kind of love you feel at 12 years old, but total, pure and mature. My feelings for her will never go away, ever....... AAAhhhh *merde!* We keep right on dancing until we drop dead, DON'T WE?

Mary

It is hard to believe that summer is over, that our glorious days in Cannes will become memories to be brought out and examined like well-loved toys of childhood. I have never been more fulfilled, so alive in every way than in these past few weeks with the ballet and with Jorge but it is time to get the show on the road. We have been paid, settled our hotel bill, and I am anxious to get on that damn train heading north before I start sniveling. Don't look back, don't stop.

Dear Mom and Pop: I am off to Egypt to dance for Nasser and the King of Jordan at a big congress in Cairo. I am not sure how long I will be there but don't worry because the ballet sticks together. I will not be carried off into the desert by the Sheik of Arabia. Love from your nomad daughter. Mary xoxo

P.S. I am going with Sally to London to stay with her mom, Lesley and visit my old flatmates. Write c/o Mrs. Lesley Seyd 9 Lyme Terrace. London N.W. 1.

Chapter Nine

London, the Swinging 60's

...Monsieur, the porter had watched over us all night while we slept on the floor of the train, our guardian angel.

WORLD NEWS

October 1964: Nikita Khrushchev dismissed as Soviet Party leader.

Sally

Rodney and I have said goodbye many times before, but this time, I feel like something deep inside is being stretched to the breaking point. How I wish we were going home together to rest before we begin again. I looked at him, so handsome, eyes sparkling and full of life and hugged him long and hard, almost wistfully. Cannes was good for him and he says he has met a lot of influential people who may be able help the ballet. I suspect that some of them are the glamorous women hanging around the gambling tables looking to help themselves. *C'est la vie!*

The train gave a lurch and I am hanging out of the window. It is about to leave and Mary is nowhere to be seen. From across the station came a whistle and the unmistakable yell "Halloo, Sal I'm over here. Wait up!" Around the corner she flies dragging her possessions behind her like a dustbin man. She leaps aboard dumping her belongings in a heap. Flopping down she pats the leather cushion like a pony and laughs "Giddy up, let's get moving."

For two little people, we have an awful lot of luggage: five suitcases, a record player, extra bags and all the usual clutter collected during the past eight and a half months of non- stop travel. Aboard the train, our cases overflow the compartment into the corridor forcing everyone to climb over and squeeze around them. There is a lot of grumbling which we ignore as we sit facing each other on opposite banquettes gazing out the window each buried in private memories. It has been a long and emotional day of farewells. The owner of *La Residence Hotel* gave us a last picnic, including a jar of his home-made apricot *confiture* as well as fresh apricots from the garden. He was a lovable man who treated us like his family. We rarely saw him other than at breakfast when he spoiled us with endless cups of *café au lait* and loaded us up for the day with *baguettes.* Often he would ignore his other guests and sit with us telling tales of all the artists who have called the Residence their home. This morning, he held my hands and confessed that he was going to miss us terribly, dabbing his handkerchief to his eyes. I think he really means it.

I will miss that impossibly beautiful white sandy beach, the breezes filtering through the palm trees, the faint smell of sun tan oil mixed with salty air and the sight of glamorous ladies lolling naked in the hot sun, but most of all, I will miss Rudy. I don't think I will ever dance '*Les Fourrures*' with such passion again. It just won't be the same with another partner. In this business it is a mistake to get too close to people because they go far away and disappear from your lives. 'Clickedy clack, clackidy click,' the rhythm of wheels on rails is getting faster and faster rocking me to sleep and making me feel safe as though in someone's loving arms.

Mary.

Everyone should have a Lesley in their lives, especially, if they are young and vulnerable and far from home. Sally's mother is a lovely, calm and gracious woman full of wisdom and humor and nothing seems to ruffle her. Of course Sally's letter announcing our arrival didn't reach number 9 Lyme Terrace before we did and it was a complete surprise for Lesley to see not only her daughter after ages and ages but me too amid a daunting pile of shabby suitcases and stuff. It was well after midnight when Sally pounded on the front door until a sleepy face appeared at the upstairs window, "Wait a moment Sally dear," and a key was tossed out onto the front step.

What a relief to be in a real home, not a hotel, not a theatre and not a bar or a restaurant. I spied a huge squidgy chair covered in a Sanderson's chintz and just fell into it, every part of my body numb with fatigue. Lez, her wool paisley dressing gown pulled tightly around her waist, poured us each a very large brandy in a snifter and we sat up for hours telling her everything, every single detail, things I could never ever confess to my own mother. She laughed and wept and cheered with us and never sat in judgment over any of our antics. I was dying for a cigarette but Lesley has weak lungs from tuberculosis and it would make her cough unbearably. In her lifetime she has spent years in a sanitarium and suffered deeply.

And the mystery of Sally's father was solved. Sally never talks about him. It was Lesley who told me that her ex-husband lived in New York and was a well-respected medical doctor. Sally was only sixteen when he died. It was about three a.m. when we finally ran out of conversation and I staggered downstairs, took off my skirt and blouse, collapsed on a small fold-out cot and was dead to the world in seconds.

From somewhere not far off the unmistakable smell of frying bacon drifts into my consciousness. Voices and laughter are coming from upstairs and I feel the ache of homesickness. Wouldn't it be terrific if I could just walk right into my own dear kitchen and see my father home and my mother in her red quilted dressing gown waltzing with a broom to music blaring from our radio? She loves to dance.

Sally

For someone who was not brought up to be practical, I am fascinated watching my mother cook in her tiny kitchen. She seems to float without effort from the cooker to the breadbox to the sink, all the while concentrating and listening intently. Nothing is held back and I tell her everything about Rodney and our financial worries. Looking around the room I think how perfect it would be if we had a warm and cozy place just like this to call our own? Lesley is sympathetic but does not tell me what to do. I love her for that.

"Wow, a real English breakfast," Mary has emerged from downstairs and gives Lesley an unexpected hug of appreciation. A bright shaft of sunlight shines on the polished table like a spotlight center stage. We dive into the bacon and eggs helping ourselves from dishes of sausages, tomatoes and toast. We haven't had a breakfast like this in months. Coffee and croissant are all one eats on the continent. Lez spreads marmalade on a small piece of toast but doesn't take a bite. "I really think you girls should spend the day downtown. Go to Carnaby Street and Kings Road. You are so wrapped up in the ballet and have spent so much time abroad that you know nothing at all. Nothing of what is happening right here in London. You will be enlightened by a revolution of new ideas." Then she picked up her toast and took a tiny nibble, peering at us over her spectacles like a wise old owl.

It takes us the whole morning rummaging through our things to find something suitable to wear that doesn't look foreign. We want to fit into the scene. Double decker bus #73 takes us right to Oxford Circus and we jump off winding our way past the Palladium and across Great Marlborough Street into Carnaby Street.

Lez is right. Carnaby Street is indeed an intoxicating new world for us. From the shop fronts music blares; the Animals, the Beatles, Rolling Stones and The Who in an all-day party. We wander about in our dreary skirts and jumpers trying not to stare. The boys are strutting along like peacocks wearing harlequin costumes in bright colours, bell-bottomed trousers in diamond patterns and others decked out in striped caftans, beads and bells smoking stubby cigarettes that smell sweet and pungent like burning rope. The street is alive with violent hues of purple, lime, hot pink and yellow. Flirty girls prance by wearing false eyelashes, showing off their legs in miniskirts up to their knickers.

The rest of the afternoon Mary and I race in and out of all the boutiques for both boys and girls: Lord John's, Lady Jane's, Mates, Ravel and Mod Male, trying on outrageous outfits. There is a white dress exactly like my costume in 'Sinner Lady' right down to the detail of the cut out front. Rodney would go mad with excitement especially seeing the live mannequins in the shop windows just like our ballet '*Les Fourrures.*'

At a quaint old pub, at the top of Carnaby Street where it joins Gt. Marlborough Street, we push our way through the crowd and order 'alfa lager' and look around. The pub, *Shakespeare's Head* looks like it has been here forever with leaded glass windows and walls of solid English oak, decorated with framed portraits faded yellow with age. It is grimy with soot and smells of nicotine, pot, perfume and unwashed bodies all jammed together shrieking and laughing. We pretend to be part of the scene gulping our beer, smoking and looking 'hip' although of course we are not. In a flash, it hits me. The dream of my teen-aged years has been fulfilled and I am no longer a Londoner but a foreigner in my own hometown. Brussels is as familiar to me as Paris, Cannes, Lisbon, Firenze and Roma. My home is with Rodney and my destiny is travelling with the ballet. Without warning there are tears in my eyes. I miss the JBR and wish they were here.

September 1964   9 Lyme Terrace, London N.W.1 England

Dear Mrs. Spilsbury:

Thank you for your charming letter – Let me say at once that, after a few days rest, both your daughter and Sally looked fine! I believe they had a trying journey – this is the sort of thing young people put up with in crowded Europe. Mary is a most delightful and I would say extremely sensible girl. I have thought of writing to you before this, but I did not see much of Mary in Montreux and did not feel justified in doing so. I do understand so well how you must feel, particularly as you are a good way away and cannot check up from time to time, as I do.

Rodney Vas is a thoroughly nice man. The reason his financial position is precarious is that he is a good artist and will not exploit his ballet. I do not think he can avoid unloading his worries on them – they are obvious and anyway one of the attractive things about the company is their cooperation and friendliness. Sometimes they get annoyed with each other and some are far nicer than others – but, they do share good and bad times and there is less jealousy than is often the case in show business.

To be honest, I think it is in many ways, a superb training for life – but of course that depends on what you want. Mary has loosened up a lot since I first saw her and has gained in self-confidence...she always had poise and great intelligence. All work in theatre – whether it is serious theatre, show business or as in this case a mixture, is full of insecurity. Sometimes they are sure of contracts for some time ahead, sometimes not. But as long as a girl has some base to come back to as Sally and Mary have, there's no great harm in it. One can cable money to them at a few hours notice! Rodney is genuinely concerned for them all and though they work terribly hard, and it is not an easy life, they usually seem to keep fit and well. Everyone gets run down at times- They are all a bit worried about finances because they all wanted to put the show onto a new level, and it is almost impossible over here to get financial backing, especially for dancing, which is out of fashion. But, this life does teach them to look after themselves and to be sensible about themselves. They soon lose false romanticism, which is the thing that leads many people into trouble of one sort or another.

As long as they do not carry on too long in this, I think it is a good experience. They grow up – and what really counts is their background and early training and the love they have had. This stands out a mile. I am very glad indeed that she and Sally are friends. Yours truly, Lesley Seyd

Mary

Just as we were leaving, Sally's mother slipped a small book into my pocket. "For later" she said, "Zen and the Art of Archery by the German philosopher Eugen Herrigel." Herr Herrigel believes that any physical activity such as dancing will become effortless after years of training and allow the mind to be released to some magical place. How different our mothers are;

Lesley living in the sophisticated center of the theatre and art world is delving into mysticism and my pioneering mother in the west is fretting about my spinsterhood. *Vive la différence*!

Sally

The trip from London to Paris went without incident and then Mary and I fell off the rails. We simply could not just pass through the most romantic city in the world without stopping for at least a few hours. Unencumbered, our belongings stored in left luggage at the *Gare de Lyon*, we crossed *Boulevard Diderot* and meandered through the streets toward the Seine. This is an area of Paris full of *joie de vivre*. The river flowing under the *Pont Austerlitz* was silver grey with flecks of sparkling gold from the sun. Dodging traffic we crossed the bridge and strolled under the row of trees along the *Quai Bernard* toward the *Champs-Elysees*.

I love watching people, the way they move, their rhythm and their posture tell the story of their lives. Are they melancholy, exhilarated or joyful or are they burdened with anxiety, sorrow and pain? The body does not lie. Some were rushing along with their heads down not seeing anything and some were just loitering like us. A man came up with pamphlets for something but he was brushed aside. Lovers were leaning on the river wall and every so often would kiss and gaze into each other's, eyes. Some were doing a lot more than that!

"Let's forget the train and go for *steak frites*," Mary said just as my stomach started to rumble. "We can catch the six o'clock, and be in Marseille in the early morning. The ship does not sail until the afternoon." What a super idea! We retraced our steps back to the *Gare de Lyon* and settled in the historic brasserie over the road from the station entrance. There we sat, as thousands before us, with a mountain of hot *frites,* and two juicy red beef steaks *'saignant.'* There is something about French cooking so simple but so perfect that is hard to surpass. Of course we washed it down with a large carafe of red wine and finished with *Mousse au chocolat.'* To us, two girls in Paris in the fall of 1964, it was perfection. A long time was spent over our meal, too long as it turned out and then we decided it best to get over to the station and replace our tickets.

The 6 p.m. train was absolutely choc-a-bloc with people jostling and shoving for places and needless to say our seat reservations were no longer valid. "Follow me," I pushed my way through the carriages to the first class compartment. This was not the time to be helpless. In very polite French I accosted the gentle looking porter who had a typically Parisian clipped mustache and well-fed waistline. With eyelashes fluttering and lips quivering we begged for a seat, a bench between the cars, the floor perhaps? I gave him my most seductive smile. I don't think we fooled him for an instant. Finally, *Monsieur* gave in to our pleas and allowed us, quite against all the regulations to stay quietly in the first class corridor. We stood by the windows for several hours talking and smoking until dark. As soon as everyone was settled and the compartments doors were closed for the night, Mary and I lay down on the floor on top of all our worldly possessions and closed our eyes. Cold drafts whistled through the cracks onto my feet and ankles. I fell into a fitful sleep.

At dawn, I awoke with the porter towering over me and holding two little cups of *café crème*. I poked Mary awake, that girl can sleep through anything. Oh the joy, the best tasting coffee ever! With a gentle smile he disappeared down the corridor. Monsieur, the porter, had watched over us all night while we slept on the floor of the train, our guardian angel.

Clackety clack, clickety click, we stretch our aching muscles, inhaling our hot coffee and gaze into the early dawn light. A man passed by smoking a Gitanes and the aroma spoke of Cannes and memories so fresh but gone forever. Too soon we have left behind the vines and flowers of the country speeding through the outskirts of Marseille.

Mary

That was a train from Hell! I thought that Sally and I were really at the bottom of the barrel but you should have seen the people in second class stagger off the train. From six in the evening until six in the morning they stood propping each other up like cattle to the slaughterhouse or else they just sat on their haunches in the aisles with people stepping over them on the way to the toilet. At 6 am we arrived in Marseille.

13.055.05 **MARSEILLE** (B.-du-R.)
L'Eglise St-Vincent de Paul, dite des Réformés.

Hello there!
We made it this
far though how is
beyond me. I left my
radio on the floor
please plonk it in the
suitcase for me.
Thank you so much
for everything —
big release, yummy
meals etc. You really
are a "super" mother!
Love Mary

Editions « La Cigogne »
7, rue de Millo - MONACO
(Exclusivité de fabrication André Leconte)

MRS LESLIE SEYD
9 LYME TERRACE
LONDON NW1
ENGLAND

Our ferry across the Mediterranean, the S.S. Kardenis doesn't leave until 4 pm. That is time enough for a very fast tour of the old town, one of the oldest ports on the Mediterranean, at least 600 BC. The port is infamous for crime, drugs, violence, and dangerous Algerian *Pieds-noir* so we were intrigued to see if it lived up to its reputation. It didn't. The *Marseillais* were utterly charming at least the ones we met. Sally and I left our bags with *Monsieur le Patron* at a bar on the dock and started up the hill to the soaring, Basilica of *Notre Dame de la Garde*. Hours later, when we staggered back to the bar thirsty and pooped and he greeted us warmly with two glasses of Pastis and a small jug of water. "Holy Cow, that could revive a dead donkey," I spluttered. After downing the first one, *Monsieur* said "Ladeees, they take eeet with *un peu d'eau*, emphasizing the first word. This 'lady' was soon to discover that Egyptian zibi, Lebanese arak, and Greek ouzo are also diluted with just a 'leedle' bit water.'

Sally and I are sitting there like two pickled fishwives when around the corner who should appear but the rest of the gang. They had been staying in nasty hotels for the week and caught bedbugs. Ha ha ha.

Covered in red spots and welts, they were whining and scratching. Sally, in an upper crust British accent cooed, "Oh Shame, *quel dommage,* we travelled First Class from Paris."

The city of Marseille on the south-east coast is the second largest city and largest port of France. The main boulevard Canebière leads from the Vieux Port to the Hotel de Ville, the city hall. In 1962 when French Algeria gained independence, there was a mass exodus of 800,000 French citizens from Algeria called 'Pied-noir', black feet after soldiers' black boots, through the port of Marseille to the rest of France. The pied-noir were tossed out of Algeria with one suitcase of possessions 'la valise ou le cercueil,' the suitcase or the coffin. One of the most famous pied-noir was Yves Saint Laurent, born in Oran, Algeria in 1936 and died in Paris in 2008. One of the staples of the JBR's wardrobe was Saint Laurent's beatnik turtle neck sweater designed by him in 1960.

Chapter Ten
Land of the Ancient Pharaohs

... Nobby just smirked." she said, "He leaned back on his chair,
blew smoke rings in the air, and rudely fondled his testicles as though
they were worry beads."

WORLD NEWS 1964

**Egypt: The Second Arab League Summit held in
Montaza Palace, Alexandria included 14 Heads of
State united to liberate Palestine from Zionist
Colonialism.**

**South Africa: Nelson Mandela Sentenced to Life
Imprisonment in a former leper colony on Robben
Island for opposing Apartheid.**

Mary

The S.S. Kardenis left from the *Vieux-Port* of
Marseille on September 2nd 1964; at least I think it was
the second. I've lost track of time. Before we actually
crossed the Mediterranean, the freighter docked to
unload and reload in the western Italian port of Genoa
and one entire day was spent in the ancient *Porto di
Napoli*, the Camorra stronghold of Italy, a city founded
in the 6th century BC. I was crazy to go ashore but we
were not permitted to *disembarque*.

Being cooped up with a bunch of high energy
dancers in third class on a Greco/Turkish boat is a bit
like being in a pond with too many frogs and not

enough lily pads. We were constantly in each other's way with nowhere to go. Rodney seems to have hopped into another class or else he missed the boat entirely. Once on board I never saw him for the entire five-day voyage to Alexandria, the ancient port on the delta of the Nile River.

After hours of playing a restless game of gin rummy and longing to be ashore, the S.S. Kardenis cast off and we headed for the open sea and a cooling breeze. I am terribly excited but a little apprehensive as to how we will be treated when we get there. From the little I know of recent history, both the French and the British were thrown out of Egypt after everybody squabbled over who owned the Suez Canal and started shooting each other. Other than Tanita, Ronáld, Xavier and Rodney everyone is either French or English so I cannot imagine what sort of welcome to expect.

Almost immediately we struck up a conversation with a very friendly boy from Cairo, also in third class. He didn't seem foreign at all but spoke fluently in French and English with a British accent. He introduced himself as Abdul. Later I find that almost everyone is called Abdul, a servant of God. This particular Abdul has been telling us about the dos and don'ts of the Arab world that we should strictly observe. Never go ANYWHERE alone and unchaperoned. Always shake hands, take food or gesture with your RIGHT HAND. The left hand is for wiping your bottom after going to the bathroom and is considered unclean. If a thief is caught stealing, their right hand is cut off and they starve to death because no one will allow a left hand to touch food. I doubt very much if this happens anymore but you never know.

He also warned that it is customary for Egyptians to stand very close to your face when speaking, and it is considered impolite to move back

166

even if they have bad breath and reek of *hilba*, a strong smelling fenugreek tea. As he said this, Abdul stepped very close to Sally to demonstrate. "You smell like *Mouchoir de Monsieur*," she said sniffing his aftershave like an English spaniel. I think he just wanted to see how close he could get before she pushed him away.

In answer to our big question, Abdul assured us that we would find henna, barrels and barrels of the stuff, enough dye for an army of flaming redheads, in the famous *Khan El Khalili* souks, the main marketplace of Cairo. Sally and I are thrilled to bits.

S.S. Esperanza, the sister ship of the S.S. Kardenis that plied the Mediterranean Sea between, France, Italy and Alexandria, Egypt during the 1960's. In this Italian postcard, the ship is sailing from the Giudecca Canal in Venice.

Sally

Land ahoy! After seven days aboard this unspeakable Turkish tub, we are finally in sight of Alexandria, the Pearl of the Mediterranean. Because we are in third class we have been treated very badly.

So many rules, we are not to go here, forbidden to be on that part of the deck, must eat horrible stew that is swimming in rancid olive oil. I HATE this sort of thing. Most of the JBR turned green almost immediately and disappeared into the bowels of the ship to their wretched berths. Only Richard, Elizabeth, Mary and I were left standing and we stayed on deck reading and teaching Richard how to play gin rummy. According to the Egyptians on board, the city of Cairo is perfection in every way and we will be treated with great respect.

Amid shouting, screeching of sea birds, crashing, scraping of metal on metal, and rattling of chains, the S.S. Kardenis docked and the long gangplank was lowered to freedom.

Nadine, who had been seasick the entire voyage, shot off as though chased by demons. The rest of us queued up and waited our turn to disembark. Weaving his way toward us through the masses was an extremely tall man in a pale linen suit. He waved; our impresario maybe and abruptly turned his back on us greeting only Rodney. "Now there's a gentleman for you," said Elizabeth sarcastically. A long conversation ensued with hands waving in the air, the ritual offering and lighting of cigarettes, little bows and finally a handshake. Rodney came back to us, nimbly dodging men in ankle length cotton gowns carrying baskets and bundles, passengers laden with luggage and poor begging children. "Dahlinks, we are staying in Alexandria awhile for an important Arab meeting." A sudden blast of a ship's horn and the cries of people trying to sell us trinkets and souvenirs drowned out the rest. "Later, later, we WILL go to Cairo," he shouted above the noise.

168

Arab Heads of State September 1964 : Montaza Palace, Alexandria – Front row from left to right. Abdul Salam,Arif (Iraq) ,Gamal Abdel Nasser (Egypt) ,Hussein of Jordan, Second row. Abdel Hakim (Amir of the Egyptian Army), Ahmed Ben Bella (Algeria)

Sept. 1964   Hotel Méditerrannée, SaBa Pacha Ramleh (sous Sequestre)
Alexandria Tel. 62707-62708 R.C.A. 26313

Darling Lezy,

I expect you are surprised to see that I am in Alexandria not Cairo. It is all a little crazy and hard to explain but don't worry, we shall be in Cairo next week.   The Méditerrannée is really a super place – outdoor/cabaret/theatre/restaurant and hotel where we are living. My room number forty-two is at the back opening onto a terrace overlooking a garden.   On the left is the stage set in a garden of white acacia trees, foxgloves, delphiniums and lychnis.   The sweet heady smell of jasmine perfumes the air.   On the street the smells are not so sweet, as you can imagine but the main hardship is the heat. It isn't like any heat I have ever experienced, even in Tunisia three years ago. In the evening the hot air crushes me and totally saps my energy. I had such a lovely time with you in London, Mary too - we both feel so much better for it. Lots of love to you, kisses, Sal xxx

Mary

Who would ever guess that learning to dance would become a ticket and passport to see the world? I certainly never imagined when I was a little girl doing my *'plies'* at Miss Wynne Shaw's ballet school that I would ever be in North Africa entertaining Egyptian sheikhs hiding behind dark gangster sun glasses. The difference is that none of us are tourists free to enjoy the antiquities of another era. All our passports have been taken away and we are classed as foreigners. Those little pieces of paper make us slaves with no rights and a whole lot of rules. We are not permitted to go anywhere without a guide. Our passports will not be returned until we leave the country and we eat and sleep where we work. I haven't yet figured out if that is for our protection or we are prisoners. But what absolutely tears me up is the hypocrisy of full body suits that we must wear under our costumes.

On our very first rehearsal the big boss man came up with a bundle of baggy, brown cotton suits that looked like men's long johns. "It is the Muslim law," he explained, "Women do not show their skin on stage." "What about belly dancers?" I protested, but he just sighed in exasperation expecting women to do what they are told without question. The first time we donned the suits I couldn't believe he was actually serious. We look ridiculous.

During the rehearsal with the orchestra, who were having a terrible time with the music, I had grave misgivings. We are certainly not in the south of France now.

Opening night, I put on my multilayered outfit; body suit, black tights, a turtle necked sweater, and boots. Without moving one baby finger, beads of sweat appeared on my forehead and black mascara pooled under my eyes like a tearful raccoon spilling over my cheeks onto the pristine white turtleneck. Yvette, momentarily speechless, stared at the spreading stains. She could barely contain herself and sucking air between her teeth, called me "*Salope.*"

Swaddled like mummies we did our very best. The orchestra, squeaked, trumpeted and banged the drums like happy children at a birthday party. It had a certain exotic charm but without any resemblance to our music at all. The audience didn't seem to notice anything amiss or else they were snoozing in the heat and awoke at the end to give us a polite welcome. As soon as our show ended Yvette snatched up the sodden costumes stained with pancake makeup and stormed out, kicking the armies of cockroaches out of her way. We all put our heads down and just laughed and laughed. What else could we do? I remember my buddy Tony Robertson advising, when things went completely haywire, "Just keep on - keeping on."

By the third night, most of the wrinkles were ironed out and the orchestra did pull itself together and to their credit managed to play our music really quite well. Thank God, *Alhamdulillah.*

Sally

Wherever we go Rodney is like a magnet. Effortlessly he attracts people who are charmed by him so it was no surprise that we were invited out to a traditional Egyptian meal, soon after we arrived. Within minutes of getting to the restaurant the assembled businessmen gathered around him asking, in fairly fluent English about the ballet and our endless travels. One of the men stared at my wooden Dr. Scholl sandals and said a little critically "bedroom slippers here." I remarked, looking pointedly at his long white nightshirt, "then that makes us even." On the street some people dress in western clothes but many of the men wear long, loose shirts *gallibaya* or striped *kaftans.* They are a lot cooler than trousers.

We are searching for fly swatters. Every morning we fly-tox the room with *Piff-Paff* but by nightfall they have reinforcements. We are going quite mad with frustration and must find nettings. After the second show is over, Tanita, Mary and I sprawl like the Beatrice Potter's flopsy bunnies on three camp beds. As the flies dance from one to the other, we swat them back and forth - an all-night game of tennis *'a trois.'*

During the day when it is too hot to dance, we have been visiting the ancient sites. For us, hiring a driver is the only safe way to be a tourist. We cannot just go off on our own, as we seem to cause a commotion even though we have been covering our heads with scarves. It doesn't help that Tanita is six feet tall and Mary and Richard are as white as ghosts. I am very much a chameleon and can pass myself off as Egyptian, Italian, anything at all.

Our drivers are a curious lot. The first one, an older man with dark skin and a moustache, seemed only interested in taking us to new buildings like the Hotel Helman built on orders of Abdel Nasser for the delegates of the Arab Summit and an aquarium full of Mediterranean fish which was too utterly boring. Ancient ruins zoomed by and he pointed out newly

172

constructed factories and industrial chicken houses. Our driver is enormously proud of Alexandria, the result he said of President Nasser's policy of 'Egypt for Egyptians,' whatever that means and the past is best forgotten.

We spotted some ruins and I said, "Please *Min fad lak* stop here!" "Oh it's nothing," he said, "You will not like, very old." But we forced him to stop and take us inside and there was a huge wall with carvings two thousand years old! Imagine that? It was far more interesting than the fish. Reluctantly, he drove us to the *Sawâre Pillar Amoud el Sawari* or column of the Horseman built around 293 AD and our first sphinx, a mythical pussycat crouched contentedly in the blazing sun with a happy smile upon its face. We leapt out leaving our driver sulking with his chums under a tattered piece of canvas and went to explore the underground site.

The much repaired sphinx of Alexandria and the Sawâre Pillar called Amoud el Sawari. The 400 -ton pillar is almost 100 feet tall with 88 of those feet one single chunk of polished red Aswan granite. Beneath the pillar (Diocletian's column) is a

*ruined subterranean serapeum or temple of the ancient God
Serapis where remains of sacred bulls have been found.*

About an hour later, we emerged again onto the
scorching gravel, found our guide having recovered
from the sulks running toward us with a posy of
jasmine to freshen the air inside the taxicab. On the
way back to the Méditerannée we were stopped by a
procession of some sort. "It's a Cinderella coach,"
Mary is hanging out the window squinting in the sun.
"It's solid gold, everyone is bowing their heads…oh for
Heaven's sake, it's a hearse," and she quickly pulled
her head back inside. The elaborate funeral was inching
its way through a throng of desperately poor people
dressed in rags; children with open sores and old men
with clouded eyes. I will never get used to the huge
gap between rich and poor. Our driver didn't seem to
notice.

There is a famous beach near the historical
battle site of El Alamein, sixty miles from Alexandra.
Another driver was hired to take us there for the day.
He was a much younger man, with the profile like a
Roman coin, clean-shaven with a long straight nose.
We whistled along the desert road like a bullet, straight
past anything he didn't want us to see. Tanita asked
him very politely to slow down in an area of once
elegant homes crumbling with neglect. Behind rusty
gates, gardens were left untended. "Why are they
deserted?" The driver ignored our questions. Later,
we shot by a collection of mud huts on either side of
the road, again empty. "Where are all the people?"
He put his foot on the accelerator staring straight ahead
like a marble bust of Julius Cæsar. "There is no one
here," he mumbled. "Slow down," I said, pointing to a
tumbled down ruin, "who is that then?" A woman was
boldly hanging up her washing and a tiny toddler

crouched next to her defecating on the ground. Two men sat listlessly watching her labours but doing nothing. "There is no one here" he repeated, "Jews, Greeks, all gone, all sent away." We looked at one another in disbelief. Why is he lying about the obvious?

The summer residence of ex-King Farouk, Montazah Palace is set in three hundred and fifty acres of rare flowers, date palms and lawns. The palace was built by Abbas Helmy II, the last Khedive of Egypt and Sudan in 1892. One of two palaces, Montaza had a private outdoor movie theatre, a teahouse and a ten-storied pink and white chicken coop. In September 1964, Egypt hosted the second Arab Summit at Montazah. (www.mideastweb.org). The palace gardens were open to the public during the summit, when the Jazz Ballet Rodney was in Alexandria.

Mary

Two hundred eggs a day, King Farouk is supposed to have consumed. Mind you the eggs here are smaller than ping pong balls, the hens being Bantams, but still, two hundred is quite excessive. According to rumor his appetite for women, was also insatiable and every pretty girl, married or single was fair game. I don't know if he was thrown out of Egypt because of the scandals, but left the country to live on a yacht near Monte Carlo surrounded by 'Les Girls.'

I am standing in front of the ex-King's ten-storied chicken coop in the three hundred and fifty acre garden of the Montazah Palace. It, the chicken house I mean, is every bit as luxurious as the palace, a fantasy in pink and white with turrets and swirls. The chickens can pop in and out of arched doors onto balconies, poop and go back into the cool interior to lay their tiny eggs. Liliane, Mireille, Sally and I took a tour of the garden but the palace itself is out of bounds because that is where the secret Arab summit is going on.

Just beyond the walls of this extravagance, scrawny children swarm the streets begging for a few miserable *piastras.* We empty our pockets into grubby brown hands.

Not far away is another summer palace *Ras-al-tin* meaning the Cape of Figs but we have run out of time and must race back to the Méditerannée for rehearsal. The palace, so we have been told, has a white marble bathroom as big as a ballroom with two sunken baths and an underground railway to get from one part of the palace to the other. It was at *Ras-al-tin* that King Farouk signed his abdication papers. He left Egypt forever with, so it is rumored, crates of solid gold bars disguised as champagne. This would be a little difficult to accomplish as King Farouk although, madly eccentric, was a Muslim and therefore expected to be teetotal.

Sally

I have a secret admirer. Without warning, a huge bouquet, at least three dozen perfect ruby red roses arrived in the dressing room with an envelope addressed to me. Everyone gathered around sniffing the blooms and cooing. "Omar Sharif I bet", said Mary as I pulled out the small white card. I was afraid to look; "the King of Jordan, a royal prince of King Saud, a billionaire oil sheikh?" Everyone is trying to guess. I turned the card over and in a neat tidy hand, was an invitation to dinner after the show but no signature. It was thrilling and even though I could not accept I was enormously flattered and must have blushed as bright as the roses because Xavier was teasing me, blowing kisses and playing the fool. On stage I do look quite fantastic in exotic false eyelashes, my hairpiece and wearing flawless makeup. It is part of the mystique of being an artist and appearing aloof and unattainable. But the JBR has an unwritten rule that if anyone in the audience, no matter how important they are, wants a date then the whole lot of us must be included. The evening flew by and I was very aware of being watched and admired and it did feel good.

Gathering up my flowers, I walked with Mary and Tanita back to our room as soon as the show was over. It was stuffy and smelled of Piff-Paff so we threw wide the terrace doors, fanning ourselves and opened bottles of fizzy water. Tap water is unthinkable. There was a knock and presuming it was Rodney I sighed tiredly, "Come in, come in, the door's not locked." In marched a dozen waiters carrying trays, platters, bowls, and baskets, piled high with food. "Who ordered this?" Of course it must be my admirer. Dishes were placed on the table, the desk, and luggage racks. We were running out of room and still trays appeared. As quickly as they came, the parade of waiters touched their foreheads murmuring, "*salaam*" and vanished. "Who can possibly eat this much food" Tanita wailed? "I can," said Mary, lifting lids and sniffing, "Allah be praised." The most heavenly scents of lamb, cardamom, cumin, chicken, and mint filled the room.

Good news travels fast in the JBR and within minutes Nicole, Liliane, Mireille and Shirley were perched on our beds, followed by Richard, Xavier, Frank, Ronáld, and Elizabeth. Finally, Rodney, Yvette, and Nadine squished into our room, spilling onto the terrace. The fifteen of us were laughing and chattering as though we hadn't seen each other in years. Richard was hilarious, telling jokes and munching lamb chops. Then he lay back and burped loudly, a sign of appreciation in Egypt. He's now one of us and has a delightfully wry sense of humor, for a boy. We ate until we were exhausted. It was a night to remember.

My not so secret admirer, a brother in law of King Farouk was there the following night, when Rodney and the manager took me to his table after the second show. He must have an important job. Normally, we would never be permitted into the audience and nor would we go. As soon as we approached, he stood up extending his hand. I was expecting a man in flowing robes and a turban but my admirer wore an impeccable white dinner jacket. We were introduced and indeed yes, Mr. X. seems to be a very important man. His bodyguard pulled out a chair for me and I sat timidly on the edge. Rodney thanked him for the generous supper and after a few polite sentences he asked me if I would be going shopping in Alexandria. "Oh yes," I enthused, "tomorrow I am looking at shoes." "And, what size do you wear?" he said as his eyes grazed my legs and came to rest on my size 39 feet. What an odd question! "Oh 37," I lied, knocking off a couple of sizes because I hate my big feet. We chatted for a few moments more and then left.

Crikey! The next thing I knew, forty pairs of shoes were delivered to our dressing room, every shape, every colour every style and all size 37. Oh why, oh why was I so bloody vain? Mary was over the moon - they fitted her perfectly.

Mary

Once, and only once, Sally and I went exploring alone but never again. Just off the main street we turned into a small alleyway and were meandering around a maze of dirt roads, *al harat,* hoping to discover the 'real' Alexandria. The streets are so picturesque with laundry strung from house to house, rusty pots of flowers balanced on walls, exotic smells of spice, tiny shops jammed with brooms and sacks of wheat and crumbling archways leading nowhere. Men in their traditional robes sit outside doing nothing at all but smoking hash in water pipes while their women swathed in black robes scurry like mice. "Why do most of the women wear black and the men wear white?" I ask. "Black absorbs the heat and those poor dears must be suffocating." Sally agrees with me but we have no answers.

The alleyway turned into an enclosed courtyard with no exit. We paused. Sally turned to me and whispered, "We are being followed." A gang of a dozen or so street urchins seven or ten years old started circling us. They were dancing around and chanting "No like flies, no like flies," and were pressing closer and closer. '*Imshi, imshi,* go away', I tried to sound assertive. Sally and I held hands and were afraid to move. Like a swarm of bees, whole courtyard filled with boys, screaming this terrible wail like a war cry and chanting "no like flies,' louder and louder, getting more excited and bolder. The laughing mob started pushing and trying to pinch us. By now, we were absolutely petrified and clung together trying not to fall over and be trampled. Suddenly, above the racket I heard a sharp whistle and a gruff male voice giving orders in Arabic. The boys scattered into doorways, behind curtained windows, until POOF, they were gone. An imposing middle-aged man emerged from the shadows. He was wearing a straw panama hat, his eyes hidden behind dark glasses. He walked quickly over to us, stood very close as the Egyptians do and said in clipped Oxford English, "Good afternoon Ladies," with a little bow, "You should not be out alone without a chaperone. Come along with me." Thoroughly chastised, we trotted along behind him retracing our route to a main street. He stopped a passing taxi, thrust some money to the driver and said "Méditerranée," opening the door with a flourish. He knew exactly who we were and where we lived. Then he vanished before we had time to say thank you. Do we have strangers watching out for us?

Sally

After almost two weeks of confinement in room forty-two we received exactly six hours' notice to move to Cairo. One would think that after all our travelling packing would be routine. But no! The room is a tip. Tanita is lolling on her camp cot painting her fingernails and haphazardly tossing items into her open case. In a white cloud of smoke, Mary is bouncing up and down on her bag that is stuffed with what should have been MY shoes, swearing like a lorry driver. She is not the timid young thing she was when she arrived at the London audition. I plan to have my own space in Cairo or shall go bonkers.

180

The Second Congress of Non Aligned Countries was held in Cairo, Egypt from October 5ᵗʰ - 12ᵗʰ 1964 and hosted by Gamal Abdel Nasser. Representatives and Heads of State of eighty five nations assembled, including the founding members: the aforementioned Nasser of Egypt, Tito of Yugoslavia, Sukarno of Indonesia, Nkruma of Ghana and Nehru of India, to discuss a middle course between the Western and Eastern blocs during the Cold War and a ban on all nuclear testing. Conspicuously absent was Israel who was developing nuclear arms. In this photo, Sally is posing under the welcome sign while Mary, the photographer with a Kodak Brownie camera stood in the middle of the avenue in danger of being run over by camels or cars.

Mary

We seem to have left the flies behind in Alexandria but here in Cairo we have mosquitoes, huge flying biters that just love white skin with freckles. All the Piff-Paff, incense, and jasmine in the world have no effect. I am a mass of red bumps that fester and itch. Richard and Nadine have come down with food poisoning or liver disease because they both look awful.   Such is the grand ballet that arrived at the *Auberge des Pyramids* at 229 Pyramid Road yesterday to impress our new boss, whose name is of course, Abdul.   We called him Mr. Nobby at first but by the end of our contract here he was 'that fat bastard.'   But, for the moment we are treated like Royalty.

Cairo, the city of a thousand minarets, is unlike any place I have ever seen.   Parts of the city appear to be very modern with office buildings for international companies and other places have a thousand years of dust.   Cars, donkeys, camels and trolleys all vying for space, share streets.   Side by side stand very old colonial buildings and half-built cement boxes that are already slum tenements before they are even finished. From my hotel room I can see the roof of one of Nasser's housing projects.   Babies with no diapers are sleeping on the roof beneath clotheslines and piles of rubbish. Molting chickens scratch about pecking at dead flies or whatever else lurks there.

I am sharing the room with Tanita in a hotel very near the newly built Nile Hilton, another project of Nasser's grand scheme for Egypt.   Sally has announced like Marlene Dietrich "I vaant to be alone," and is staying across the hall in a room all by herself.   She likes her privacy and tends to be a bit grumpy when she gets sick of us, especially me.

The big Congress of Non Aligned countries is about to begin and security was everywhere.   Rodney warned us not to write anything controversial, no smart remarks, even made in jest, in our letters home because not only would they be censored, but we could be in serious trouble with the dreaded secret police, *Al Mukhabarat.*

Five times a day, the city comes to a sudden halt. From the top of the thousand minarets comes an unearthly, primitive cry, up and down the scales. It is the call of the parish priest or *muezzin* to all the faithful Muslims advising them to stop what they are doing and pray. And that is exactly what they do.

The *Auberge des Pyramids* where we are performing is where the Muslims, at least the wealthy ones, come to play, not pray. The prices to get into the *Auberge* are more than we make as performers. Isn't that madness? The cabaret was built in the middle of the war and we were told that the infamous 'Salle Dore' the downstairs bar was a favourite watering hole of British officers as well as, ex-King Farouk, Noel Coward, Gore Vidal and other *bon vivants*.

From the outside it is not at all impressive, a sprawling white plaster building with a flat roof but the interior is like walking into a Turkish harem of gold, mirrors and curlicues, a fanciful salon with an open courtyard. King Farouk, who was actually Turkish not Egyptian must have felt right at home, but the décor did not make me feel like I belonged, quite the contrary. Last night we officially opened at the *Auberge des Pyramides* in front of President Nasser, known as 'The Giant of the Middle East', Tito of Yugoslavia, the very handsome King of Jordan and a whole lot of bodyguards all armed to the teeth. I was intimidated dancing in front of a roomful of men hiding behind dark glasses.

From Al-Ahram Weekly established in 1875. Issue No. 548: "The Auberge des Pyramides with its infamous 'Salle Dore' bar opened in the summer of 1943 and was closed in late 1986 after it was set on fire by rioting Central Security forces. Egyptians have always had mixed feelings about nightclubs and bars, suspecting them to be linked somehow to institutionalized prostitution. In the 1960's during periods of unrest, the population's first act of defiance had been to set nightclubs ablaze, thus eliminating the most obvious symbols of Westernization: the consumption of alcohol, lack of segregation and indecent acts performed in public." August 23-29 2001.

Sally

It was brilliant! The opening was fabulous and the audience loved it all. Well, to be perfectly frank, not '*Black Saint and Sinner Lady*.' I warned Rodney that it was a rotten idea to do a ballet in Egypt that began with Xavier's voice reciting *en Français* from Genesis Chapter one Verse twenty six, the story about Eve and the Serpent, with Shirley dancing in nothing but a flesh coloured unitard and an asp slithering around her body. What did he expect?

Right after, I made my entrance dressed as a nun, representing the established Church of Rome and then Mary the Temptress portrayed the 'Fall from Grace.' Ha Ha! At least her tummy button was covered but one leg was bare to her hip. Rodney argued, "This is beeg international Congress and they vaant modern dance so modern dance is vaat they get. Daahlink, I know what I do." Well, this particular international congress was completely mystified by the American/Chinese/Scottish jazz of Charlie Mingus and when we got to the 'machine age' dancing with abandon to *Black Saint and Sinner Lady* blasting from the speakers in the ornate harem, I think they all wished they were downstairs in the infamous *Salle Dorée*, drinking goat's milk or whatever.

Mary playing 'Temptation' in "Black Saint and Sinner Lady." Photo taken in Beirut, Lebanon by Garo. 1964. Photo: Jazz Ballet Rodney

Yesterday was the most ghastly day of my life and it started out so innocently. It was a rare day off and I had planned to henna my hair in the morning and then join Rodney for lunch at the Hilton Hotel. We need to talk. Plans evaporated at seven o'clock when there was a tap on my door and unlocking it saw Nadine her face ashen and her eyes pleading like a puppy. *"Viens avec moi au medicin,"* she begged. Oh No! It's not possible. I looked at her waistline in horror, and despite the heat, I felt icy cold. She is *still* very pregnant. Somehow I thought this problem had been dealt with in Marseille. Damn, she must be four months maybe four and a half months along. Oh why me? Why does she not trust one of the French girls to help her? *"Je ne peux que te faire confiance pour m'aider."* I don't want to have any part of this but I have no choice. She cannot be left alone. I pulled her into my room and quickly dressed.

In front of our hotel, Nadine hailed a taxi and we climbed in. She handed me a scrap of damp paper with an address and with trembling hands she lit a cigarette inhaled deeply and settled back into the seat. Silence, we have nothing to say to one another, nothing at all. Nadine is the girl who lusts after my roles in the ballet; the girl who flirts outrageously with my man and now it is me that she turns to for help. For almost a year we have been dancing together every night and I realize that I know nothing about her at all.

The taxi squeezed down a narrow alleyway and braked in front of a stone archway. I opened the taxi door, "Wait for us, please" and he nodded. Nadine carelessly dropped her cigarette on the threshold and crushed it with the sole of her right foot. With a show of bravado she walked quickly through the entry to a shabby door with peeling green paint. It was ajar. I followed as she disappeared up a stone stairway to a landing dimly lit by a slit in the wall. A door opened.

Obviously we are expected as a woman silently beckoned us inside. She was not Egyptian but looked central European, Russian perhaps and was wearing a long faded blue skirt and a clean apron with a pocket.

On the right hand side of the room there was an alcove, with a high narrow bed partially hidden by a curtain that was yellowed with age. Nadine strode in, handed the woman an envelope of money. Counting it carefully, she shoved it into the pocket and gestured toward the alcove. I felt faint and started to head for the landing. "*Ne me quitte pas,*" Nadine implored. At that moment she looked terrified. "I am right here Nadine" and pulled the door closed behind me.

Outside on the landing, I plugged my ears with both hands and hummed. I willed myself to disappear to another place. Minutes passed, I waited. There was just one horrible scream like a wild animal being torn apart and then silence. I was sick into the cleaning bucket.

Reluctantly I went back into the room. Nadine unsteadily took a few steps toward me. I couldn't help myself I looked down at a small bundle of newspaper laying in a basket. "What are you doing with it," I whispered tonelessly. We will throw *him* in the Nile was the reply. And then I cried. Nadine stood like a granite pillar, rigid, staring at nothing. She will have to be on stage tonight or none of us will be paid.

Mary

No one goes to Cairo without visiting the *Khan El Khalili* market, a square mile or so of teeny, tiny, narrow shops, with factories above where workers beaver away on any conceivable object that might sell.

187

Sally and I had to drag Richard off his bed because he claims to be dying of food poisoning, dropsy or something weird. But we need him to be our escort so we ignore his groans and protests.

Khan El Khalili, market or caravanserai of Khalili is built over the Tomb of Za'afran, the burial place of the founders of Cairo in 960 AD. The Khan itself was built around 1380 and is the largest market in Egypt. To enter is to step back in time.

I will be censoring my weekly letter home but today will be remembered as long as I live. The three of us set out on foot with vague directions intending to spend an hour or so at the souks before heading out to Pyramid Road for our two nightly shows.

The streets were jammed with people bustling here and there shouting and arguing. Cars and trucks rushed along the streets avoiding the trotting donkeys and camels standing by the side of the road in their own dung - a normal day in Cairo on this October morning 1964.

One minute we were out in the scorching sun and the next we were plunged into the shaded labyrinth of narrow, tight alleyways, hundreds of years old and falling under the spell of the Arab bazaar. The sounds, the sights the smells were intoxicating and Sally, Richard and I dashed about from stall to store touching beads, trinkets, curios and pottery, stroking camel hair blankets and soft leather and inhaling the perfumes, incense, coffee and spices. "My friends, I make good *brice*, only for you." Come in come in, to my poor shop." Sally and I went in behind the beaded curtain. There were piles of embroideries of cross-stitch in red, orange and saffron gold and hand-woven rugs, thousands of them piled on the floor like folded rainbows. Richard called from outside "Come look at this" and we dashed out again to the next stall of worry beads, amber necklaces and gold chains. There he stood wearing a *Keffiyeh* a white scarf with a black and gold woven black cord, and a big grin. He looked... well, like a silly English boy with a napkin over his head, not a dark, dangerous and thoroughly irresistible Arabian sheikh. "My friend, you want, I make good *brice*." "Yes, yes, buy it," and Sally got into a corner and haggled with the poor man until he practically gave it to Richard. "*Bleese* you my friend, lady make good *brice*, I am poor man.

Nobody can bargain better than Sally. "It's my Jewish blood,"... Shhhhh. She clapped her hand over her mouth remembering Rodney's warning. Everywhere we stop even if just to browse, thick coffee with grains in it will appear in tiny cups on a brass tray. It is very sweet and strong.

Sounds bounce off stone walls like a melody as old as time, loud, exotic and pulsating. Vendors call out their wares in Arabic, German, Russian and English and kids howl as their exasperated mothers swat them around the ears with little sticks. Music blaring from small radios competes with hammering on metal and sawing on wood. A faint far off trill of a solo flute is barely audible over the tinkling of bells, and growling of dogs scrapping over small bits of food. Deeper and deeper we explored into the heart of the souks inhaling the sweetness of jasmine, sandalwood, cinnamon, saffron, the earthy smell of henna leaves, and Bay laurel and the sharp stink of urine mixed with tobacco and unwashed sweat.

Sally

Of the thousands of small trinkets and jewelry on offer, Mary insisted on buying a useless three-foot long brass hubbly bubbly that must weigh ten pounds. "How on earth are you going to pack that?" "Oh I'll mail it or something. I dunno," she replied. I bought a necklace, the most beautiful turquoises ever seen, five strands of them with a real gold clasp. Just when I though our shopping was over, Mary found a huge round metal tray with legs, the top etched with geometric Islamic patterns. "It's the perfect wedding present for my sister Dale," she thrust it into my hands "will you bargain for me?" The three of us went into the shop to have yet another cup of grainy coffee and talk about price with the owner, a short wiry man with all his front teeth missing and a wonky left leg.

The rear of the shop was a workshop, a circular gallery of niches each containing two or more men working on various pieces. They were hunched over, making tables, vases, lamps some painstakingly etched with silver threads pounded into a pattern. Others were working with mother of pearl cut into tiny bits fitted like a jig- saw puzzle onto trays and boxes of all sizes.

"My friends, I show you something special, yes." our toothless shopkeeper wanted to be our guide. "Leave table, *sheesha* here." Without hesitation Mary and I jumped up. Richard was reluctant. Our guide held open a curtain and pushing Richard ahead, we entered a world that few tourists ever see.

We crowded into a small warehouse jammed with souvenirs on floor to ceiling shelves and metal chandeliers crusted with semi-precious stones, thousands of them dangling from the ceiling. There was no exit except a ladder of wood and rope. Despite his leg, our guide scampered up like a monkey and through a hole to the roof. "You go next Richard" and with a sigh he climbed cautiously, one foot after another until he was almost out of sight. "It's brilliant, the rooftops…" and he was gone.

The roof is like a bed of burning coals stretching for acres. Mary and I are clattering along are trying to catch up to Richard in his flying *Keffiyeh.* I feel like the cat burglar in "To Catch a Thief" with Cary Grant, except that I am in a tight cotton skirt and clumsy Dr. Scholl's. We stumbled across a board ramp with no rails to the next building and then the next. "Don't look down," and I don't. Our guide is waiting looking very pleased with his 'special' treat but I am beginning to have doubts about this scene as we descend into a sort of open air pit with walls all around. Our friend remained on the roof watching delightedly.

The sunken pit is whitewashed but not terribly clean. About six gentlemen of varying ages and dress are sitting around having a hubbly bubbly party. They showed no surprise at our arrival. A very old man in a long sleeved *gallibaya* was in the corner playing an eerie solo on a reed flute. "You want *sheesha* yes?"

Now, I should explain that saying yes and no in Egyptian is more difficult than you might guess. If you shake your head up and down and make a kissy "laaa" with your tongue on your front teeth, it means no. If you shake your head no - that is more like yes. My answer was a definite NO! I tossed my head in the air and hissed Lah LaLaLa!

Richard giggled and Mary said "I wanna try it" and she plunked herself down with the men in the pit. A woman knelt in front of a pipe and filled the bowl with a burning coal, added a brownish rope of tobacco and handed the hose to the first man or last man, who knows? He inhaled deeply eyes lost staring into space for a moment, then exhaled and spat in the center of their feet. The second man took the same pipe and inhaled, exhaled and splat a great gob into the center. This went around the walls until it was Mary's turn. She grinned wickedly at us and then put the filthy thing in her mouth, inhaled, rolled her eyes dramatically as if she was drugged, exhaled and then spat as hard as she could into the mess. Richard immediately rushed over and peered deeply into her eyes, "Can you see me, hear me, are you stoned?" She laughed like a hyena. "I feel nothing at all."

"Merde, Look at the time!" We all jumped up searching for our toothless friend but he was nowhere to be seen. "Oh bugger, we're lost" shouted Mary. The roofs look all the same. In the distance we saw a striped robe "O.K. Let's follow that man" and we turned back across the roofs. Mary tore her shoes off and started running in bare feet on the burning tar. She stopped short, put them on again and we struggled along in our bloody Dr. Scholl's. Richard, for some unknown reason exploded into barbaric war cries. In a burst of euphoria, he soared through the air in a series of *grand-jétés* and airborne turns all the while hanging onto his *keffiyeh,* which had fallen over one eye. For a brief euphoric moment our boy was drunk with happiness.

On the next roof we found a very steep staircase and scrambled down into private home among astonished strangers who were sitting around a table eating. *"Shukran, Shukran"* Excuse us, please" and we went through an open arch into an alleyway. "Taxi, taxi," Richard was now frantic again. A sweet little child with dark round eyes took him by the hand gently as though he were Methuselah and calmly led us through the maze into the main street exactly where we started hours ago. With only enough money for a taxi to the Auberge des Pyramides, Mary and I stuffed cigarettes into his baby hands and he ran off. Richard doesn't smoke. Just as we were climbing into a taxi, our guide came limping up with the brass table and hubbly bubbly. Our last sight of the bazaar, a grinning black face, pressed up against the window *"salaam aleikum"* Peace be with you too old friend!

Gamal Nasser, born (Gamal Abd El-Nasser) was the first truly Egyptian head of state in 2000 years which explains his mania to nationalize everything and create an 'Egypt for Egyptians.' On July 21st 1960, he gave a speech on the first ever television broadcast in the Middle East. "Under his nationalization and centralization policies, Egypt became the uncontested media hub of the Arab Middle East for radio, film music recording and television." James R. Grippo, Music and Media in the Arab World: ed. Michael Frishkopf.

Mary

"Fill the space, Daahlink," Rodney calls from his position behind the camera. I look around. The space is the size of an arena and I wonder how on earth I am going to fill anything more than a few square yards at full gallop let alone *en pointe*, in broken down shoes. How I wish I had bought new ones when I had the chance in London. The JBR are assembled in an enormous whitewashed room rehearsing for a television special to be aired on the final day of the Congress. With the eyes of the world focused on Egypt, President Nasser has pounced on the opportunity to show how modern the country has become. Perhaps he should have heeded his predecessor, the chubby ex-King who once said "Never count your eggs after they are scrambled," or something like that.

We are rehearsing the two chosen ballets, *'Les Fourrures'* and *'Adagio, Allegro & Beat'* on the first day and 'shooting' on the second. The vast floor is marked with chalk to indicate the camera range. Rodney is re-choreographing both ballets in a fit of artistic inspiration. Needless to say it is exhausting. We work through the full heat of the day and then rush off to the *Auberge* for our nightly performances.

The next day I am buoyed up. It is the first time in my life I will be dancing a solo on national television or any television for that matter. We do a run through of *Adagio,* a most demanding ballet. Changes are made - a second run through, this time in full costume and without body suits, "one more time daahlinks." Rumbles start growing like an impending storm. "This is impossible," Sally tries to reason with him. "We cannot go on and on." Sweat is pouring off me soaking my white unitard and I take this moment of controversy to lie on the dusty floor with my poor feet in the air, ignoring Yvette screaming, "filthy *dégueulasse* get up *putain*."

Finally it is filmed, 'in the can'. Back in the tiny dressing room, my battered point shoes are removed and I carefully pull off the white unitard. Every toe is blistered – no, every toe is *bleeding*. The skin sticks and gets ripped off. I pull on my cotton shift and cannot even get my sandals on my feet. *"Godverdomme"* thunders a voice from the other side of the door. Rodney never swears unless something horrendous happens. Sally pokes her head out, "Rodney, what is it?" "There is no film in the camera." They have no film." It is the will of Allah and so - no film. *Insha'Allah.*

Richard, Sally, Elizabeth and I fall into the taxi in silence. After fourteen hours dancing on concrete in a furnace we cannot think of one thing to say and are shaking with shock and fatigue. The taxi driver speeds off toward the *Auberge des Pyramids.* We have two more shows before we are finished for the night. Suddenly it is all too unutterably funny. Richard starts to laugh, at first a just a snort and a snuffle and then he is overwhelmed and howls clutching his sides, We all fall apart then, much to the astonishment of the driver, begin shrieking out of control, holding our tummies, tears running down our faces. Finally we start to sing. We feel so hated here, and launch into every bloody British song we know. "Roll out the Barrel"♫♫ I guess it's because I'm a Londoner – That I love

London town. Even the taxi driver is hollering "La la la la love Lunnnen, I sing, me too.' Hah, Hah, Hah. God Save the Queen!

Sally

It doesn't seem to matter how hard we work or how much praise we get in the newspaper, our boss at the *Auberge* is dissatisfied. We are not treated with respect. A clause in our contract clearly states that no photographs are allowed during the performance. Right from opening night, flash bulbs popped and when Rodney rushed out into the 'house' to put a stop to it, he came face to face with a stony- faced bodyguard who spat '*la a*' with that spastic jerk of the head which means emphatically no, buzz off. Mr. Nobby pulled him aside and sneered, "they have every right to take photos."

The door to his office is always open and we must pass by on the way to the dressing rooms. Invariably he is sitting with his feet up watching and waiting, like a wolf circling a flock of lambs.   Just before our day off, Mary went into his den and asked very politely for her passport so she could take a tour to the Valley of the Kings before it was flooded. He agreed on the condition that he personally escorts her on a private tour. Well, you can imagine the red headed rage that provoked. She shouted that she would rather cut off her right hand than get into a car alone with a sleazy bugger. "Nobby just smirked." she said, "He leaned back on his chair, blew smoke rings in the air, and rudely fondled his testicles as though they were worry beads."

Just as I was thinking that Egyptian men are not particularly charming, my admirer from Alexandria,

Mr. X turned up and invited me out for an entire day, riding camels at the pyramids and then feasting in a bedouin tent at Sahara City. He knew jolly well that the whole ballet had to be invited too because we do not go out alone. The day turned out to be one of the most memorable of my entire twenty-four years on earth.

Early in the morning several cars with drivers picked us all up at our various hotels and we met on the desert sand near the pyramids. There was a herd of camels, some standing, some lolling about looking bored and I inspected at each one making my choice. The one that caught my attention had beautiful eyes with long curved lashes half closed like drowsy shutters. Unfortunately she was lying down chewing something disgusting but she was the one, my choice.

I hoisted my skirt up to my thighs because unlike Liliane, I did not think to wear trousers for the day and climbed into her saddle. With an enormous groan the great brute lurched to her feet, sneezed and blew air out of her thick lips, which sounded like and elephant breaking wind and plodded along a track. My camel driver was a tall and unusually skinny man with a face that looked like a dried fig. He tapped the rump of my girl with a stick and encouraged her undulating walk. ♫♫ "The Camels are coming Hoo-Rah Hoo Rah. With the sound o' trumpet, pipe and drum, The Camels are coming Hoo-rah ♫ He sang the Scottish marching song, laughing merrily at his witticism. The inside of his mouth was black and yet again, the poor man had no teeth.

A day to be remembered, October 1964.   Sally posing with her singing camel driver on the plateau of Giza.

Mary in front of the 65 million ton Pyramid of Cheops and the Great Sphinx of Giza. (The Terrifying One), 1964.

Though we arrived at Sahara City, rumpled and smelling of camel, we were treated royally. Rodney and Mr. X were waiting to escort us into a magical, carpeted tent, open on one side and hung with bright blankets in the reds and yellows of a sunrise. I was seated next to my admirer in a semi-circle of cushions like the Queen of the Nile. The tent, he explained, was made of finely woven goat's hair, which my nose could well believe. Behind the tent there was a cluster of smaller cooking tents and dozens of women in Bedouin robes. The lovely smell coming from the open fire pit was way, way out. After a ritual washing of hands, a parade of white robed men brought more food than I have ever seen before, enough for ten ballet companies.

I picked bits from little plates of hors d' oeuvres with my fingers. Dozens of different olives, red, green, brown and black, were offered also small pottery bowls of pickled chillies, some burning hot and others mild, sour turnips, baby onions, and a mixture of exotic vegetables called *torshi-ye-leeteh.* More and more dishes kept coming, extraordinary little hamburgers called *kubbat maraq,* that Rodney loved but burnt my mouth, they were so spicy. I can't believe the amount of food that was prepared just for us; heaps of salad, breads and a yummy lemony pigeon stew that is an Egyptian favourite, in fact they love pigeons every conceivable way, fried, boiled or stuffed, which is what I am right now.

Just when we thought we could not eat another morsel there was a fanfare of clapping and a platter the size of a table arrived with a whole roasted unborn baby lamb lying on a mattress of rice strewn with all manner of things, nuts, dried fruits, and desert herbs. It would be very rude not to eat more. My host leaned close to me and whispered, "*Kharouf Mahshi* is for very special occasions only, weddings, days of joy like today because," and he gestured toward me his eyes twinkling. I didn't say anything but I must have blushed. He is certainly very generous and kind but I don't fancy him at all. I glanced over at Rodney but he was happy drinking red wine called 'Omar Khayyam,' with his own personal harem, the girls of the ballet.

Mary

Uncle Ben's precooked Converted Rice, is the only kind of rice served back home, white long-grained and usually boiled to mush. My mother insists on "killing the bugs and weevils" and overcooks everything. So I almost swooned when a giant brass platter arrived with a fluffy golden mountain, dripping in buttery herbs, almonds, dates, diced giblets and kidneys, mixed spices *za'atar*, saffron, crushed *summāq* berries, and perched on top, a whole lamb, head, tail, legs, even baby cloven hooves, which had been roasted over hot coals. It tastes of paradise. Holy Cow! I'll never want plain old Uncle Ben's ever again.

Luckily, burping is not rude but a sign of satisfaction because I heard plenty of them as we all rinsed our greasy fingers and settled back on our cushions. Before we had time for a quick snooze in our exotic cocoon, a figure appeared from nowhere like a '*djinn*,' a Genie in front of our semi-circle and with graceful fingertips of his right hand on his forehead, gave a deep and dramatic *salaam*. While he was bent almost double four musicians drifted through the opening in the tent and stood poised to begin the *Chehata* dance. Slowly he stood upright, a smallish man with an enormous turban that trailed down his back, wearing a full red skirt with dozens of petticoats or underskirts of different colours. He was handed four round gypsy tambourines but without cymbals. We waited. He stared without blinking, stared through the goat's hair walls into a far off space in the Sahara desert or maybe beyond searching for inner peace. The music began filling the tent with rhythms as old as time, of stallions galloping across the sand, sensual plodding of camels, and high pitched whistles and flutes of ululation, the unmistakable cry of the desert, once heard, never forgotten.

With a start, the Chehata dancer began to twirl counter clockwise around and around not moving from one small spot in the sand. He balanced the tamborines in patterns as he whirled on his left foot, his skirts becoming a *tutu* sticking straight out like a dinner plate. Around and around he spun, head thrown back in a trance. Like Salome and the dance of the seven veils, the red top skirt whirled off and became a scarf, the tambourines having been tossed to one side. Flutes, zithers whistles keep up the throbbing pace and we were all getting hot and excited. He kept spinning on and on – another skirt came off, then another. We were mesmerized; the rhythm intensified as he built to a climax. Faster and faster he twirled in a primitive strip tease until he was down to a simple belted earth coloured kaftan. His turban loosened and was cast to the ground and his long hair, never cut since birth, swung round and round. He worked himself into a frenzy - us too, we were going crazy. And then he stopped dead in his tracks – no sweat, no dizziness, no panting, but perfectly calm after the storm - he stood arms wrapped around his body at one with the universe; earth, air, fire and water. La la la la la, we trilled the Arab call yodeling with the back of the tongue on the uvula, la, la la la la the cry of exaltation!

The amazing 'Whirling Dervish' who performed a Chehata dance at Sahara City, the tent retreat of ex-King Farouk out in the desert. Sally is on the dancer's right and Mary on his left.

Sally

Darling Lez: WE HAVE BEEN TOSSED OUT!   I can't believe the cheek of the manager. Without warning we are no longer working in the Auberge des Pyramides and our contract was literally THROWN in our faces.   The reason that Nobby gave is that we refused to work downstairs in the horrible Salle Dorée after the shows as cocktail girls, hired to chat up the customers and encourage them drink and spend lots of money. Of course Rodney wouldn't let us set foot in the place and he knew it.   It was just an excuse not to pay us now that the Congress is over and the dignitaries have all gone home. Don't worry Lez, we should leave anytime now as soon as we can get our passports back. I'll send our next address soon. Love Sal xxx

Rodney did everything possible to make the manager of the Auberge honour our contract but there was nothing to be done. I went with him to lawyers and various government ministers, even the Governor but apparently he cannot or will not interfere. I must say Rodney seemed quite calm about it all and rang his agent in Paris or maybe Sciavoni in Milano. We will be leaving for Teherān next week via Beirut, on the first available flight out of here.

One last time I went with him to the *Auberge* to see if Nobby would pay us what we were owed and already there was another group of three dancers in leotards warming up on stage and one guy in tights and a bare chest. Our replacement had all been planned in advance and I was incensed with rage. To my utter surprise, Rodney gave a great cry of joy and rushed over to the tall man in tights obviously the ballet director. They hugged one another like the best of friends. "Sally, come here and meet Ben, a remarkable dancer." He beckoned me over and practically pushed me into his arms. I look up into a handsome smiling face. He had Rudy's dark glittering eyes, slightly mocking, cocky and sure of himself. And Rudy's hard, muscular dancer's body, but instead of Indonesian olive skin, he was the colour of glossy chocolate and simply luscious. I'm sure my mouth dropped open. He took my hand and squeezed it and our eyes locked. Standing so close to him I could feel his heat. I was instantly attracted. Rodney doesn't miss a thing but he just smiled, wrote down the hotel number and told him that the JBR were not leaving immediately. I could not let go of his hand, so warm in mine and simply stared at his beautiful white teeth.

Rodney and I never discussed Ben although he knew perfectly well that we had a sizzling affair. It was almost as if he wanted to set me free so that we could both move on to a different relationship not sexual but based on mutual respect and working together for the ballet. Of course it didn't work out like that...

Tomorrow noon, the JBR are leaving Egypt forever. The costume skips, speakers and recorder are already at the airport in a storage room. Richard, Mary, Liliane and I intend to spend our last moments in this mysterious land at the very top of the pyramid of Cheops and watch the sun go down over the desert. Actually, it was Richard's idea and a jolly good one at that. Our lanky English lad is becoming more daring.

We drove past the sleeping sphinx and stopped at the base, quite deserted at the end of the day. Our taxi driver has promised to return in a couple of hours. Waiting at the bottom of the great pyramid was Abdul our guide, who would lead us up the four hundred and fifty foot climb to the summit. There is only one possible route and it is forbidden to attempt the ascent without a guide. "*Salaam*, my friends, you stay close, me climb, you climb, stay very close," and he pocketed our money into the folds of his tattered robes. And we did stay close to him. Step by step we hoisted ourselves up the battered blocks. Abdul hauled and we pushed each other up the treacherous rock face slowly and carefully. One false step and we could tumble like rubble down a cliff. Our legs are limber after a lifetime of balletic exercise and we have no trouble keeping up. "I wonder how many slaves died building this thing," Mary called out cheerfully, "Keep moving, for crying out loud." Richard is getting worried that the sun is setting. Abdul's strong black hands grasp mine as he pulls me onto yet another flat rock. I reach out and hold onto Liliane as she stumbles briefly. "Don't look down." We are almost at the top and the ground below looks miles away. Bits of rock and debris careen down the face and disappear into the gloom below. It is eerie and yet, majestic. I am almost tearful with anticipation. The wind is blowing off the desert and slapping our faces as we finally reach the pinnacle – built over two thousand years before Christ. We are on top of the world, laughing, hugging each other even the surprised Abdul, and flinging our arms in the air...triumphant acknowledging the silent applause of the empty desert. Sitting on flattened stones we gazed at the sunset absorbing every nuance of colour, the sky, slowly changing from a pinkish blue, before the artist's brush turns it pinky, orange, dissolving into purple. The only sound is the lonely melody of the wind. "We go now." Abdul is watching the darkening sky and points to the headlights of our taxi far off in the distance. "Stay close, please, I go down, you go down too."

Mary

I am flying over the desert, as though on a magic carpet. Below there are miles and miles of golden glittering hills and plains, stretching far beyond the horizon. Peering down through my little porthole in the side of the airplane, I can just make out miniature figures like toys in a sandbox. I squint. Now, more clearly there are three camels in a row with their riders looking like three wise men, late and lost. It takes my breath away.

Oh how I wish my grandmother were beside me. She is ninety-two and has never, ever flown in an airplane. My grandmother has encouraged me since I was a child to travel the world and to see and do everything possible in my lifetime. Somehow she managed to send money through to me in Egypt with a message in her lovely scratchy handwriting, "Please visit the Valley of the Kings for me, before it is too late." I can hear her in my head saying, "You have only one short life. Go, seek, explore, learn and grow and then you will be ready to come home. I may not be here, but I will be with you in spirit." My grandmother was right. I never saw her again but, she lives forever in my heart.

Well, damn it, I would have loved to have gone to the Valley of the Kings, and visit the famous Temple of Abu Simbel, but the fat bastard that runs the *Auberge* refused to give me my passport. He waited until the last possible moment.

We were all at the airport and our plane was on the runway before he sent his bodyguard to return the passports and visas. He tossed the precious envelope at Rodney's feet, and left without a word.

Chapter Eleven

1001 Nights on Vodka and Vitamins

...the five year old Crown Prince of the Imperial State of Iran, teetering on his gilded chair, squeals with delight... He is loving us ... begging to see the little tramp (Le Charlot) again. ...he had a fifth birthday present he will remember always. I know I will never forget it.

WORLD NEWS 1964

October 1964: Teherān, Iran. Shah of Iran has the Ayatollah Khomeini arrested by CIA backed secret police SAVAK and incarcerated in Evin Prison for opposing his 'White Revolution.'

Mary

A wise old poet, Alexander Pope, once wrote 'a little learning is a dangerous thing.' However, a little learning is a whole lot better than none at all and might have kept me from heartbreak in the capital city of the Imperial State of Iran in the late fall of 1964.

The plane banked steeply, descending quickly between the mountains and landed at Mehrabad Airport in Teherān. We have arrived in an ancient land, one of the world's oldest civilizations, 2800 years BC and I am tingling with excitement. My knowledge of Persia or Iran as it is now called is limited to carpets, caviar, some verses of erotic poetry by Omar Khayyám and like every ballet student, the tale of the plucky legendary Persian Queen Scheherazade.

Greeting us in the airport lounge were two giant twenty foot coloured posters of Mohamad Reza Pahlavi the Shah of Iran and his third wife an exquisite twenty - six year old Empress Farah Diba. They were splendid, costumed in a fantasy of jewels and velvet-embroidered robes. I was captivated. As it turns out the Shah like the sultans of old, had three wives and each of them lovelier than the last. His first was a stunning seventeen year-old Sultanic Highness Princess Fawzia of Egypt who happened to be ex-King Farouk's sister. Their only child was a girl. At the second nuptials celebrated in Golestān Palace in Teherān, a sixteen year-old bride Soraya wore a Dior cape of white mink and a gown of pearls and stork feathers. The stork failed to bring a son to succeed to the throne and so another divorce. His third wife produced the son and heir. Who could have predicted that by 1979, there would be no throne to sit upon and the Pahlavi family would be in exile?

Mohamed Reza Pahlavi, Shah of Iran and the Crown Prince Reza Cyrus Pahlavi. It has been estimated that the absolute monarch's fortune amounted to ten billion dollars, mostly acquired after the nationalization of the British Iranian Oil Company in 1951. His love of fast cars was legendary and he had a fleet of at least 140 classics, the Mercedes Benz 500 coupe, one of only two ever built.

In Teheran the Royal family owned the Golestan Palace compound of fourteen castles, the Saadabad complex in Shemiran area with eighteen palaces and the Niavaran summer palaces and pavilions. In October 1964 Xavier and Sally performed the mime 'The Little Tramp,' at the palace of the Queen Mother, Todj ol-Molouk, in honour of the Crown Prince Reza Cyrus' fifth birthday celebration.

Photocredit www.iranpoliticsclub.com

Sally

At first glance, Teherān looks like a modern bustling city and the Persians, like the Egyptians wear a mixture of western clothes and traditional robes. As in Alexandria, we are living and working in the same place, Hotel Miami on Avenue Pahlavi at Shemiran

Road in an area in the north of Teherān called
Shemiranat. The avenue, according to our taxi driver,
is the longest street in the world and runs straight
downhill cutting the city in two. On either side of the
wide boulevard there are posters of little Prince Reza
Cyrus Pahlavi that hang like flags from the trees.
Underneath there are open drainage ditches, poor mans'
sewerage and home to wild dogs that look like they
have mated with wolves

Almost all the taxis in Teherān seem to be
Mercedes Benz. Some of them are so old that they have
no doors but old carpets hanging in their place. You
just nod to the driver and fling yourself in.   Not so
good if it is already full and you land upon an occupied
seat.   The drivers must be trying to save on petrol
because they fly straight downhill in neutral gear,
completely out of control. A last moment gear change
brings the taxis smartly to a halt, narrowly missing the
throngs gathered in Ferdowzi Square in the centre of
Teherān.

©*Left to right, Sally and Mary in front of The Miami on the north end of Avenue Pahlavi, the longest street in the world, ten miles or 17.3 kilometers. After the revolution in 1979 the name Pahlavi vanished forever and it became Valiasr Street (a reference to the 12th Shi'ite Imam.) Photo taken in November 1964 when the Jazz Ballet Rodney was in residence.*

The Hotel Miami is a large cabaret/theatre that famously caters to wealthy Persians, American Air Force families stationed in Teherån, diplomats and royalty. On the floor above the stage there are offices, a private salon for our exclusive use where we can read, write letters home or just unwind after the show. Down the hall is Rodney's suite, well actually one and a half rooms that, as it turned out became a love nest just when I thought our affair was to be platonic. I am rooming with Mary on the second floor and we share a pale green room with floor to ceiling glass doors leading to a terrace overlooking the Avenue Pahlavi. We have the best room and it suits us perfectly. An old fashioned dressing table with full-length oval mirror takes up one corner and every day the maid puts out a

bowl of fresh oranges and a glass carafe of *vodka*.
Mary thought it was water at first took a large glug and
almost fell over.

The manager of the Miami is very professional
and unlike the randy old goat at the *Auberge des
Pyramids* in Cairo, is honest and straightforward with
Rodney. He assures us that Iranians are very
sophisticated. "Persians are Aryans not Arabs," he
says although to be honest I don't know what
difference that should make. It is terribly important
that we are successful here. All of us are flat broke
because we have not been paid for more than two
weeks.

Ever since we got here we have been
rehearsing, non-stop and making last minute changes.
It is very tiring and I am fighting bronchitis. Yvette is
in full command, ironing, sewing and snarling with a
mouth full of pins at anyone who has torn their
costumes or missing hooks and eyes. Opening night I
peeked through the curtains and yes, Iranians do look
very sophisticated, very European in dinner jackets and
much to my surprise after our masculine audiences in
Egypt, there are lots of beautifully dressed women
chattering and sipping champagne. It is almost as if we
were back in Cannes. Rodney came up and kissed me,
"*merde*" he whispered in my ear and I knew he meant
much more than good luck. He has the most sensual
eyes. Oh! Here we go! Our music is starting –
discordant notes that make you sit up and take notice.
I glance over at Mary looking limber and aloof in her
sheer white leotard, yawning as she always does when
she is nervous. Right on cue she glides on stage like a
swan and takes her pose. There was a spontaneous
burst of applause that was welcoming and warm and I
knew we could win them over. Brilliant!

Rodney is prancing around like a circus pony with a glass of vodka and a cigarette in his fingers. He is ecstatic. They loved 'Black Saint and Sinner Lady'. This is the first time an audience other than the students in Cannes, have understood the ballet and realize that we are dancing evolution from primitive man to robotic machines, dancing to the music of one of the most inventive jazz musicians of the decade, Charlie Mingus. They 'got' it.

Rodney Stephan Otto Felix Vas, the choreographer and maestro of the Jazz Ballet Rodney. Photo taken in the Greenroom of the Miami Theatre/Cabaret in Teherān. Oct 1964.

Rodney put his arm around my waist and said *"Ba'Salâm ati"* to health, as he raised his glass in a toast to all of us. We are gathered around two long tables that had been set up in our salon. The tables are laden with bottles of Iranian vodka called *Sabnam*, Coca Cola, huge bowls of oranges, breads and crackers and an ornate silver tureen filled with ice with an inner glass bowl of dip. What luxury! Rodney poured me a shot of vodka, which I tossed it back like a native without coughing and spluttering. Peeling a segment of orange into the glass, I topped it with more '*Shabnam*' and toasted "to vodka with vitamins - for my sore throat." Everybody laughed and rushed to fill their glasses." *Ba'salâm ati!*

The 'dip' turned out to be the best Beluga caviar and we were stunned at the extravagance. The bowl would cost as much or more than we will make in a week. I peered at the little greyish green eggs about the size of an English pea. Hesitantly, I nibble one little egg and it burst into my mouth, a salty explosive droplet of pure ambrosia, food for the Gods. So I heaped a big spoonful onto some toast and was in heaven.

Mary

Sally has another admirer, Dr Edouard G, dentist for the Shah and the endless members of the Royal family. As you probably have guessed, Sally has a special magic about her that attracts men like bears to a honeypot. She looks seductive yet innocently shy, confident but cool and whether she is onstage or off radiates sex appeal. She has 'IT.' The day after our opening Dr. Edouard invited the whole ballet to his home for lunch just so that he could meet her. We are all thrilled to be invited to a home not just another restaurant and Rodney accepted on our behalf.

Sally

A short time after our arrival in Teherān, the Shah's dentist sent a car to take Rodney and me to his home for lunch. The JBR were all invited and they followed along in taxis, proper taxis with doors. As soon as we turned off the Avenue Pahlavi, the streets became like tunnels with high walls on either side. These walls hide the houses and villas from the street and it would be very easy to get lost. Small doors presumably go into gardens because I can see tops of trees reaching to the sun. It is very mysterious and exciting.

Dr. Edouard's house is like a museum, modern but filled with antique treasures; rare silk carpets, ancient pottery, wall hangings, paintings, maps and old swords. He is charming, a bit of a flirt and like Rodney speaks many languages; French, English, German, Armenian as well as Persian. Most of the French girls are flirting with him but I think Dr. Edouard fancies me. We are invited again for lunch on Friday, a much bigger party to meet lots of important people.

Darling Lesley: Hotel Miami, Teherān

Thanks for your letter, the books and the French grammar course. The weather here is most peculiar – hot days and exceedingly cold nights. I find myself embarrassingly 'unclad.' Could you be a dear and get me a nice suit and a dress, warm and yet smart? – Remembering, I only possess black and brown accessories. I need these things desperately. I am having quite a gay social life – the Shah's dentist is taking me out and I have nothing to wear, it's awful.

Would you like some caviar for Christmas?   Lots of love, Sally xxxx

Wearing my cream blouse and Liliane's skirt with my Egyptian turquoise necklace, I sailed into the house. Dr. Edouard nodded his approval.   I was introduced to the Shah's brother or half-brother and some royal cousins. Crikey, this is all very exciting but to tell the truth, if I didn't know he was a prince I would never have guessed. He was just a regular bloke and very easy to talk to. A title doesn't mean very much to most people. Even my sister has an ancient title.   She is married to Earl Haig of Bemersyde, Scotland so is a Countess, yet, she is just my big sister Adrienne.

The afternoon was a grand success, talking, joking and having a laugh. It wasn't long before Rodney was the center of attention with the royal guests clustered around like long lost friends. He has that natural ability to make everyone male or female to feel excited about life and all it offers. Rodney would have made a splendid diplomat, if only he had a country to be diplomatic for. That's one of the things I love about him.

The banquet table set up in the dining room was sumptuous with platters heaped with colourful and exotic meats and sauces smelling of cinnamon, cardamoms and fresh sweet herbs. There was pink rice, made with pomegranates, a wonderful chicken *khoreshe* with peaches, a decorated mountain of potato salad, oval meat patties with lemon and saffron called *Kotlete Kubideh,* cold meats, salads and fruits; a brilliant feast and terribly elegant.

Mary

Oh crap - a lunch from Hell! Sally and I have *food poisoning* or else we were just plain piggy. Thank God I made it through the show but later in the middle of the night, I had diarrhea so badly that I lay down exhausted and slept on the tiled bathroom floor. Sally hammered on the door, charged in and ralphed. All night long we played "lemme at the bathroom." I blame the sliced meats. We have resolved to cook for ourselves and actually bought a new hot plate that has knobs that work.

Sally

A day or so after our lunch party, Dr. Edouard sent his car and driver to take four of us to the Bank Markazi to see the crown jewels. An armed guard guided Mary, Elizabeth, Liliane and I to the solid metal door of the vault that was at the bottom of a steep staircase padded in a musty carpet. The door was wide open which was a bit of a surprise and I stepped inside and the others followed into a fairyland. We were like wide-eyed children. The vault was filled with treasure. Tiny spotlights lit up glass boxes containing the most amazing things you could ever imagine. Jewels sparkled - some so big that I thought they must be cut glass. Every case contained an object entirely encrusted with diamonds, emeralds the size of eggs, topaz, rubies, sapphires and pearls. Cabinets were filled with jeweled eggs, knives, paper openers, belt buckles, thimbles, a sword embellished with three thousand precious stones according to a small cardboard plaque, brooches, rings, crowns and boxes of loose stones and pearls. We are all 'ooohing and aaahing'.

The spectacular gold coronation belt first worn by Shah Nasser al Din (1848-1896). The belt is a giant 175 carat oval shaped cabochon-cut emerald surrounded by diamonds. Photocredit. www.Iranpoliticsclub.com

"I think Queen Vicki was in love with an old Shah." Mary whispered in my ear. "Look at all the stuff she has given." And sure enough there are goblets ringed in diamonds. 'Gift of Her Majesty Queen Victoria of Great Britain,' a set of chinaware studded with gems, 'Gift of Her Majesty the Queen of England."

Suddenly there was a shriek from the other side of the room. The guard dashed forward and "*sshhhh*" as though we are in some sort of holy place. Really! There, nestling in a burgundy velvet box was a bejeweled fly swatter! It was covered in diamonds and an emerald the size of a gobstopper encircled with seed pearls. "Don't tell me Victoria gave him a fly swatter." We all started to laugh like lunatics and ran around the vault trying to count all the gifts from Queen Victoria to the Shah whose name was Nasser al-Din (1848-1896) according to the white card.

"Look at the crown," squealed Elizabeth, I peered over her shoulder and gasped. It was as big as the Pope's mitre but entirely encrusted with pearls and precious stones and topped with a feather made of diamonds with a giant emerald in the middle. It looked to me like a giant headache. A discreet little plaque read KIANI CROWN."

La 'Darya-i-Nur' est par ici" called Liliane. We rushed to the other side of the vault to gape at the largest diamond in the world. There are no words to describe the colour and size - just magnificent. I guess we were making too much racket because the guard became all uppity and important. He had finally had enough and said, "No more, you must go now, time is up" as though we are visiting prisoners in a jail.

We took a final glance at the 186 carat diamond, the sea of light, and then all trouped into the street blinded by the sudden daylight, the spell broken by the chaotic bustle of a restless city centre. Very faintly above the sounds of traffic, the call to prayer promises the faithful that God is good.

Mary

Well there is nothing like a smelly old leotard and tights to bring us back to reality. Tanita had begun class by the time we returned and changed into our work clothes. I hurried through *plies* and a few warming *battement tendus* and then continued exercising with the others. *"Grand battements en cloche,"* called Tanita, "ten on each leg" *s'il vous plaît, developpé, en avant, à la seconde, en arriere."* The music started and all thoughts of rubies, pearls and diamonds disappeared. We danced for an hour or more and then stretched into the splits, until loose and limber with muscles warm and tingling. I stayed behind and practiced *pirouettes, fouetté en tournnant* and *chaîne* turns until I was dizzy. My tired old pointe shoes are completely broken but there is no use complaining because there is nowhere to buy new ones. I stuff the shoes with sheepskin and hope for the best.

Shahnaz Square, Teheran. Postcard 1964. The square is named in honour of Princess Shahnaz whose mother was the first wife of the Shah. When they divorced Queen Fawzia returned to Egypt but was forced to leave her six year-old daughter behind in the tender care of the infamous Queen Mother who has been described as a "tiny, feminine woman with the personality of a bulldog." Venus "Life and Times of Princess Fawzia."

Sally

Everyone is in a right royal tizzy, even Yvette. Xavier and I have been summoned to the palace of the Queen Mother Todj ol-Molouk to perform for the birthday of the Crown Prince Reza Cyrus at 7p.m. There was no warning at all. It was an order that we perform "The Little Tramp (*le Charlot*). It is the perfect little ballet mime for a child, innocent, funny and loving. Yvette, ironed, quite unnecessarily my mauve satin costume with white fringe and folded it between tissue paper and put it in my holdall. A limousine arrived in front of the Miami at a quarter past six and Rodney, Xavier and I were whisked off to the palace. There was no time to be nervous or intimidated. We entered through massive arched doors and found ourselves in a long marble hallway. It quite took my breath away – the lavish carvings, tall ceilings, mirrors, mirrors everywhere and chandeliers, but most of all, the exquisite soft and silky Persian carpets. I floated down the hall in a dream. We were ushered into an ante chamber where we changed into our costumes - Xavier with moustache, bushy eyebrows and big black circles under his eyes, and me wearing wide-eyed false eyelashes and dressed in a 1920's fringed frock.

As soon as Xavier and I were ready, a tall and rather pompous servant led us through a maze of hallways to a towering double door. He didn't say one word to us but just nodded toward the door. It opened like magic. I peeped in and there was the entire royal family sitting upright on two rows of gilded chairs as though posing for a formal portrait - the Shah, Farah Diba with the little prince between them, an older woman who must be Queen Mother and about a dozen others solemn, serious and expectant. They were all exquisitely dressed as suited the occasion of the birthday of a Crown Prince. Rodney gently nudged me forward and heart pounding. I stepped boldly into the room.

Instead of our shabby park bench and street lamp, there was a satin brocade settee as our prop. All of a sudden I had an attack of stage fright. My throat squeezed up, both hands trembled and I thought I had to go to the loo. I glanced toward Rodney who was fiddling with the tape recorder placed just inside the door. Our tinny, honky-tonk, piano music began, he turned and smiled, with eyes full of love and pride and I slipped into character. Clicking across the polished floor in my silver heels, I sat on the edge of the settee modestly pulling my fringed dress over my knees, took out my handkerchief and a letter and started to silently sob. After a few seconds Xavier wearing oversized shoes, paddled in to the rhythm of the honkey-tonk, in his Charlie Chaplin gait, swinging his cane with an exaggerated twitch of his moustache. He saw me, stopped dead in his tracks, plunked himself on the other end of the bench, and furtively withdrew a sandwich from his enormous pocket and nibbled on it like a rabbit.

The little Prince, teetering on his gilded chair, squealed with delight. He loved us and would you believe it, at the end of the sketch where I end up with the sandwich and the tramp begins to cry, he jumped up and down, begging to see it again. And so we repeated it. The five-year old Crown Prince of the Imperial State of Iran had a birthday he will remember always. I know that I will never forget it.

Mary

Within walking distance of the Miami, there is a sort of tumble down market where Sally and I shop. Down the hill and on the left there is a steep canyon that looks as though there was an earthquake, a monster bite out of the middle of the city. No fence or anything to protect people from falling over, never to be seen again. No one pays any attention. On the very edge of the cliff are hovels made of old bits of wood and tin just hammered together and roof of fragments of canvas. I guess people live inside but it seems impossible. To reach the shops you must jump over the drainage ditch where the dogs live. A string of bare light bulbs shine on each hut going down, down, down, the hill. If you squint your eyes, it looks like Christmas. Posters of the Crown Prince dangle like ornaments from the trees at the side of the road. There is an ungodly gap between the rich people hanging around the royal family and the desperately poor people who live right here.

Our meat shop consists of a lopsided table covered in scratches and gouged with use and one glaring light bulb. Behind it stands a man, clutching a sword. Usually he has a sheep carcass laid out like a corpse, attracting flies. The first time we saw the meat, Sally held up two fingers. "Two pieces" she tried. *Deux, zwei*, then Arabic, *'te nen.'*" He threw back his head and howled with laughter. A curled up bundle in black scuttled by and murmured *'do.'* He immediately lifted his sword and with a 'swoosh' the flies vanish and crack he carved off a chop, then another. These he wrapped in some brown paper and held up six grubby fingers. Six *rials* were handed over and it appeared to be correct. *"Moteshakker"* we said hoping it meant thank you – 'got to learn more words' and off we went to the next stall for a few flat breads called *nâne lavâsh* - another stall for a lemon *'limu* and our shopping is done. Sally has figured out that we can have supper of *'do'* mutton chops cooked on our new hot plate, bread toasted on the end of a knife, some goat's cheese *'panir'* washed down with tea and lemon for a few shillings. And of course we have free vodka and orange after the show.

I was settling in nicely to the rhythm of life in this fascinating city, window shopping, exploring the bazaar, admiring exquisite Persian carpets, looking at the architecture of the buildings, writing letters home telling of our discoveries, and dancing to enthusiastic audiences every night. It was too wonderful to last.

One fateful night, after the show I went upstairs and lay on my bed reading and eating oranges, content and ready to fall asleep. Elizabeth tapped on my door and said, "there is a bloke in the salon who wants to meet you. He spent ten years at Ohio University and wants to hear a North American accent." "Ten years? He must be a moron! Forget it," and I went back to my novel. Fifteen minutes later, Sally arrived and begged me to come down, "just for a minute." Reluctantly I snapped my book shut and pulled on a skirt. I absolutely refused to change into shoes and slid into my big puffy bedroom slippers, yanked my hair into a ponytail and slopped downstairs with "a face like a boot" as my mother would say. I have never been able to figure out why people in any audience are so crazy to meet the performers. Without stage make up, false eyelashes and costumes, the fantasy is over and we are just people like anyone else.

The Green Room was filled with our group and a few odd people chatting and smoking. I plonked myself down, someone handed me a glass of vodka and ungraciously I took a gulp. Without turning my head I growled, "So rich daddy sent you out to learn English at Ohio State." I tried to sound sarcastic but a cheery voice said "Hi, I'm Chris" and you must be the feisty Canadian. We spoke briefly, I excused myself and left. The next day there was a note and an invitation to lunch, which I ignored. It is not that I found him ugly or creepy, in fact he's kind of cute except for thick glasses. But what is the point of ever going on 'dates' or getting involved romantically, because nothing can come of it and we will be gone in a few weeks. Besides, my intuition tells that he is just a playboy who wants to be seen with someone in show business. The next night he was in our private den again. Damn who is inviting him anyway? I glared at the room at large. Everyone was laughing and chattering but I stomped back to my room.

It was all kind of sneaky; Ronáld and I were invited to join Sally and Dr. Edouard for dinner on our night off. The dinner party was at the home of the Second Air Attaché for the American air base stationed here in Teherān. I am not quite sure why the Americans need an air force base in Iran, no one is at war. Perhaps I'll ask our host. The four of us walked in and there he was swooping down on me like a hawk. Immediately, Ronáld drifted off with a rather effeminate looking young man, and sat engrossed in conversation with him the whole evening. And so I was seated next to Mr. Ohio who pulled his chair close to mine until our knees were touching and I could smell his aftershave and it was thrilling.

The meal floated in as if in a dream. A steaming mountain of buttery white rice was dotted with half egg shells like tiny cups with the yolks. Slices of broiled lamb were piled on top and the lot was sprinkled with a dark red spice called *sumac* that is sour and stringent like cranberry. I loved it – I was crazy mad about it. We ate with our fingers using a piece of flat bread to coop up the ingenious combination of flavours and textures. *"chelo kebab"* he translated in a husky voice, making the words sound exotic and somehow a lot more exciting than rice and meat.

I don't quite know quite how it all happened but after days of lunches at the Teherān Hilton overlooking the snowcapped mountains, late dinners at the Paprika restaurant, parties at various friend's homes, I fell for him hook line and sinker. When he took me to meet his mother who was very sweet to me but spoke only a word or two of English, I began to fantasize what it would be like to live in Teherán. I could always learn the language.

One night, he invited me to a late party after the show. As soon as we finished the finale and the applause died down, I dashed upstairs to dress in my most sophisticated black, raw silk sheath that I made myself. I wore a single string of pearls given to me for my twenty-first birthday, twisted my hair into a bee hive and put two dabs of Balenciaga '*Le Dix*' behind my knees. At eleven he arrived in, what looked like a limousine and whisked me off through the streets, until we arrived somewhere in the northern residential part. We stopped in front of a tall, narrow, house surrounded by a wall with a small metal door - the entry to a secret garden? There were no lights anywhere and seemed deserted. The driver was sent off and Chris took a key out of his pocket and unlocked the gate. "I thought we were going to a party" I began as another key opened the main door. He pulled me into his arms whispering, "We are - a party for two." Without warning, I felt a rush of warmth all over. He held my hand tightly and led me up a narrow staircase and into a small bed-sitter. Whose place is this?" What if someone comes back?" I have a million questions, '*shhhh*' "Don't say another word." He has that unmistakable look in his eye and there is no more time for talking. I leaned over, took his glasses off and allowed him to strip me down to my birthday pearls. I am feeling a little shy but I want him to touch me.

Overnight we went from golden autumn sunshine, no coats and flies buzzing around to icy cold, the first snowfall, and dead flies. I began to see that there were two sides to this mysterious and exotic capital city and it was not all music, dance and romance. While we are swanning around in limousines, with the snowflakes twirling like white fairies in a ballet, the people outside are freezing - some in bare feet, no warm coats no shelter. I saw an older man getting a shave on a broken kitchen chair outside in the slush. Bundles of black were curled up in the snow, not moving - asleep or dead? No one seems to notice, or if they do, they do not care. I am seeing it all for the first time. The wind or is it the wolf dogs, howl. How can some folk have everything and others live worse than animals. I am feeling very uneasy.

Sally

Of all our ballets, the 'Afro Cuban' is the most fun to dance and the most exciting for the audience. I guess because it looks so wild and free but is as controlled as a sword fight. Every movement is precise but it appears as though we are out of control leaping through the air, collapsing on the floor in splits and backbends, swinging our hair like the whirling dervish and in danger of crashing together in a heap of arms and legs, a battlefield of broken limbs. The climax is a tropical storm, thunder, and lightning as the rain comes down umbrellas appear in the ultra violet light.

Fortunately for the JBR our white-fringed umbrellas got lost somewhere between Cairo and Mehrabad airport in Teherån. Only later did we learn that opening umbrellas inside brings very bad luck. However, Yvette was outraged and Rodney spent hours rechoreographing the second half of the ballet thus avoiding evil spirits from falling upon the Miami and all who were in the audience which happened to be half the Royal Family on the night we performed our 'Afro Cuban'.

Later that night in our lounge Rodney strode in and clapped his hands for attention like a ring-master, "Dahlinks listen, I am going to cook my goulash, the most famous in zee world for the prince's birthday." His eyes sparkled just like a child. Someone else is making the rest of the dishes so there's nothing to fuss about. Between thirty and forty guests will be arriving at Dr. Edouard's house at the end of November. That's a lot of goulash!

Hotel Miami, Teherān November 1964

Darling Lezy

The most extraordinary thing happened late Friday night after the show. As usual we had a full house – the people here are crazy about us. As soon as the finale was over I went straight to my room, had a snack and then started reading "The Anvil of Civilization" by Leonard Cottrell – this book is not too great, it hops about a bit and is vague, but I am learning. Here I am Lez trying to improve my mind when I was summoned downstairs to meet 'an admirer'' – a powerful and wealthy man from the hills who loudly demanded to meet me and he is not be refused. Very reluctantly I went to meet him. Lez, he was horrible, a great tall, pig of a man, swarthy with gray gnarly teeth, dressed in sheepskin and leather trousers, reeking of raw onions. I was frightened that he was going to grab me but Rodney planted himself like a rock between us. The dialogue in some weird dialect, between the manager and this apparition was translated "Tell the girl," snorted the pig, that I have fallen in love with her and want her to come with me." I just stood there; mute, unable to say a word. Rodney translated back that a 'date' was quite out of the question – whereupon he turned bright red and roared and slobbered that he would to cut my tummy out and break my knees if I went out with anyone else or ever tried to leave the hotel. So now I am a prisoner here. Don't worry Lez, and lots of love and hugs. Sal xxx

Every night after that, four burly figures stood across the street, staring our balcony window, watching and waiting for me to try to leave. Damn, I am going to miss the party.

I feel like Cinderella sitting in rags by the fire. Everyone has disappeared in his or her finery and I am left with the sodding Anvil of Civilization and a carafe of vodka. Sitting on my bed, I imagined the scene which is taking place over at Edouard's house. Rodney stirring a great vat of beef, paprika, sweet onions and peppers, the smell intoxicating, smoky, buttery, '*jouissant*', no other word to describe it, orgasmic. He will be the master chef, a one-man show, having a ball with Nadine drooling all over him that French tart. I bet she is having a fling with him.

My reverie is broken. Rodney in person is standing in front of me, like the fairy godmother. "Get dressed Sally Anna. You are going to Dr Edouard's house. We have cooked up a plan to get you there without being seen." With that he grabbed some clothes, a pillow, a chair and a blanket and while I dress he fashioned a life-like dummy which he propped up on a chair with my book. On its head, is a woolly hat with my false pony tail. Rodney took my hand and we crept downstairs to the staff entrance. I heard a long low whistle and held my breath. A few seconds later Rodney stepped into the alley just as a milk van slowly pulled up with no headlights and its side doors open. He turned and shielded me as I climbed in. The door slammed shut as we roared off and lurched around the corner toward Dr. Edouard's party house. It was thrilling.

Music was blaring, lights were low and everyone was wild. If I didn't know better I would think I was back in the *Whiskey a Go Go* not in a Muslim country in the middle of the Middle East. We danced for hours, the twist, rock and roll, the twitch and mambo. We taught everyone the moves – the shimmy and the shake with a couple of the JBR specials thrown in - no palace protocol here. When it was time to go home everyone was quite tiddly and his highness staggered out clothes damp with sweat shaking Rodney's hand and thanking him over and over for the fab goulash. It turns out it was his idea about smuggling me into the milk van. On our return, the van pulled up to the staff door and I was able to sneak back inside. Meanwhile on the avenue, our shadowy dummy was bent over the Anvil of Civilization still on the same page. Sometime later we heard a rumor that the watchdogs from the mountain had been removed by the Shah's dreaded secret police.

Mary

I have made a complete fool of myself and can't wait to leave this crummy city. It is an old, old story and I should have seen it coming. Boy meets girl, girl not interested, boy continues pursuit until finally girl capitulates, boy drops girl like bloody "hot potato" no longer interested. I thought he was about to propose to me. He even introduced me to his mother for crying out loud. How could I have been so blind, so misled that I thought we were just two people falling in love. All he wanted was to go to bed with me and brag to his buddies. Oh God, I am such a fool.

The goulash party was ghastly, absolute torture. Everyone had a blast, except me. I waited and waited and every time the door opened I looked up to see if it was Him. Finally, when it was almost time to go home, he cruised in cigarette dangling from his lips like a gangster in the movies and walked right passed me as though we had never met. Suddenly I felt icy cold, faint, mortified, humiliated - it was a sharp slap in the face and I wanted to die.

Sally

On our last night in Teherān we were invited to join the audience and see the opening night of the new show featuring Panteleón Pérez Prado, King of the Mambo and the George Reich Ballet. We were stunned by what happened - they were actually booed. We thought their first ballet was really clever, a perky dance, very appealing with brightly coloured umbrellas weaving in and out, opening and closing to the music of 'Unsquare Dance' by Dave Brubeck. We applauded enthusiastically but the rest of the audience was outraged and then someone called "boo" like a cow in distress. Rodney muttered "Oh no! They shouldn't open umbrellas inside – very bad luck." In a Muslim country it appears that evil spirits will fall upon you and your house like rain from the sky if you open one umbrella and tonight the ballet opened eight of them. A hailstorm of rotten luck must be thundering down on the ill-fated Miami. That night they all got pie-eyed on vodka and vitamins and we joined them.

The next morning we were all packed, anxious to leave the country and far away from the threat of the pig man. As planned, Rodney and I jumped in a waiting taxi and he shrouded me in his arm as I hid my face. I was terrified as we sped toward the airport. Rodney, watching nervously out the rear window. It was a horrible trip but finally we screeched to a halt at the terminal and zig-zagged through the chaos of people and luggage toward the waiting ballet. They closed around me protectively like a loving family and I am safe.

Mary

I am standing in the middle of Mehrabad Airport studying the larger than life photo of the Shahbanou in her excessive jewels and futile opulence wondering how long she will last before getting dumped, when who should come staggering in but '*him*' so completely sloshed that two of his buddies are holding him upright. He is swaying in front of me struggling to say something profound, but ignoring him I muster all the dignity of my ancestors, stand erect, gather my bags and exit stage right like "Lady Macbeth." Richard, dear, dear Richard rescues me. He takes my arm propelling me toward the plane and in a stage whisper crows, "I have lost my virginity" and we all fall over laughing, congratulating him and patting him on the shoulder. I do not look back.

Chapter Twelve

Beirut, Paris of the Middle East

"our contract has been cancelled. Everyone is in the worst possible mood. So just before Christmas we sit without work and probably won't even be able to afford a turkey"

WORLD NEWS

January 20 1965, Washington D.C. Lyndon Johnson is sworn in as President of the United States of America.

January 24 1965. London: The World Mourns the 'Greatest Statesman of the 20th Century', Sir Winston Churchill who died today in his London home.

Sally

The costumes got left behind! Someone did not load our skips into the cargo hold of the plane in Teherān. I am wondering if it was on purpose. Blimey! We have the worst luck. All our suitcases, tape recorder, Kitchen, boxes of junk everything arrived safely in Beirut, except the most important thing, our four skips with all the costumes. Rodney is dashing about like a whirling dervish but there is nothing to be done. Of course, our contract has been cancelled. Everyone is in the worst possible mood. So just before Christmas we sit without work and probably won't even be able to afford a turkey. I have invited all the ballet and the lift attendant in our flat that we have rented for Christmas dinner. I want to show how Christmas is celebrated in England with or without a bloody bird.

It doesn't feel a lot like Christmas in Beirut with sunshine all day and warm nights right until midnight. There isn't a decorated tree in sight but since half the population is Muslim, that is to be expected. I am sharing the flat with Mary, number 16 in the Chehab Building on Commodore Street in the French, half of the city. This is where we intend to 'dry out' from the excesses of the past month and get ourselves sorted out. I want some time to myself after the frenzy of living in Teherān. The French quarter, which is more like half the city looks over the Bay lined with very chic hotels. The Muslim half looks older and mysterious with narrow streets stone archways, and a spider's web of shaded passageways. There is a souk just like in Cairo where we buy our vegetables and spices but here we speak French of course because Lebanon used to be French colony.

Beirut or Bayreuth in 1964/5 was a sun-worshipping playground for the Westernized Arab world. A former French colony, Lebanon was dominated by the Christian right although the majority of the population was Muslim. Who could have guessed that within ten years a vicious and bloody struggle for power that lasted 15 years would see 120,000 dead and 78,000 homeless and Beirut the jewel of the Mediterranean in ruins?

Our days are spent taking classes and in rehearsals. We cannot just sit around getting out of shape because our muscles like musical instruments must stay in tune. The rehearsals are held in an abandoned machine shop that has been loaned to us by someone Rodney has met and charmed. If anyone peeked through the grimy windows they would be astounded at the sight of a dozen or so dancers working hour upon hour, using rusted engine parts or bits of machinery as a *'barre'* while outside these four walls is a whirl of extravagance, snazzy hotels and chic clubs, least for some, in the Paris of the Middle East. As we are without work, Rodney is rechoreographing "Asphalt" which he wants to make more abstract and dynamic for our return to Europe. Our publicity stills are being shot by a friend of his introduced only as Garo who is supposed to be tops. His photgraphs of celebrities have appeared in America in Newsweek and Time magazines. How are we going to find the money to pay his 'friend', God only knows. Rodney doesn't look worried in fact he is over the moon with enthusiasm.

Publicity still of Xavier and Sally in 'Asphalt' by celebrity snapper Garo Nalbandian who was an Armenian photographer based in Jerusalem but orking in Lebanon, 1964-65.

Our flat has become a hang-out for a group of guys who arrive unannounced and just pop in. They seem to like the atmosphere or else they are bored and we offer a diversion. As far as I can guess most spend their time gambling, smoking hashish, drinking and gossiping. Mary is driving me absolutely bonkers weeping and moaning over that creep in Teherån and calls my new friends, *flâneurs*.

Mary

These past few days before Christmas have been spent alone, pacing the famous *Corniche,* the Grand Promenade in front of the new Hotel Phoenicia and the Pigeon Rocks, where usually tourists and lovers stroll, depressed and suicidal. I gaze out to sea and wonder if I should throw myself in, drown and done with it. How could I have been so gullible as to fall in love with someone so unsuitable? Our apartment is like a zoo, filled with a group of strangers who wander about at any hour. I think I am going crazy with grief. I blame the vodka and have sworn off the stuff for my entire lifetime.

Even though I don't feel like it, I am going to visit the five thousand year old ruins of Baalback as they are only two hours away by bus and I will never get the chance again in my lifetime. Baalback is the most famous and holy place of the ancient world and is a shrine to the Goddess Astarte who is Venus, the goddess of love.

236

A Roman Temple, sixty-eight kilometres northeast of Beirut is the largest stone construction in the world. Even today scientists, both engineers and archaeologists alike are amazed and mystified as to the transportations and construction of the massive stone blocks that is "beyond the technological ability of any known builders, ancient or modern."

This photo was taken in 1965 by fellow dancer Richard Gough of Sally and Mary in Baalbek, Lebanon.

It was bitterly cold even in my boots and hairy coat but I was glad I went. Baalbek was not to be missed. It is a very old and holy place, a giant arena of temples larger than anything in Egypt and quite overwhelming. The massive rock formations were temples worshipping ancient gods and goddesses Jupiter, Bacchus and Venus. Richard smiled and said wistfully, "sounds useful to me, those Gods. I could do with a little love." It was then, amid the ruins that Richard told us that he was brought up in an orphanage and had no idea who his parents were. He spoke slowly at first and then his whole story came tumbling out almost with relief. I think we are his first real friends. I have danced with him for seven months almost every night and suddenly find I know nothing at all about him. Richard, suddenly embarrassed, leapt up and we charged around the massive rocks like Fred Astaire. There was not a soul there but us so we just climbed up and down giant staircases feeling very small. My troubles seem trifling and I resolved to "buck up" as my father would say and start anew.

Sally

Darling Lezy,   *January 1965*

Happy New Year to you all. I am just recovering from New Year's Eve and also from the flu and a very bad cold. I got thoroughly run down and have decided being the 'housewife' over the festive season is 'intolerable.' Turkey dinner for thirteen people was just too much. . Rodney found a twenty-pound turkey, goodness knows from where. When it was all over I was exhausted and promptly got ill. It could be the change in climate and altitude – leaving Teheran 1500 meters above sea level and biting cold, snow on the ground then living by the sea. There's bright sunshine all through the day here but it is extremely damp, very bad for old ladies with rheumatism like me! The only thing that ruined my Christmas and New Year's celebrations was the realization that this year I shall be 25! Lots of love. Sal xxxxx

P.S. Our next address from the end of January until the end of February is the Theatre Astoria-Bremen, Deutschland.

Love Sal xxxx

Mary

At this time of year, there are not too many passenger ships heading out of Beirut to Europe because of the weather but Rodney has found us third class passage on the MS Lydia leaving soon. It is going to take eight days from here to Genoa in Italy with brief stopovers in Port Said and Piraeus, then west across the Ionian Sea to Italy I am hoping I have enough money to change from steerage to second class so I don't have to watch everyone throw up for a week.

One of the flâneurs hanging around the apartment said we were *complêtement fou*, 'out of our minds' to cross the Mediterranean in January. After those encouraging words, I went out and I bought a tiny Saint Christopher medallion to hang around my neck. Maybe I should buy a great big gold one and become a Roman Catholic.

MS Lydia was built in 1931 in Copenhagen and acquired by the Hellenic Mediterranean Line in 1955 as a sailing vessel for a route from Marseille, Genoa, Piraeus, Alexandria, Lemassol, Beirut and Port Said. After changing hands many times Le Lydia, now74 years old was reborn as a grand casino, disco bar, spa and exhibition centre. The Jazz Ballet Rodney set sail from Beirut to Genoa on January 17th, 1965.

Sally

Nothing is ever boring with our lives.   This ship, the Lydia looks fine from the exterior but the inside, is horrible. The stench of the kitchen grease is nauseating and our cabins are right next to the bilges. One deck above us is the cinema where we all met on our first night aboard. The film was aptly, "The Cruel Sea" with Jack Hawkins. It seemed an amusing choice at first.   As we watched the film, the 'Lydia' gently rocked us from one side to the other. But, not for long!   After about 20 minutes into the film, not only were we watching the waves battering a boat on the screen, but it as happening to us as well! The first person left, holding hand over mouth. As it got worse we were hanging on to our seats watching the film. I thought it was great fun. Together Mireille, Liliane, Tanita, Frank, Rodney and Richard shot from the theatre.   After another ten minutes of tossing and crashing through the waves, the theatre was completely empty except for Mary, Xavier and I, who were sitting there puffing away on our fags, quite pleased with ourselves and feeling just fine......

M S LYDIA. BEIRUT to GENOVA

17 January 1965 MS LYDIA, BEIRUT TO GENOVA VIA PIRAEUS

Darling Lez

I am reading the books you sent me. There is nothing to do on this crazy ship so we play a lot of cards. I eat masses and sleep like a dead dog as they say. That is, of course, excluding our one night stopover in Athens.

The 'Lydia' docked in Piraeus about 9.30 p.m. and having already eaten some revolting stew, we all got dolled up, disembarked and took the bus into Athens to see the sites at night.

Our first stop was the main square where everyone meets. It's called Syntagma, or Constitution Square. Looking around there is not much to see except a water fountain in the middle. Xavier pointed out a livelier looking street and we found a coffee bar that had real 'expresso', not the awful brown water on board our ship. Everyone ordered coffee and Greek cognac, which is quite good and very cheap. I stood by the bar and got friendly with the owner who spoke maybe ten words in English and ten words in French – by jumping around miming and being a better actress than any school could ever make of me, he understood that we wanted, which was to find the 'old district' of town with the famous taverns that have guitarists and singing. "Ah hah" he said, "You mean THE PLAKA." I gathered it was quite close but he insisted that we take taxis to be safe and he warned us that the taxi driver might try to make us pay three times the normal price (mind you, he was probably charging us double for our coffees!).

So we set off, all jammed into two taxis, piled out and into the Plaka. The tiny streets all had dozens of taverns so we just followed out noses and chose one in a basement. Down we go, and we were met with the most amazing sight, the whole room was blacked out – except for one spotlight shining on a half-coloured boy sitting on a chair at the top of some stairs, singing and accompanying himself on his guitar. The whole scene was enchanting. Lez, it was the most aesthetically beautiful thing I have ever seen.

One felt it was a minute theatre – the stage was the staircase. It was perfect. At the end of the song, there was an eerie silence. No one wanted to break the spell. Then the lights came on and we all clapped and whistled. Looking around, we were in a completely different atmosphere. The tavern was old and worn, with wood tables, and chairs all very slightly carved. The walls were roughly plastered and there was a bar at the back. Without warning or announcements the lights were turned off again except for the staircase, which was lit by a couple of spotlights. The boy was not alone this time. He sang and at the bottom of the stairs was a girl, her hair covering her face. They sang alternately which reminded me of the Portugese Fado. The boy then played a solo on the guitar that left me breathless it was so beautiful.

He finished abruptly, put his guitar on the chair, bowed and went down the stairs to sit and have a drink with his friends. Retsina wine was flowing. His last song was with the girl and a narrator standing half way up the stairs playing a sort of 'vibrophone' as he recited. It was quite moving and I felt uplifted.

We left the tavern with everyone arguing where to go now. I got fed up and said to Liliane "I don't care what anyone else does, I am going this way" and off I headed.

Almost immediately I found myself looking down some old stone steps into a mixture between bistro, workman's cafe and tavern. It was just chairs and tables with dirty old cloths and the toughest looking characters all sitting around with one guy playing a guitar. Just like a Greek film, there was a gangster's moll lolling over her man.

242

The rest of the ballet followed likewise – retsina started flowing again. Everyone was singing, and I remarked that we too had a singer. Poor Ronáld was forced to sing, mind you he was completely in his ambiance. By now, the people realized we were 'artistes'. Ronáld began with a Spanish song and then much to our surprise the Greek singer joined him in a duet!

They then looked upon us most haughtily and continued singing Greek songs. It was a challenge. I said to Ronáld, '"God damn it, sing your Greek song " He waited and at the right moment he got up and walked over, had a little chat with the guitarist and the boss of the bistro, then stood up and started to sing in Greek – WELL – all hell broke loose. The boss stood up and started throwing plates and glasses over his shoulder – everyone was jumping around screaming with delight. The moll went into a trance and before we knew it was on the table, dancing and she was joined, Lez, you will not believe this, by our Richard. Our little suburban English Richard was undulating on the table with her. By the time the song ended we were all sitting at one table which went from one end of the room to the other – another guitarist had arrived – more retsina – more "underworld characters" and the night was well on its way!

At 5 a.m. one of these types had the idea to transport the whole lot of us to 'his' tavern up the street. We couldn't refuse. There he put on records and we danced, talked (those who were still capable) drank (likewise) till six o'clock, when after sad farewells– we went back to the Lydia in several taxis.

I slept for about one hour and was heaved bodily out of my bed at seven in the morning by Richard and Mary to visit the Acropolis.

Heading back to Italy we just passed 'Stromboli', the volcano and tonight we arrive in Naples. Ohh lovely spaghetti and Chianti & saluti a tutti! Tomorrow Genoa – where we spend a day.
Well, must close now, lots of love to you all

Sally xxx

Mary

It is not recommended in any guide book that one should sail across the Mediterranean in January especially third class on a Greek ship with a Turkish cook unless you are seriously considering suicide. Even for me, with my Canadian cast iron stomach it was a challenge to remain upright with eyes focused on the rocking horizon that was the coast of Egypt. A kindly steward kept bringing steaming cups of very strong coffee until he was convinced that I was not about to jump overboard but just waiting to glimpse the entrance to the Suez Canal.

As the MS Lydia steamed closer and closer, various members of the ballet staggered on deck and hung over the rails. Engines slowed, a lot of shouting could be heard and then as the anchor splashed and sunk, a flotilla of tiny boats appeared from nowhere like a swarm of bees. They were darting in and around the freight barges that were unloading and reloading giant boxes from Lydia's starboard side. "You wanna buy gold?" called voices from below. *"Bon prix pour vous."* "Hello, hello, *bonjour* lady" antiques from the pyramids?" "Look here, I have fresh fruit" holding up a basket of molding figs. The little boats started bunting each other out of the way like frolicking Billy goats. It was a floating market of men with bushels of bracelets, toy mummies, little statues of Nefertiti and alabaster pipes – all shouting about their wares to the passengers.

With the ship at anchor the breeze died and the heat grew oppressive. I turned to go onto the shady side when a voice shouted "you like camel, lady" and I saw a huge stuffed camel that was adorable. Liliane, who was beside me, urged, "take *eeet* Mary" How much" - I was not really serious. He said "what you have" and I took out the last of my Christmas money and called out " five dollars". Well, he moved like lightening and the next thing I knew the camel was being hoisted up the side of the ship with a thick noose around its neck and swung onto the deck. I undid the noose, put the five dollar bill into a little brown leather pouch and it was lowered back down to his waiting hands. Only then did I really look closely at my purchase. It stood about four feet tall, had a body of molting fur, probably rabbit stuffed with rags. Around his neck was   a small brass bell. Rodney arrived on deck, at that moment. "I am going to call him Chris," I said. Rodney rolled his eyes and groaned, turned and went below.

For the rest of the voyage, except for a night in Athens, I stayed bundled up in a deck chair beside Chris the camel, put my nose in a book and refused to speak to anyone.

Chapter Thirteen

Europe – home again

♫♫…passengers will please refrain from flushing toilets while the train is in the station, darling I love you…♫♫

WORLD NEWS 1965

Paris France: France begins underground nuclear testing at Ecker, Algeria.

Sally

I have had my hair bobbed and there was almost a revolt in the JBR especially with Yvette. Everyone except Nadine has very long hair and I suddenly decided to be mod - a complete change.   As soon as the SS Lydia docked in Genoa I was the first to disembark and disappeared into the throngs. A taxi dashed me and all my bags, boxes and paraphernalia to the old town where I found a *'peruquieri'*, who managed to squeeze me in for a wash, cut and set. I feel reborn and drifted into the railway station like a film star, arriving on the platform at the very last second.

Rodney looked harassed and then amused when he saw me with a porter following with all my belongings. When Yvette caught sight of my hair she raged and spluttered, *"merde,"* turned her back and stormed onto the train. Nadine gave me a quizzical look. Rodney came over and looked at me very closely and whispered, "Dahlink you are so beautiful." Well! I think I have shown Nadine who is Rodney's leading lady.

246

Breathing in the familiar smells of leather, perfume and cigarettes, I pressed my nose against the carriage window watching northern Italy slide by like a travel film. Lake Como, Modena, Milano, Verona passed before my eyes until my lids got heavy and lulled by the movement of the train I slept like a kitten.

The delicious aroma of a café latte placed on the pull out table, pulled me back to the present. Rodney was waiting for me to waken. He is actually flirting with me after all these months. The feeling made me a little giddy. "We are crossing the border in a moment or two" he said. And I knew what he was thinking, the man without papers, a man without a home. He disappeared.

Theatre Astoria, Bremen February 1965

Darling Lezy Wezzy

There is a HUGE write up and PHOTO of me in a Bremen newspaper. I've ripped it out and will send it but of course it's in German. Rodney translated it is roughly as...."English dancer Sally Seyd has appeared 5000 times around the world" She is a ballerina with the international Jazz Ballet Rodney etc etc and the journalist calls me 'graceful, beautiful, elegant as well as funny in our 'Charlie Chaplin' parody. Strangers stop me on the street! They recognize me and I am famous, at least, for the moment. Did I tell you Lez that Rodney Junior and Francis have arrived with all their belongings including drums and intend to stay? As well as doing two shows a day, we are re-working the "Asphalt" and rehearsing madly for a television special. If it is brilliant, it will be Germany's entry into the Prague Film Festival. Isn't this thrilling! – What is NOT thrilling are some nasty Germans – especially when they are in a group or drunk. Individually they can be quite charming. The other thing that is really bugging me is my birthday – I will be 25 NEXT WEEK and it scares me to death.

What am I going to do about my future? I am worried, so don't you. Love from your famous daughter   Sally Anna xxxxxx

The world famous 'Rathaus' in the Marktplatz in Bremen Germany with the 32foot high statue of a medieval knight Roland, the symbol of the city standing in front. This is a modern photo. When the JBR was performing at the Astoria, the Rathaus and the 11th century Cathedral of Saint Peter were black and sooty' and Roland was covered in grime. During W.W.II Bremen was the target for a ruthless and methodical destruction of German military power by the Royal Air Force and the US. 8th Air Force. The RAF's '1000 bomber raid' took place in June 1942, which destroyed much of the ancient seaport. The Rathaus was spared and is now a Unesco World Heritage Site.

Mary

In the Marktplatz, near the Astoria theatre, there is painted cart on wheels with a roof, a mobile kitchen that sells hot dogs. Every time I walk by the 'Rathaus' and the famous statue of Roland, I am tantalized by the smell of those dogs. They are making me crazy. One day there was no line-up so I ventured over. The cook, as plump as a sausage, had the kindest face. This is a big relief because some of the people here are so brusque and scowly. I looked into his twinkly eyes and asked slowly and firmly *"Bitte, ein weiner, danke shon"* He peered down at me and said *"Wurst"* *"Nein, nein der beste,"* I replied in what I hoped was a very Germanic accent for I have studied one semester 'German 101'. *"Wurst"* he repeated as he speared a big fat juicy wiener and waved it in front of my nose, trying to look stern, *"Das ist ein Wurst"* Now I get it! The *wurst* is the name of the hot dog. *"Ja"*! With the flourish of a conductor in front of an orchestra, he twirled the sausage in the air and delicately placed it into a small bun. It was wrapped gently in shiny paper and handed over. On a narrow shelf, jars of sweet relish and mustard are poised waiting to be spooned on. I took one glorious bite. Hot juices spurted into my mouth dribbling down my chin and I closed my eyes in ecstasy. *"Das wurst ist der beste."* Herr Sausage is beaming at me. He knows I am going to be back again and again.

At long last I have a single room four walls all to myself. Tanita is with Frank, Elizabeth is staying at another hotel and Sally is off in hibernation all by herself. "I have to think about my future" she tells me. Mine is looking bleak so I am not thinking at all.

This morning we finished filming the "Asphalt" for the Prague International film festival. It was quite a production

249

with new scenery of a downtown New York back street. We rehearsed it over and over with Rodney changing details and bits of choreography to fit the camera angles and the scope of the small screen. We would just get it right and voice would ring out from the dark, "*nein*" and a long discussion would take place in German and then Rodney would change it all over again. Thoroughly confused we did the final 'take' in costume; black faux leather dresses, and thigh high boots. The film crew was aghast when they saw us in our outfits and false eyelashes and not in our horrible leotards and wooly tights. We looked very glam and they couldn't believe we were the same people.

Filming is not as exciting as one might think. It is just a big room filled with cables and cameras and guys running around plugging things in and looking through lenses and chattering. And then the music is piped in from somewhere and you perform to a blank wall. I much prefer a living breathing audience any day. If they like you they applaud and if they don't, they don't and that is that.

The new 'Asphalt' filmed for the German entry into the Prague Short Film Festival 1965. It didn't win the grand prize. From the left Sally, Xavier, Richard (back) and Elizabeth.

Sally

My relationship with Rodney cannot go on as it is. Every time I try to discuss our future together he makes jokes or else changes the subject. We don't ever argue. It is intolerable and now that I am turning twenty-five and he almost fifty, I must think about what to do with the rest of my life. Dancer's careers do not last forever. Finally, on my birthday he agreed to give it some serious thought. Happy Birthday to me! *Alles Gute Zum Geburtstag.*

Mary

Mein Gott! I have just mastered enough words and phrases in German to get along and we are leaving for Madrid. Now I've got to start all over again in Spanish. By Friday after the second show we are packing and heading straight to the Bremen *Hauptbahnhof* boarding the overnight train to Paris and changing trains for the Spanish border. For once we have sleeping cars.

Clutching my ratty old camel, I found my upper berth and wearily climbed in with all my clothes on. I am absolutely dog-tired but the buzz of the final show keeps me on edge-the music, the applause, the costumes and chaos. Instead of counting sheep, I sing to myself a crazy song from school to the hypnotizing rhythm of the train …

♫♫ Passengers will please refrain from flushing toilets while the train is in the station, darling I love you. We encourage constipation while the train is in the station, moonlight always makes me think of you
♫♫

Wouldn't Antonín Dvorák have laughed to hear his Humoresque in G flat turned into this ditty? In the deepest recess of my mind, I remember getting my passport stamped at the German/ French border then fell into a dreamless sleep until we jerked to a halt many miles later at the *Gare de l'Est* in Paris. Sally is up and shaking me "Hurry, for heaven's sake – we are in Paris, get up. I leapt up, Paris, oh, yes sirree!

Rodney helped me pile all our suitcases, kitchen, stuffed camel, hubbly bubbly, and record player on a *chaiot* marked with our logo and I dashed after Sally, or rather clip clopped along in my high heels and tight skirt to the closest taxi. *"Bonjour monsieur. à la Louvre, Les Jardins des Tuileries et Champs-Elysées, TOUS s'il vous plait."* I instructed in my flawless French. Ha Ha. Just try to say '*Tuileries*' as the French do with an adorable little twitch in the back of the throat and light a cigarette at the same time. It is not easy. The driver smirked.   The city of light waits!

Sally

At noon, Mary and I climbed the worn stairs to a humble little flat in the Stalingrad area, in the 19th arrondissement – which is not the fanciest part of town. This is where Madame Lavegi, Liliane's mother has lived forever. The intoxicating aroma of food, glorious food met us on the landing. We were starving. The door was ever so slightly ajar so I pushed it open and squeezed through.   Crowded into the tiny one room flat, the entire ballet including Rodney Junior and Francis were standing about, clutching glasses, cups and mugs of wine, giggling and talking at once. Liliane was gushing, so proud to have the JBR at her home.

On the small gas stove in the corner a casserole simmered *"Poulet braisé aux eschalottes"* beamed Madame Lavegie lifting the heavy lid a crack. Oh! the aroma! Pot-roasted chicken in white wine with baby onions and mushrooms. Home-cooked food, I almost wept. Madame Lavegie laughed as we entertained her with silly stories of our travels and insane adventures. She dotes on Rodney and he charmed her as only he can. Huge platefuls of her divine *poulet* were devoured as we perched on every seat. The flat is minuscule and the loo is a 'Turks Head' on the landing above and shared by the whole building.

You cannot imagine how absolutely fabulous it is to be in a REAL home no matter how humble– a home is a home. *'C'est tout!'* Liliane began sobbing and kissing Pénélope smack on his slobbery lips.   The dog is not coming to Spain. Thank Heavens Madame Lavegie consented to 'camel-sit' for Mary so I won't have to look at that disgusting thing again. *"Au revoir, merci, très sympatique, bisous"* kiss, kiss, kiss, - we head off in taxis to the *Gare d'Austerlitz.   Atención,* Madrid, and watch out, here we come!

Chapter Fourteen

The Sun Also Rises in Spain

"...I have fallen in love, or at least I think I have...he is gorgeous, irresistible....a divine mixture of a matador and a flamenco dancer"

WORLD NEWS

Viet Nam, February 6, 1965 'Rolling Thunder' sustained Bombing of North Viet Nam by the U.S.A. started today.

Mary

Rodney Junior is a flirt just like his father except that he is a married man. After being away in Amsterdam for the past six months he started stalking me and was my shadow for the entire trainride from Paris to Madrid. I gave him no encouragement, as the tears of Teherān still haunt.

The moment the train pulled into '*el estaçion*' in Madrid, Sally announced that she would live by herself to meditate and study Spanish although she is quite fluent. We all like our privacy. Elizabeth and I reluctantly patched up our differences and agreed to share a room in a student boarding house in the old center on *calle Jacometrezo 14*. "It's within walking distance of work," she assures me as I stooped down to enter the strangest room I have seen in all my travels. Perhaps 200 years ago it was a washhouse of a nunnery. Two single cots on one wall, a giant cement washtub in the corner and that is all. My head brushes the ceiling and at eye level there was a tiny barred window with a worm's eye view of the paving stones. It gives me the creeps and I hate it. We are headlining at the El Biombo Chino or Bamboo Curtain located on la Calle de Isabel la Católica. Although it is quite famous and has hosted many international stars, my mother and father would not be ecstatic that their daughter was dancing in a 'club nocturno' no matter how well known. All mail is being addressed to the American Express.

Sally

Immediately behind the *El Biombo Chino* is a tapas bar that we call *Olé*. It is probably the most popular one in all Madrid and is always packed with artists, musicians, singers, dancers, matadors and also the staff from clubs of Madrid. It stays open all night. The smells of the food, the noise and the laughter is a magnet and I love it here. The bar immediately became Rodney's office; clubroom and meeting place and we could find him there day or night between rehearsals and shows.

After the first show, the 'Aperitivo Show' at about 10 p.m., I would pop round to the bar to relax with a glass of local wine and munch on my favourite tapas *Gambas al ajilo*, prawns with garlic and chillis served in earthenware bowls and small slivers of local crude *jamon* cut from the haunch on a stand.

One night, while I was waiting to be served, a delicate glass of sherry, *fino* – the kind I like - very dry and very chilled, was slipped into my hand. I glanced slowly up, curious to see who was the owner of the fingers on my glass and encountered a pair of dark brown extraordinarily sensuous eyes looking straight into mine. I felt a crush of animal attraction! It was instant. His face was alarmingly handsome and I was mesmerized and honestly quite weak at the knees. The long and short of this little story is that my Spanish improved greatly over the next few weeks. Pablo was gorgeous, irresistible and I had fallen madly in love. For me he was pure Spain – a divine mixture of a matador and a flamenco dancer!

April 1965

Darling Lez.

A life! Oh – long walks in the country – visits to the Prado, Toledo for the bull fights – I love it all. I have gone and fallen in love – at least I think I have and it has made things ten times more complicated because I want to come home. Trust me! I am furious with myself it just is not the right moment. This has been influencing me day and night – I am at the same time happy and sad. By the way, I read the bit in your letter to the girls about sending the HORSE GUARDS to fetch me home – Well, they all think that is a perfectly fabulous idea, send especially the good looking ones. Ha ha Your love-sick daughter Sally xx

P.S. By the way did I mention his name is Pablo and he's a waiter at El Biombo Chino?

256

A 1965 postcard of Manuel Benitez Pérez, the famous El Cordobés. Although he was born into poverty, grew up in an orphanage and was a teenage petty criminal, he became the most famous matador of the 1960's bringing show business theatrics into the bullring and by the time he retired in 1971 was the highest-paid matador in history. On October 2002 he was awarded the crown Quinto Califa del Toreo, by the city of Córdoba.

Mary

Plastered about Madrid are posters of three handsome matadors all in their twenties, Manuel Pérez known as *El Cordobés*, Santiago Martin Sánchez, nicknamed *El Viti*, and *Paco Camino* who full name is Camino Francisco Sánchez. They are wildly popular and treated like Gods. *El Cordobés* looks like the boy next door with a sweet smile and hair flopping in his face, *Paco Camino* has a round baby face with dark bushy eyebrows and *El Viti* is sultry, haughty and dangerous looking. I know this because I have met them all at our hangout. Normally we would never dream of eating between shows but here in Spain night becomes day. The '*aperitivo*' show starts at seven and the next one isn't until one a.m. so we have hours to sit around doing nothing and don't drag ourselves to our caves until three in the morning. Weird eh? Class and rehearsals begin at four in the afternoon so I am putting in eleven-hours every day but Sunday. Hallelujah! Sunday is a day of rest or as it turns out a day at the bull fights.

At about ten o'clock one night we crowded into the bar to choose some tapas. Rodney, all smiles and charm met us at the door and ushered us upstairs to a private dining room, which was a complete contrast to the rowdy stand-up bar below. Oil paintings in gilded frames and ornate mirrors decorate the wood paneled walls rather like a grand mansion and running down the middle of the room a trestle table, laden with dishes and platters of food. Within minutes the place was crammed with people all laughing and telling jokes in Spanish and in the chaos I was introduced to *El Viti, El Cordobés* and several other matadors, their managers and hangers-on. It was all-thrilling but just a buzz in my ears because I understood not one word of Spanish and no one was speaking French or English. I slunk into the shadows to be an onlooker. "Hello, my name is Paco said a soft voice at my elbow. *"Yo me llama Paco"*. Everyone seems to be called Paco. This particular Paco filled my glass to the brim with *vino rioja* and standing very close to me, in fact breathing right into my face, told me his life story in an amusing mix of three languages. He is a banker for the matadors and not at all flamboyant like his clients – the quiet, pensive type. I was glad of his company for this one moment. He had other ideas for later but they were quickly squelched.

Sally

Thank Heavens I have been studying Spanish because it caused quite a stir at the fiesta. Imagine little old me surrounded by the most famous matadors in Spain actually listening to my attempts at conversation and laughing uproariously at my pronunciation. They thought I was hilarious and I had a ball. *Vino tinto* flowed, probably far too much and flirting with sexy and conceited bullfighters went to my head - or maybe it was the wine. All too soon it was time to return to El Biombo Chino for the one o'clock show. Rodney gathered up his 'family' and we trooped around the corner to the *entrada de artistas* staggering in like a gaggle of geese, giggling and shushing. Yvette was raging mad probably because she had missed the fun and was hostile calling us *soulards,* drunks and worse.

That night I was to introduce the ballet in my best Spanish, wearing my Finale costume, a long, dove grey chiffon coat edged in bright orange feathers. "It's a full house," Rodney whispered as he handed me the microphone. An enthusiastic fanfare blared from the orchestra pit as I stepped through the soft black velvet curtain. The spotlight encircled me and with a wide welcoming smile I started down three small steps. Almost in slow motion I saw myself lassoed by the microphone lead, thrashing about to free myself and landing splat on my tummy with my bottom in the air and a pile of bloody feathers over my head.

The audience went wild. *Olé Olé, Arriba, Arriba*, they shrieked as though I was a fallen bull and they swooned all over each other in hysterics. Scrambling to my feet, untangling myself from the lead and trying to regain my composure, I began, *"Señoras y Señores* Welcome, *Bienvenida,"* and peered past the spotlight squinting into the gloom. No one was paying the slightest bit of attention. People were crying with laughter, heads thrown back and howling like hyenas. Oh sod it! I might as well become a comedienne. With one shoe strap flapping, I clumped back up the stairs and disappeared behind the curtain.

Mary

My first bullfight and I am hooked, becoming what the Spanish call a *taurino*, a fan of the sport. Or is it a sport? It seems to be pure show business, music, dance, costumes, and a theatrical ritual that is centuries old, deeply rooted in the Spanish soul since the Moors first introduced it in the 11th Century. Liliane refuses to go. She loathes the fights, calling them cruel and barbaric. Sally, Richard and I are spellbound.

I was introduced to the '*Corrida de Toros*' in Madrid on our only day off, the first Sunday that El Viti was fighting. It was hot, blistering hot by ten in the morning. *Madrileños* were swarming like bees around the wicket wanting seats on the shady side for the late afternoon fight. We were too excited to care about sun or shade, which proved to be painful.

260

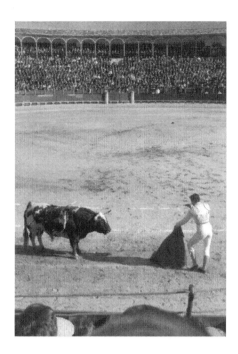

Seconds before 'tercio de muerte' - the death of either the bull or the matador, Mary took this photo with a Kodak Brownie at the La Plaza de Toros de Las Ventas in Madrid. (May 1965) The coliseum of Moorish design holds 25,000 people and was built in 1931. Five gates open into the 200-foot wide arena where the bull fights take place. The building has two hospital rooms to patch up the wounded and a chapel.

After a lot of shoving and jostling in the late afternoon, the three of us settled on our small hard stone seats. The air was alive with anticipation and the audience was building into a frenzy, squirting wine from leather *botas* and calling to one another. From the expensive seats in the shade came a roar and we all stood up cheering and straining to see what happened. It was nothing at all, just collective madness.

Finalmente comenzó, let the circus begin. The trumpets rang out the familiar "ta taaa ta, ta, ta, tum" the drums exploded into a rumble like thunder and the spectators roared like lions mopping perspiration and wine stains off their faces. The cheap seats were burning hot. Suddenly from one of the five gates below, strode the matador and his team who waved to the crowd and saluted the dignitaries seated opposite. This parade is called the *paseillo*. We recognized the matador at once as he preened and waved to his fans looking gorgeous in skin tight, white satin pants with a wide stripe of gold embroidery down his skinny legs and a sleeveless open bolero encrusted with jewels. Without the costume and the bull, he was just one of the guys hanging out in our bar.

It all became a blur of excitement after the initial parade. The huge snorting bull rushed into the arena stood absolutely still; his head lowered. Seconds passed, no one moved a muscle. From stage right the *picadors* on horseback pranced into the ring and everybody took their places. The *banderilleros*, as agile as dancers, teased the bull with sharp batons. Tension rose as the wounded beast gushing blood from lances and flags became enraged. I put my hands over my eyes hardly daring to peek between my fingers. The trumpet sounded the final fifteen minutes. With a bright red cape called a *muleta,* the bull was worked to a hypnotic stage with a series of more and more dangerous poses until, the climax, the moment of death, eye to eye, man verses beast, the matador plunged a thin sword into the bull's shoulders, he shuddered, swayed and dropped on his knees.

'Olé, Olé, the crowd shouted, me too, I yelled hysterically until I was hoarse. I have never been so gruesomely excited in all my life. We watched three bullfighters that evening and the third matador was El Viti. He was magnificent, cool, elegant and sexy. Richard and I were burnt raw almost purple. Next Sunday we'll splurge on posh seats in the shade.

Sally

The JBR is leaving for Barcelona in forty-eight hours and I have still so much to see and do. With enormous relief Rodney has found us two weeks work at the Apollo theatre and then a month as part of a variety show called *Campagnie Espectaculos Colsada.* We are called '*Las alegres chicas*' the happy girls of Colsada. Isn't that a hoot? Yvette refuses to be a 'appy *chica*' for any bloody Spaniard and is indignant. I guess Francis is not particularly happy either because she is staying behind in Madrid without Rodney jr. who doesn't appear to be terribly bothered. In fact he is already dancing attention on her replacement Julie, a lovely redhead from London who was trained at the Royal Ballet School and is begging to be in our company.

Meanwhile Mary and I are having a last dash around the Prado to see our favourite paintings of El Greco, Velázquez, Picasso and the disturbing work of Francisco Goya's 'Saturn Devouring his Son', which I don't understand at all. My favourite is '*La Maja Desnuda*' painted when Goya was in a much more wholesome state. The beautiful Maja's ginger-coloured pubic hair caused a great fuss when it was first displayed. The Catholic Church was horrified and the public titillated, making it one of the most beloved paintings in the Prado.

Postage stamps of The Naked Maja in commemoration of Goya's work were privately produced in 1930, and later approved by the Spanish Postal Authority. That same year, the United States government barred and returned any mail bearing the stamps. This was the first time that any stamp represented a naked women.

My Barcelona home for a month is a flat on the sixth floor of *Casa 18 Calle Marqués del Campo Sagrado.*' Richard, Mary and I can just afford it on our salaries. We are pretending to be a family: cooking, shopping, playing records, reading together, the three of us flopped like a pile of rag dolls onto a chesterfield and for a brief moment, living a normal life. Of course it is not terribly private because everyone in the ballet descends on us at any time of the day, hanging out and listening to our records of Enrique Guzman and Shirley Bassey. Rodney arrives at all hours bursting with new ideas and larks around the tiled lounge like Gene Kelley doing the 'old soft shoe' with an imaginary top hat. Ta tum, ta tum, ta tatatata ta tum! Oh we do have a laugh!

We all long for a real home, at least I do and now I think I am pregnant. When I told Rodney that we should make plans for our new life together as he promised in Bremen, he was distracted or pretended to be, with a new ballet to be called '*Cityscapes*.' I wrote to Lesley and told her everything.

One suffocating night, after the show I climbed in a scalding tub with Mary perched on the khazi reading Ernest Hemmingway's "The Sun Also Rises" and Richard in the doorway telling really bad jokes to make me laugh. He cranked the music up full volume while I drank an entire bottle of cheap gin and we put that right. Who knows? Maybe I was never pregnant in the first place. In any case, lying on my bed in the middle of the night I made up my mind to leave Rodney and the ballet by the end of the summer.

Mary

On our very last night in Madrid I met Paco my serious, somber banker. I think he has a bit of a crush on me as he is always hanging around me like a puppy. I finally agreed to go out to a farewell dinner but there is no hope for him. I do not want to end up a Spanish housewife stuck in Madrid till the end of my days. Well I'm glad I went because he took me to a madly expensive restaurant just off the *Plaza Mayor* called '*El Botin*,' dating from 1725. The restaurant is world famous for pig on a spit and I've just read in Ernest Hemmingway's book 'The Sun Also Rises,' that his character 'Jake' "lunched upstairs at Botin's…had roast young suckling pig and drank three bottles of *rioja alta*." And that was after he had polished off three pre - lunch martinis. Always ravenous, I gorged myself on mounds of pork and greasy strips of crackling but, unlike Mr. Hemmingway's hero Jake, did not drink martinis and three bottles of *vino rioja alta* or I would have been under the banquette or worse. Gluttony did not seem to put Paco off. He wants to write to me in Barcelona.

Generalissimo Francisco Franco controlled Spain from 1939 – 1975. During what is referred to as the Franco Era, Spanish law prohibited wives from almost all forms of economic opportunity including, employment, ownership of property, even travel away from home, without 'permiso marital.' The government directed a policy of 'perfecta casada' keeping women subordinate in the house. Abortion and adultery were crimes punishable by imprisonment until 1978 and divorce was only legalized in 1981. The thought of being a Spanish wife did not appeal.

The *Teatro Apollo*, in Barcelona is creaky with age, complete with old fashioned trap doors, a bank of footlights and a strange wooden apron called the *passerella* that is a narrow ramp built from one side of the proscenium arch around the orchestra pit into the audience and ending on the opposite side. I've never seen anything quite like it. It is a Spanish custom that at the finale of the show, each performer dances along the *passerella* and takes bows. You cannot look down but smile bravely and pray that you do not tumble onto some unsuspecting lap.

Opening night I tottered along the plank, squinting through mascara laden lashes at the swaying boards quite terrified but, after a few performances could skitter along like a prancing pony. Just like spectators at a bull fight, the audience roared their overwhelming approval. Newspaper reviews called us the most modern ballet ever to come to Barcelona and that endorsement guaranteed packed houses. Of course the tickets are very cheap especially the seats in the top balcony, only two pesetas. The price increases at the lower balconies to fifty and the main floor, wealthy patrons pay three hundred pesetas. I have to pinch myself to believe I am actually part of this.

There is a certain magic about Barcelona, a hodgepodge of rich, poor, historic, modern, traditional and rebellious. We actually have time to explore the winding cobbles of the old town and parade down the wide avenue *Las Ramblas* shaded by arching rows of sycamore trees. It is only six blocks from our theatre and follows the route of an old stream or flowing water *la rambla* of the city sewer. During the daytime the avenue is a vast outdoor marketplace that sells everything from fruits and vegetables, to parrots in cages. At night *putas* with bright pouty lips, loiter in the shadows hungry for customers. I told Rodney that I wanted to buy a lime green parrot to sit on my shoulder like Long John Silver and train it to scream "Beat it Buster." He shook his head and muttered that I was crazy, *completamente loca,* and would get TB.

In the center of Barcelona stands a monument to creative energy, The Temple of the Holy Family known as 'Tempio Expiatorio de la Sagada Familia.' The temple was begun in 1882 by Catalan architect Antonio Gaudi and worked on until his death in 1926. Its unique design is a fascinating fusion of traditional and avant-garde ideas that has never been completed. The unfinished masterpiece became a UNESCO World Heritage Site. This photo is from a 1965 postcard.

Sally

Darling Lez:

I am writing this in the Apollo theatre – reason for lipstick marks - It is deadly having such a long time between ballets but we are happy to be in a theatre. The show itself is a bit 'corny' and old fashioned but WE got fabulous reviews, much to the disgust of the male star also director who immediately cut two of our ballets. We still come out on top with the female star (soubrette) who is a dear and an 'artist.' I just received a note from the post office to collect a parcel. Whoopee, Lots of love to all, Sal xxx

On May the first we had a spontaneous celebration that turned into a disaster for that French tart, Nadine. It began late at night on stage after the final *passerella* with the whole Colsada troupe, orchestra and all. Someone brought massive kegs of *vinto tinto.* Before many glasses were drunk, the night turned into what the Spanish call a *zambra.* Jazz music was blaring from our speakers over the whole theatre right to the top balcony. Rodney junior and Paco, the Spanish drummer who wears dark glasses day and night, battered away on two sets of drums each taking turns with solos. Everyone was improvising, dancing themselves into a frenzy, strutting, spinning, doing high kicks, we are good at that, and tearing across the passerella airborne in a *grand jétés.* Nadine who is usually so agile, leapt through the air and landed straight into the orchestra pit with a crash and clanging of cymbals. We all laughed delightedly.

The following afternoon, a sober and defiant Nadine met me on the same stage, now swept of debris, her broken arm in a sling. She has been told that I will take over the lead role of Emile in '*La Rue Verte.*' "*Je mon fou*" she said rudely tossing her blonde hair from her forehead and wincing. I know she does care very much. Secretly I am thrilled to play Emile, a plum of a role and my chance to take the comic lead from my rival.

Rodney arrived and we began rehearsals putting Nadine in the back row. Broken arm or not, she must be on stage or she will not be paid.

That night in the wings, Rodney stood beside me and gave me my cue to make my entrance. I feel his hand on the small of my back. "NOW, is said under his breath and gave me the tiniest nudge. Wearing high heels for the first time, ankles falling over, awkward and smiling foolishly with my bum sticking out, the audience roared with laughter and I hadn't done a thing yet! Well from that moment on, the role was mine.

Making people laugh can be a lot more difficult than you imagine but I seem to have a knack. Even standing still, with a certain look on my face and my posture and the timing or just blinking my eyes, I can make an audience laugh right out loud. Nicole was VERY put off. *'Rue Verte'* was a hit.

Photo from the JBR archives taken during the tour of Spain with 'Campagnie Espectaculos Colsada' in the summer of 1965. From left is Richard Gough playing 'Johnny the Pimp of Paris,' Sally Seyd as 'Emile' and Xavier as Arturo the Marquise in La Rue Verte.

Mary

As a child, I used to dream, like all children of joining 'the big top' of running away to join a circus. Our tour of Spain was exactly like a circus but performed in old opera houses rather than tents. We travelled like gypsies not in caravans but in a gaudy red and yellow wreck of a bus that broke down every day. Our bus was the laughing stock of the entire 'Campagnie Colsada'. The show toured from town to town, a different theatre every few nights with each town trying to outdo the previous one in hospitality. Crowds greeted us at the stage door and more than once we needed a police escort to lead us to a restaurant. Our lives were chaotic, exhausting, exhilarating and never to be forgotten.   In the space of six weeks the JBR performed in Murcia, Elda, Vitiel, Castellon, Reus, Manresa, Huesca, San Sebastián, Vitoria, Logroño, Bilbao, Granada, Palma de Mallorca and back to the beginning in Barcelona.

On May 21, 1965 my twenty-fourth birthday, alone in my hotel room, I re-read my letters from Canada. "Come home and get a real job," my father pleads.   My mother's letters are more hurtful as she implies that the ballet must be hopeless if it has to be part of a variety show.   It's very difficult to explain to her, especially in a flimsy tissue air letter, the differences between theatre in North America and Europe, from a society that is rich with endless sources of entertainment and government subsidies for the arts, to poor Spanish towns with one theatre, no television and diversions tightly controlled by the Catholic Church and a fascist dictatorship.   What is a 'real job' anyway? Happy Birthday to me. *'Feliz cumpleanos a mi!'*

Colsadas, not so 'happy *chicas*' finished the second show late one night in the port of San Sebastián near the French border, staggered aboard the bus, half dead with fatigue and at about three in the morning rattled southward toward Granada, that ancient Moorish stronghold to be part of the celebrations of *Corpus Christi.* We had been promised a newer bus in Madrid. Well, of course we should have known better. On the outskirts of the capital we pulled into a machine shop. There were mutterings and mumblings, lots of cigarettes smoked and our driver threw his hands in the air, shrugged his shoulders and climbed back in muttering *'a perro flaco, todo son pulgas'* which I think translates as the bloody bus is a flea-bitten dog.

A Postcard of San Sebastián from 1965. The harbor of San Sebastián, or Donostia in the Basque language is in the 'parte vieja' or old town. Up on the hill, Monte Urgell, a giant statue of Christ gazes over the city.

Sally

Ghastly! There is no other word to describe the appalling journey. We suffered through an overheated engine, a punctured tire and screaming brakes and stopped for cup after cup of coffee and queues for the loo. Eventually I fell asleep sitting bolt upright.

The final rumble and splutter through the streets of Granada was a blur but the shabby hotel looked as good as the Ritz on Piccadilly. We had travelled for over twenty-four hours from the most northerly Basque town on the Bay of Biscay to Andalusia in the south, without a proper break.

"Wakeup, rehearsal in twenty minutes," screamed Mary. I felt as though I just flopped into bed. And so it all starts again in another theatre, a fresh audience and renewed energy, that is our glamourous life with the Jazz Ballet Rodney and we wouldn't change it for the world.

The fiesta of *Corpus Christi* which means the Body of Christ, is supposed to be a religious celebration but the streets are rollicking all night long with Spanish music, folk dancing, eating and squirting rough red wine from leather *'botas'*. All ages parade the streets, some heading toward the Church and others just having fun.

The first night Sally and I took Paco, our drummer with the *Colsada* orchestra along with us to translate. We wove our way through the chaotic cobblestones decorated with green garlands and flowers where stalls lined the way selling shrimps and spiny lobster straight from the Mediterranean. I've never seen so many different kinds of fish and don't know what they are, eels maybe and little silver fish, plump red fish and ugly blue fish with gaping mouths. From cones of paper we munched deep fried shrimp and *calamari,* with sea salt, pieces of squid, tentacles and all. The smells of the sea, of newly pressed olive oil, sizzling garlic, and bread fresh from outdoor ovens is intoxicating.

We drink brandy in paper cups right out in the street. At home you would be arrested immediately. All of a sudden Sally was surrounded by boys dancing around her faster and faster like a traditional Greek circle dance. They put a necklace of flowers and garlic around her and she twirled laughing around in the middle of the crowd until she disappeared from sight. The music and the madness got louder and more boisterous. At one or two in the morning it was still hot, and sticky. Paco put his arms around me and pulled me close. Momentarily I felt wildly out of control and stood swaying with him in the street. He is a married man with a child for Heaven's sake and I pulled away.

I awoke with a Technicolor headache. Outside the shuttered windows the fiesta rages on with beating drums, singing and laughter. Our room is a mess of laundry; of dripping bras, blouses, dance belts and stockings. Sally is like an Irish washerwoman scrubbing every stitch of clothing she owns in the small basin by the door and humming cheerfully. "What time did you get in?" She didn't answer the question but just grinned and sang "I had a *BALL*."

Sally

The González family, who seems to own half of Granada, invited the whole ballet and the orchestra to their private villa near the *Plaza de Bib-Rambla* for the last evening of the *Corpus Christi* celebration. They must have known how lonely it is to be constantly on tour, always moving, never getting to make friends. That night Xavier, Tanita, Yvette, Mary, Richard, Paco and I arrived at the Gonzáles home after the last *passerella* and the costumes were hung up to air. There we were welcomed into a great hall that was simply breath taking. The walls were great chunks of rock, tables of unfinished wood and the ceiling was made of intricately woven straw like a tapestry. Bunches of dried red peppers, onions, sausages, hams, braids of garlic and all sort of Spanish fruits hung from metal hooks and overhead were polished copper buckets, pans and kettles. Antique swords, oil paintings and primitive farm implements were displayed on the walls. It was a museum, absolutely brilliant and I wandered around taking in all the amazing details and dreaming that one day I would have a magnificent kitchen like this, maybe even better.

Our host Señor González had the face of a man who had seen much tragedy but he had little twinkle about him. Large, sad, El Greco eyes were the first thing I noticed, then a bushy graying moustache that almost covered his narrow face and big ears that stood out from the side of his head. He was the man of the house and led us in with the sweep of his arm and introduced us to three grand dames who smiled with no teeth. Grandpa was curled up in a chair asleep and about twenty other odd aunties and uncles were in seated in a circle. No one spoke a word of English but they beckoned us to us and made us feel welcome.

While we were all helping ourselves to endless platters of food and the finest sherry, a lone guitarist was playing in the corner until one by one family members got up and performed either a song or folk dancing or recited poetry. For the first time I didn't feel like a stranger, an outsider but a part of Spain and its people. They wanted to entertain us. They were expressing their joy, their sadness and love and I revelled in the tradition of Spanish hospitality. When Señor Gonzálaz finally picked up his classical guitar and played 'Malaguena,' we all wept with emotion, completely undone.

Mary

The night of *Corpus Cristi* passed in a gentle dream but just before dawn, the aunties hurried us out to join in the final moments of the festival. Stepping into the street was like being thrown into a boiling river of people all pressing toward the plaza and crowding into narrow cobbled side street bars jammed with singing drunks squirting plonk from their *botas* into eager mouths. It was a glorious mad and hysterical party. Almost immediately, Sally was swallowed up into the sticky mob of people, laughing and dancing.

Paco grabbed me by the hand and didn't let go until we were through the plaza and in the fairground. At the gate to a giant Ferris wheel he found a kiosk called an *aguardiente,* where an old lady was selling 'firewater.' *"Sol y sombre,"* he said. I know enough Spanish to translate sun and shade but this explosive stuff was anise and cognac. Yikes! I took a gulp and felt the creeping burn throughout my body. It felt wonderful.

The Ferris wheel slowly, slowly circled up and up until at the very top it seemed to pause and we sat like two little specks and watched the dawn break over the city of Granada and peered down at the tiny figures far below whooping and cheering as the day replaced the night - the triumph of light over dark. We kissed. *Corpus Christi* has been a party of a lifetime. We are off in a few hours to the island of Mallorca. As I lay on the bed, one foot on the floor to stop the room whirling, a voice in my ear sniggered, "There's no rest for the wicked".

One of the many beautiful beaches (Badia de Palma) on the island of Mallorca near the main port and largest city (Ciutat) of Palma de Mallorca. The name comes from the old Roman settlement of Palmeria dating back to 120 B.C. Roman ruins remain unearthed in the city of Palma. Between 902 and 1229 Palma de Mallorca was the Arab stronghold of Medina Mayurqa. Constant, invasions, conquests, piracy and vandalism have given Mallorca, the largest of the Balearic Islands, it's romantic and multicultural history and unique architecture. During the 1960's Mallorca was fiercely pro Franco, religious and conservative. Then, its exquisite beaches were invaded by endless hordes of tourists.

Sally

Teatro Lyrico, Palma Mallorca.

Darling Lezy

I am writing this on my special spot in the sand on a beach on the island of Mallorca. This is our last week of the Spanish tour in the Teatro Lyrico in the main port of Palma. The whole island is gorgeous. At first glance Mallorca is not very Spanish because it is so full of European tourists and more people seem to speak German than anything else. It could be an island anywhere in the Mediterranean.

The natives make it unique, they or many of them are descendants of Moorish pirates and are swarthy, very handsome and speak a dialect of Catalan, which I don't understand at all. The opening was two nights ago and it was quite nostalgic – everyone felt it - being the last week of the tour. I told you that the show was a little corny at first but all the artists have become united like a family and it will be difficult to say goodbye to them forever…happier news… yesterday I bought a new bikini, very tiny (for Spain). It is white with blue polka dots and it is not going unnoticed. I am lying here soaking up the warmth and feeling the faint breeze blowing like kisses on my skin. Perfection! Soon I will be coming home. The moment we have finished our contract in France, Juan les Pins, I will pack up and be coming back to London. I know my decision is right. Don't you think? I will send you the time and the exact date I will arrive at Victoria Station. I can hardly wait. Lots of Love Sal xxx

I adore being by myself here on the beach in the warm sand feeling the sun on my face making me drowsy and nostalgic. Everyone else is at the *Teatro Lyrico*, rehearsing 'Cityscapes' which will open in Juan les Pins. Mary has the lead, and I am happy for her, yes really I am! The music is wild; motorcycles revving, horns honking, whistles, sirens, big city noise, and the costumes brilliant, sort of space age, geometrical *Courrège* dresses in black and white plastic, with helmets and visors. They are not like any costumes ever seen, very avant-garde. The ballet is about a motorcycle gang wedding, gritty and disturbing but with no real story and the ending is superb. I would be lying if I said I didn't mind not dancing in it. The choreography is fabulous. But, my mind is made up and I am going home to Lesley.

As the warm sun beats down, I think about all my years wandering around Europe, North Africa and

278

the Middle East, touring with the ballet. I left home when I was only nineteen years old, so full of hope for my grand career and my future. I smile to myself remembering meeting Xavier and Liliane who gave me my first job in their little troupe of dancers, The Rainbow Ballet that they formed in 1960 in Brussels. If it were not for Xavier, I would never have met Rodney. Xavier insisted that if Rodney wanted to hire the Rainbow Ballet for his tour of Europe, it was *'tous ou rien',* all of us or nobody. I was not to be left out. It was me who introduced Rodney to Martha Graham's innovative ideas and incorporate them into his vision. Liliane and Xavier live with such passion, such drama, with endless scandals, their wild separations and the reconciliations. They are two explosive people just made for each other. I will miss them both.

I muse about Rudy, the most sensual and expressive performer that I have ever had the honour dance with – our beautiful unfulfilled love affair so short but so intense it was painful. It will live inside me forever. I think about his career now, dancing with Zizi Jeanmaire and other ballerinas in Paris. I think about the dancers who have left over the years and wonder what happened to them, beautiful tall Susannah who wanted to be a film star at *Cinecitta i*n Rome and handsome Remo who ran off with Puck after our success in Cannes.

Of course I think about my wild and woolly Mary. We have done and seen so much together that she will always be my friend and confidant. In three years she has grown in every way and with all the travel, footlights and adventure and is a completely different person than when she arrived so fresh and uncomplicated at my audition in Max River's Studios in London. She will go back to Canada eventually when she is ready; confident and fulfilled.

I try not to worry about Rodney but I do. My mother and our family have become his anchor and support and soon, he will have only Nadine clutching at him and Yvette mothering him. I am too young to be responsible and must turn my back or be forever be wandering homeless across the stages of Europe. He will always be in my heart of hearts no matter what happens in the future.

Chapter Fifteen

Juan les Pins and All That jazz.

…With a whoosh almost a sigh, the heavy red velvet curtains
wearily sank to the dusty stage floor and it was over…

NEWSFLASH

Vietnam: August 1965 Operation Starlight. First ground strike against the Viet Cong. The fighting begins…

Sally

There is a general air of gaiety as the train speeds across the Mediterranean coast of Spain into France with a brief stop at the border crossing of Cerbere. The French are finally home again and rattling away *en francais* with the speed of a machine gun. Spanish is forgotten. We are all brown as walnuts and jubilant after months in the sun, well perhaps not me. I am feeling a little sad.

Gazing out the window of the train, the sun sparkling on the *Golfe de Lyon* between clumps of Mediterranean pines. It is very lovely. In a few hours we will be on the *Cote d' Azur* and I am remembering that it is almost a year to the day that we were in Cannes all twenty-five members of the ballet. So much has happened, in one short year. I pull down the window just a little to smell the salt air tinged with the scent of the *garigue*, the dry scrubland, of lavender, wild herbs and pine.

Mary

Sally is a little quiet, probably nostalgic as Juan les Pins is her last contract with the JBR. I cannot bear to think about it so I don't and concentrate on writing long overdue postcards with scenes of Palma de Mallorca, bathing beauties and the caves of Porto Cristo, about thirty miles from Palma where I dragged Richard one day.

Eventually the motion of the train lulls me into a trance and I don't wake up until our arrival in Marseille at the *Marseille Gare Saint Charles*. *"Vingt minutes"* calls the elderly porter in his traditional blue uniform, as he marches like a soldier up and down the platform. *"vingt minutes'*. With that everyone piles off the train in a frenzy to gather around the mobile bar ordering hot café and *croissants* that disappear in seconds leaving a trail of pastry flakes on the ground. Oh Bliss!

Holidaymakers and business men climb off the train and others almost identical climb back on. A shrill whistle from up the track signals departure, *"en voiture"*, all aboard, calls our porter his face a mask of boredom. He must have been doing this job for decades, *"en voiture'* and we scramble back on the train, settling down into well-worn corduroy seats facing each other.

There is a game of rummy in a compartment down the corridor and feeling restless, I decide to join the game, starting down the passage, climbing over our excess luggage. At that moment the train lurches around a corner and I stumble onto my own suitcase, which happened to be the only one with a hubbly bubbly sticking out like a sword. I feel a sharp pain down the front of my left leg on the shinbone. Ow! Damn, damn damnation, blood is running down my leg as I inspect the damage. I have an eight-inch long

282

valley of skin missing. Rodney comes out and is concerned I suspect more for my appearance on stage than if I am maimed for life. I am bleeding like the Niagra Falls, blood gushing on my clothes, my shoes and my hands as I hobble to the carriage where Yvette has the first aid kit. *"Merde"* she growls with no sympathy at all, zee tights, zee leotard, *salle canadienne, vraiement stupide."* I let her rant on about the dirty, stupid Canadian until she bandages my leg with lots of padding and tells me to put pressure on it.

Toulon, St Tropez, St Raphael and Cannes whizz by with me holding my throbbing leg in the air until we arrive in the tiny old station in Juan Les Pins, the town made famous by Scott Fitzgerald in his novel of the 20's 'Tender is the Night.' *"Quatre minutes,"* calls the porter. Four minutes, Crikey! I hobble off the train and leave someone, anyone, to get my bags off. Frank, our muscle man does most of the catching as Rodney sprints down to the baggage cars with Xavier and Ronáld to oversee the unloading of the costumes. Three and three quarter minutes later the ballet and the massive pile of luggage are off the train once more. *"En voiture"* calls the porter" and the train with an exhausted groan, pulls out again heading eastward toward Nice on the *Baie des Anges.*

Sally

An impeccably dressed gentleman was walking his little dog, along the platform when Rodney stopped to ask him directions for the casino. They chatted away for ages as though they were old friends. An obviously contented Rodney returned and said it is just across the boulevard a few minutes away. "Daahlinks, you have one hour and then we meet in the Casino for rehearsal" "Quickly now" and he handed me the names of two hotels with a list of who is booked into which one. I notice that his name was not on the list. Where will he sleep?

A taxi pulls up in front of the small station. Mary, Liliane, Richard and I squeeze in with our bags piled around us and just a short distance away, an easy walk really; find ourselves at a small hotel on *Avenue du Docteur Fabre*. It is an old fashioned villa with shuttered windows, perhaps twenty rooms in all. Just down the avenue, a very inviting little bar beckoned. That will probably become our local, I think to myself. The entire area has the atmosphere of a summer holiday and the smell of good food, *Gitanes* tobacco, French perfume and suntan oil fills me with nostalgia. I hadn't realized that I missed France so.

Mary and I are on the top floor of the hotel just under the eaves, in a clean whitewashed room with simple oak furniture. It is smaller, and cheaper than all the other rooms downstairs. I am saving every centime for my trip home to London in two weeks. It's hard to imagine what it will be like, to live away from the ballet. I won't think about that now as I want to enjoy my every moment in the here and now.

The JBR are performing at the Casino Eden Beach for a fortnight including several galas with our old pals; from the Casino Montreux, Sacha Distel, Gilbert Bécaud from the Lido Excelsior Palace in Venice, and the boys from the Pantelon Perez Prado orchestra that we met on our last night in the Miami Hotel Cabaret in Teherān. What a strange circuit we follow. We will be closing with a new French pop star, Johnny Hallyday who is younger than we are and has everyone in a dither.

*August 11, 1965. The Jazz Ballet Rodney performed
at a Gala opening at the Eden Beach Casino in Juan les Pins.
It was the premier performance of the ballet 'Cityscapes.' The
evening was hosted by Sacha Distel, not only a French singer
songwriter, but an accomplished jazz guitarist. The Gala menu
offers Cantaloupe frappé with port wine, Filets de Sole
'Nantua,' Poussin, or little capons stuffed with duck liver pâté,
garnished with buttered green beans and to finish a frozen ice
cream 'Eden Beach' and petit fours. The champagnes included;
Ruinart Tradition, Tattinger Brut and Moët et Chandon. The
total price; 95 French francs plus a 15% service charge.*

Dropping our bags in our tiny attic room we
pulled out a few dresses put them on hangers in the
wardrobe and left the hotel, incognito in our new
Spanish sandals and Audrey Hepburn sunglasses. The
Eden Beach Casino is just down the boulevard near the
beach. When we came tripping in the stage door we
found Rodney and Sacha Distel on stage, deep in
conversation. Sacha nodded in my direction, gave me
his famous smile that makes the girls melt, and glanced
around. I wonder if he is looking for Francis who is
left behind somewhere in Madrid. He had eyes only
for her at the Casino in Montreux. At that moment, our
Julie came striding in with her carrot red hair in wild
disarray. She stopped in her tracks and stared at him

almost devouring him. I wonder if there will be flowers in the dressing room tonight.

And so we begin with the Prologue. Rodney wants to make some changes that he thought up on the train. "Dahlinks, we must startle them, make a beeg bang, everyone, come, come, okay. Start with tat a tum TUMMMM. Stan Kenton's orchestra booms out from our recorder into the empty casino ballroom. Now the rehearsal begins in earnest. For some odd reason Yvette actually looks cheerful. I do a pirouette, Xavier catches me about the waist and I fall into a backbend. Upside down, I think 'that silly old cow is quite happy that I am leaving the ballet.' Run, run, run, grand jeté, "Stop," shouts Rodney, *"doucement, encore, mes cheries, et, un, deux trois,* Ta ta, tum de de dum," the music starts again.

Mary

"Cityscapes" opened last night and boy! Did it shock them? There is a blackout to begin. My cue is a barely audible tap on the podium and then I slip to a small 'x' center stage. This is more difficult than you might imagine because I am wearing dark glasses and a plastic sort of motorcycle helmet and I can't see a thing. One, two, three and on four a spotlight hits from behind and in the light I spin like a top in total silence. The second I finish there is an explosion of a dozen motor cycle engines bursting to life and headlights dart straight out toward the audience. They were gasping and applauding. What a start! From then on we had them and the ballet was a triumph. Even with my wounded shin, which was hidden inside white boots, I felt very sure of my *pirouettes* and danced with a new confidence that I didn't know was in me. For the first time since I left Canada in September 1963, I wished that my family were in the audience watching. The hours, days, months and years of dancing suddenly all

286

seemed worthwhile. An inexplicable swoosh of sadness washed over me and then the moment passed. Ten days later the fateful letter arrived from my father, the gentle sweet lady who was my grandmother and my biggest fan died in the evening of August 11, 1965.

Photo from the Jazz Ballet Rodney archives of Cityscapes © a ballet choreographed by Rodney Vas in 1965. It was one of the most innovative ballets seen in Europe at that time with Space age costumes patterned after the latest fashions of Mary Quant's plastic mini skirts, Yves St Laurent's 'Mondrian dress' inspired by Dutch painter Piet Mondrian and white boots, the signature footwear of André Courrèges.

Sally

Of course the creaky old lift has conked out so Mary and I had to clamber up the steep stairs to our quaint little room under the eaves of the hotel. She was ahead carrying the large iron key with an oversized metal medallion designed so that guests do not forget to leave it on the table downstairs. Suddenly she stopped turned to me, fingers to her lips, and whispered, "Our door is open."

I looked in horror and pushed it wide. The door crashed against a chair. No one was inside but we saw immediately that we had been robbed. Stunned silence! *Merde*! All our suitcases were open and our clothes strewn about with abandon: on the bed, the floor and in the corner sink. The drawers were pulled out of the wardrobe, underwear, jumpers, dresses, shoes, make up thrown everywhere. I am sickened. With my stomach climbing up my throat I rush to my case and unzipped compartment where I keep my jewellery box hidden. In my heart I already know that it is empty and everything taken. All my mementos of my years of travel and memories of my life with Rodney are gone. Everywhere we have travelled for the past seven years he has given me lovely mementos, gold charms, a wristwatch that was my Christmas present in 1963, rings and bracelets – from Algeria, Italy, Tunis, Egypt, Iran, and Greece. Even my turquoise and gold necklace from Egypt has been nicked.

Mary sat on her bed in shock, quite speechless. All her savings and a gold charm bracelet with irreplaceable family heirlooms and her sapphire sorority pin in the shape of a key - gone. "Who could have done this?" she wailed. Immediately it is all very clear, at least it is to me. There is only one person who knows our exact whereabouts when the ballet is performing, what hotels we are in and who would do anything to hurt me. There is a one girl who is so insanely jealous of my special relationship with Rodney that she would steal his gifts to me and only one member of the JBR who lives near here, and has a creepy gang of cousins. "Nadine!" Mary nodded. There is no point in going to the French police. What a joke. The lot will be miles away by now. I think both of us would welcome a large glass of *pastis* and so we left the scene of the crime, slammed the door so hard it shook the house and trooped back to the streets to *la belle vie.* Ah Yes! The good life lets you hide all the sadness you feel. Oh the good life's so full of fun and seems ideal.

Mary

Who is Johnny Hallyday? I really haven't heard of him but he must be "someone" because he had a police escort to the casino. There is no rehearsal today, which is unusual but Rodney seems very distracted and has spent the entire morning on the telephone. Tanita gave a long and very tiring class and we were just preparing to spend the rest of the afternoon on the beach when Xavier announced that we were invited to an after show party with Johnny Hallyday and his entourage. Well! The French girls almost swooned with delight but Sally and I are not very happy to be anywhere with the others. Suspicion is a very nasty thing. We didn't tell anyone about the robbery hoping that some little hint might drop, a careless word might be as good as admitting guilt.

Our part of the show went over surprisingly well considering they came to see Johnny not us. After our finale and a short intermission, Sally and I crept backstage to watch and listen to him sing. Against all rules, she photographed him from the wings. You could hardly hear the music because everyone in the audience was cheering, yelling and making a racket, especially when he sang. ' *Pas cette chanson.*' He sang and played a lot like Elvis Presley which I thought was really cool. Sally did too but is pretending to be much more sophisticated than the crowd of yelling teenagers.

Jean-Philippe Smet (1943 -) whose stage name is Johnny Hallyday was known in the 1960's as the French 'Elvis Presley' singing rock and roll in the French language and selling millions of records throughout Europe and the province of Quebec in Canada. He headlined with the Jazz Ballet Rodney in August 1965.

With her trusty Brownie Box Camera, Sally photographed Johnny from the wings backstage at the Eden Beach Casino in Juan les Pins. August 1965. He was 22 years old.

Sally

Rodney walked stiffly into our dressing room without knocking and just stood there looking at me. This is unusual as he always knocks first, and strides in filling the room with energy and an easy confidence. This night he looked nervous and very tired. I thought he was sick. "what is wrong?" Yvette rushes over. He sat down suddenly on the nearest chair almost falling and put his hands over his face.

Liliane called Xavier from the other dressing room and everyone came rushing in.

"Daahlinks, our ballet is finished, gone, fini, kaput." What? I couldn't believe it. He shook his head from side to side and he kept saying over and over. "I have tried so hard but there is nothing more I can do, nothing, nothing." I tried to comfort him but felt helpless. "I have no one left to turn to. I have nothing but debts, no contracts, no hope of anything more. "You see my Daahlinks, television has taken over and our ballet is a luxury that no one can afford. Sciavioni says that all the movie theatres in Milano, are closing and no one is hiring ballets for '*Avant spectacle.*' The young people - they don't want to see modern dance, they want to dance themselves, watch television and rock and roll. Our time is up and we are finished." He looked at his watch, gave a great sigh and said sadly, "It's time, daahlinks, let's give them the show of their lives. And so we did. "*Je vous dis merde,*" break a leg."

Slowly I pull on my tight orange boots and gloves as I have done a thousand times before. Automatically, I check in the mirror to see that my makeup is still fresh, slip into my fine dove-coloured silk coat and head for the wings to wait for the now familiar music of Stan Kenton's *Artistry in Jump for* the last 'Finale'. Taking a deep breath, I step forward just to the edge of the curtain, stand completely still, waiting. My heart pounds almost painfully. Rodney junior's starts the drum roll and I count, one two three and go. Opposite me, Mary leaps onto the stage like a frightened deer with her red ponytail flying and we are caught up in the music. The others join in but we do not notice them, not this time. Mary and I are really dancing for ourselves; for the pure intoxication of our art and for the years and years we have trained our bodies. From our souls to the very tips of our fingers, we dance together for the last time.

In a flash of orange feathers, gloves, sparkling earrings and tuxedos, we take the final pose, a tableau of artists smiling as though they are the happiest people on earth.

The heavy fringed curtain descends. The applause starts slowly and builds into a crescendo. The curtain rises again and we take a bow. The orchestra stands and acknowledges the audience and then turn back to us and we bow again. From stage left Rodney emerges and takes Mary's hand and then mine. The applause grows and we clap with them ignoring the tears and sweat streaking our cheeks.

As the audience rose to their feet, Rodney stepped forward on his own, the spotlight following his every gesture. He stood very tall, elegant, aristocratic and confident for a few short, very short seconds; a lifetime? With a whoosh almost a sigh, the red velvet curtains wearily sank to the dusty stage floor and it was over.

Curtain Calls

Rodney Vas – After years of travelling and enjoying his gypsy lifestyle, Rodney settled in Milan and opened his own dance studio. He choreographed for individual artists and television shows, however, in his heart the JBR was his 'family' and his greatest achievement. Rodney died of cancer in 1981 in London. Sally was at his bedside with their son René.

Sally Seyd - Worked in Holland with comedian Toon Hermann on stage and television for a year and eventually reunited with Rodney. In 1968 they had a son René Vas who now resides in Los Angeles and works as a film production designer. She later opened one of London's first wine bars, Peachey's in Belsize Park. Sally met her future husband Baron François Faverot de Kerbrech and together they owned two very popular restaurants in the City of London. Sally, now the Baroness Faverot de Kerbrech, and François, moved to France and restored a ruined 18th Century *'mas provençale'* into deluxe guest cottages and produced award-winning wines on the Estate. Today they divide their time between London and the Luberon.

Mary Spilsbury - toured Italy as a dancer with *Compagnia Carlo Dapporto,* The Claudio Villa Show and the island of Sicily with RCA recording star, Michele Maisano and company until she had saved enough money for a ticket home. In 1966 she returned to Canada and fell in love with Michael Ross, a surgeon and has been married to him for over forty-five years. They have two children and two grandchildren. Mary is an accomplished artist, the author of Doubleday's best-selling cookbook, *Frugal Feasts* and was a journalist. She and her husband frequently visit Sally and François in Provence.

Rudy Wowor - returned to Paris and worked on television until he joined Zizi Jeanmaire. He married Femina and has children and grandchildren. Eventually he left Europe for Jakarta, Indonesia where he is still very much a dancer, teacher, television personality and choreographer. "Dancing with the JBR was one of the happiest times of my life."

Xavier - had a short career as a solo act and eventually moved to Switzerland where he owned and managed a nightclub called the Pussy Cat. He died of a heart attack in the 1980s surrounded by his kittens.

Liliane Lavagie - Xavier broke her heart and she returned to Paris and took up her mother's job as an usherette in a movie theatre "*Aux Champs Elysees*". The ballet was her only love and she died alone in her mother's apartment in the 19th arrondissement.

Ronáld - disappeared after the final curtain and was never seen again.

Elizabeth and Julie, returned home to England and we lost touch.

Richard had a career dancing on television in Paris.

Frank and Tanita - went to Paris as a "double act" and were last seen working in the Moulin Rouge.

Remo Schiavi – left the ballet in Cannes and went to Paris and later Las Vegas where he danced in all the major shows. Eventually Remo opened a restaurant in Las Vegas, a 'hit' with Italian entertainers Frank Sinatra, Dean Martin etc. Remo and his wife Anna own *'That's Italian"* a popular trattoria in California. They have a son and twin grandchildren. "My time with the JBR was a highlight."

Rodney Junior – was a professional drummer in the orchestra of the *Teatro Smeraldo*. Later he toured with the Gino Santoro Band throughout Europe. After many loves and adventures, he escaped to the island of Santorini and lived a quiet life. He had children and grandchildren. Sally and Mary kept in touch via email and Skype until his death from cancer in 2012.

Francis remained friends with her ex-husband Rodney junior and lives in Spain.

Mireille, Nicole and Nadine - we hope they kept dancing somewhere in France and read this tribute to Rodney. They all adored him.

Yvette - had a brief affair with Rodney whom she loved for years. Later she went to Switzerland and opened a florist shop. She is married and doesn't keep in touch with the '*sale anglaise*."

Susannah - had some success as a model in Rome but we have lost contact.

Thank you for reading the story of the Jazz Ballet
Rodney (1963-1965).
Merci beaucoup, Danke shon, Grazie Mille,
Egészségere Daahlinks!

Sally and Mary

Printed in Great Britain
by Amazon.co.uk, Ltd.,
Marston Gate.